Reconceptualising Eva
in Higher Education

SRHE and Open University Press Imprint

Current titles include:

Veronica Bamber *et al.*: *Enhancing Learning, Teaching, Assessment*
Catherine Bargh *et al.*: *University Leadership*
Ronald Barnett: *Beyond all Reason*
Ronald Barnett: *Higher Education: A Critical Business*
Ronald Barnett: *Realizing the University in an Age of Supercomplexity*
Ronald Barnett and Kelly Coate: *Engaging the Curriculum in Higher Education*
Tony Becher and Paul R. Trowler: *Academic Tribes and Territories (2nd edn)*
John Biggs: *Teaching for Quality Learning at University (2nd edn)*
Richard Blackwell and Paul Blackmore (eds): *Towards Strategic Staff Development in Higher Education*
David Boud *et al.* (eds): *Using Experience for Learning*
David Boud and Nicky Solomon (eds): *Work-based Learning*
Tom Bourner *et al.* (eds): *New Directions in Professional Higher Education*
Anne Brockbank and Ian McGill: *Facilitating Reflective Learning in Higher Education*
Stephen D. Brookfield and Stephen Preskill: *Discussion as a Way of Teaching*
Ann Brooks and Alison Mackinnon (eds): *Gender and the Restructured University*
Sally Brown and Angela Glasner (eds): *Assessment Matters in Higher Education*
Burton R. Clark: *Sustaining Change in Universities*
James Cornford and Neil Pollock: *Putting the University Online*
John Cowan: *On Becoming an Innovative University Teacher*
Sara Delamont, Paul Atkinson and Odette Parry: *Supervising the Doctorate 2/e*
Sara Delamont and Paul Atkinson: *Successful Research Careers*
Gerard Delanty: *Challenging Knowledge*
Chris Duke: *Managing the Learning University*
Heather Eggins (ed): *Globalization and Reform in Higher Education*
Heather Eggins and Ranald Macdonald (eds): *The Scholarship of Academic Development*
Gillian Evans: *Academics and the Real World*
Merle Jacob and Tomas Hellström (eds): *The Future of Knowledge Production in the Academy*
Peter Knight: *Being a Teacher in Higher Education*
Peter Knight and Paul Trowler: *Departmental Leadership in Higher Education*
Peter Knight and Mantz Yorke: *Assessment, Learning and Employability*
Ray Land: *Educational Development*
John Lea *et al.*: *Working in Post-Compulsory Education*
Mary Lea and Barry Stierer (eds): *Student Writing in Higher Education*
Dina Lewis and Barbara Allan: *Virtual Learning Communities*
Ian McNay (ed.): *Beyond Mass Higher Education*
Elaine Martin: *Changing Academic Work*
Louise Morley: *Quality and Power in Higher Education*
Lynne Pearce: *How to Examine a Thesis*
Moira Peelo and Terry Wareham (eds): *Failing Students in Higher Education*
Craig Prichard: *Making Managers in Universities and Colleges*
Stephen Rowland: *The Enquiring University Teacher*
Maggi Savin-Baden: *Problem-based Learning in Higher Education*
Maggi Savin-Baden: *Facilitating Problem-based Learning*
Maggi Savin-Baden and Kay Wilkie: *Challenging Research in Problem-based Learning*
David Scott *et al.*: *Professional Doctorates*
Peter Scott: *The Meanings of Mass Higher Education*
Michael L. Shattock: *Managing Successful Universities*
Maria Slowey and David Watson: *Higher Education and the Lifecourse*
Colin Symes and John McIntyre (eds): *Working Knowledge*
Richard Taylor, Jean Barr and Tom Steele: *For a Radical Higher Education*
Malcolm Tight: *Researching Higher Education*
Penny Tinkler and Carolyn Jackson: *The Doctoral Examination Process*
Susan Toohey: *Designing Courses for Higher Education*
Melanie Walker (ed.): *Reconstructing Professionalism in University Teaching*
Melanie Walker and Jon Nixon (eds): *Reclaiming Universities from a Runaway World*
Diana Woodward and Karen Ross: *Managing Equal Opportunities in Higher Education*
Mantz Yorke and Bernard Longden: *Retention and Student Success in Higher Education*

Reconceptualising Evaluation in Higher Education

The Practice Turn

Editors
Murray Saunders, Paul Trowler and Veronica Bamber

Society for Research into Higher Education
& Open University Press

Open University Press
McGraw-Hill Education
McGraw-Hill House
Shoppenhangers Road
Maidenhead
Berkshire
England
SL6 2QL

email: enquiries@openup.co.uk
world wide web: www.openup.co.uk

and Two Penn Plaza, New York, NY 10121-2289, USA

First published 2011

A catalogue record of this book is available from the British Library

ISBN-13: 978-0-33-524161-3 (pb) 978-0-33-524160-6 (hb)
ISBN-10: 0-33-524161-1 (pb) 0-33-524160-3 (hb)
eISBN: 978-0-33-524162-0

Library of Congress Cataloging-in-Publication Data
CIP data applied for

Typeset by RefineCatch Limited, Bungay, Suffolk
Printed in the UK by CPI Antony Rowe, Chippenham, Wiltshire

The McGraw·Hill Companies

We dedicate this book to Dr Joan Machell who was a good friend and colleague and spent most of her professional career evaluating aspects of Higher Education policy and practice

Contents

Figures

Tables

Contributors

Veronica Bamber is Director of the Centre for Academic Practice at Queen Margaret University, Edinburgh. Previously she was Director of Educational Development at Heriot-Watt University. The Centre for Academic Practice is responsible for enhancing learning, teaching and research at the University. She has worked as an educational developer for ten years, and has participated in numerous national initiatives, including the Scottish Enhancement Themes. Prior to this, Roni was a lecturer in Spanish for 18 years, teaching in four different universities around the UK. Roni's current research is in universities as organisations, the development of staff, and the evaluation of development programmes.

Margo Blythman is a visiting research fellow at the Centre for Learning and Teaching in Art and Design at University of the Arts, London. She was formerly Director of Teaching and Learning at London College of Communications at the same university. She has published with Susan Orr on such topics as retention, development strategies within higher education contexts and the development of student academic writing, particularly in the context of art and design. She is currently working on the evaluation of teaching and learning projects that make significant use of social networking tools and the experience of international students.

Val Chapman is Director of the Centre for Inclusive Learning Support at the University of Worcester, has an international reputation in the field of Disability and Inclusion in Higher Education having been recognised in 2004 with the award of a National Teaching Fellowship, and in 2005 by the designation of her Centre as a partner in the LearnHigher Centre for Excellence in Teaching and Learning. From 2006 to 2008 she held a UNESCO funded Chair in Special Education at Qatar University alongside her UW responsibilities. Val has presented at numerous national and international conferences and has served on a range of national committees and working parties.

Bernadette Charlier studied psychology and educational sciences at the University of Liège (Belgium) and was Professor at the Ecole Normale pour enseignants du secondaire I Saint Barthélemy in Liège. She gained a PhD in educational sciences at the Catholic University in Leuven on the topic 'Apprendre et Changer sa pratique d'Enseignement'. She is currently Professor (Professeure associée) at the Center for Higher Education didactics at the University of Fribourg.

Rob Cuthbert is Professor of Higher Education Management and Director of the Centre for Authentic Management and Policymaking in University Systems (CAMPUS) at the University of the West of England, Bristol. With 20 years' senior management experience in roles including Deputy Vice-Chancellor and Acting Vice-Chancellor, he has worked in universities, further education colleges and national government agencies as a manager, academic and consultant. His six books and many reports, articles and papers on HE policy, management, teaching and learning include Management for a Purpose, Going Corporate and Working in Higher Education. Rob was Chair of the Society for Research into Higher Education in 2002 and 2003.

Harry Hubball is a curriculum consultant from the Faculty of Education of the University of British Columbia, Vancouver, Canada and is a portfolio reviewer for the Faculty SoTL/SoCP Leadership Program at UCB.

Kerri-Lee Krause is Chair in Higher Education, Director of the Griffith Institute for Higher Education and Dean (Student Outcomes) at Griffith University. Her role connects the student experience and outcomes with support for academic staff and curriculum enhancement. Her research expertise spans broadly across higher education policy areas, with a particular focus on the changing student experience and the evolving nature of academic work. Her research also includes a focus on institutional performance and quality enhancement in higher education. She regularly provides advice to the sector on the implications of her research for national and institutional policy and practice.

Neil Lent is a Senior Research Associate in the Department of Educational Research at Lancaster University. He is currently working as the Research Director of an evaluation of the Quality Enhancement Framework for learning and teaching in Scottish Higher Education. His research interests derive from experience in higher education as an administrator and researcher, particularly higher education policy, change and evaluation.

Alan McCluskey has worked on change management in educational and industrial contexts, peer learning in research and policy-making and technology-assisted learning in both formal and informal education. Recently, at Fribourg University, he worked on methodology and evaluation in a number of international projects including the European Palette project aimed at facilitating and augmenting individual and organisational learning in communities of practice and P2V, an international project about valorisation and peer exchange in ICT policy-making in education. He is also a novelist and artist.

Ian McNay is Emeritus Professor of Higher Education and Management at the University of Greenwich. He has previously worked as a policy advisor, manager and academic in Scotland, England, Belgium and Catalunya. He has written extensively on research quality assessment and was a member of a sub-panel in the 2001 RAE in the UK. He has also acted as an assessor for the national Teaching Fellowship scheme and is senior external examiner for the Association of University Administrators. He edits *Research into Higher Education Abstracts*. Other research interests include policy analysis, strategic management of universities and culture and values within HEIs.

Joan Machell was a long standing member of CSET in the Department of Educational Research, Lancaster University, in which she had a leading role in some 20 evaluative research projects. In recent years she had worked extensively in Scotland, in which she had a distinguished career in policy evaluations within Higher Education. She died in March 2010 so her contribution to this book is published posthumously.

John M. Owen is Principal Fellow in the Centre for Program Evaluation at the University of Melbourne. He is interested in the dissemination and use of knowledge created through research and evaluation and other forms of social enquiry. In particular he is concerned with the design and conduct of studies to inform decision-making by individuals and groups. He also has a strong conceptual understanding of change theory, particularly how technical and social innovations are adopted and used within organisations and systems. A feature of his more recent activity has been to work with organisational leadership and management to improve the delivery of innovative programs, using the principle of strategic interactivity. This principle assumes that ongoing cooperation between evaluator and management increases the use of funded knowledge in decision-making. This principle been applied in long-term partnerships with national agencies such as the Asia Education Foundation, and Emergency Management Australia. He is a regular contributor to journals and at international evaluation conferences in Australia and overseas. His book *Program Evaluation: Forms and Approaches* provides an integrated framework to evaluation theory and practice that has had favourable reviews worldwide.

Marion L. Pearson is the Director of the Entry-to-Practice Program of the Faculty of Pharmaceutical Sciences at the University of British Columbia, Vancouver, Canada. For 27 years prior to accepting this appointment, she was an instructor of pharmacy practice. Marion is an award-winning teacher, with interests in teaching and assessing for outcomes, peer- and self-assessment, portfolio assessment, and curriculum evaluation. She has served on faculty curriculum review, teaching evaluation and development, and program evaluation committees, and is part of the portfolio assessment team for the university's SoTL Leadership Program. Marion is currently pursuing a PhD degree in Curriculum Studies, with a research focus on the scholarship of curriculum practice in higher education.

Michael Prosser is the Executive Director of the Centre for the Enhancement of Teaching and Learning in the University of Hong Kong. Before his present appointment he was Director of Research and Evaluation in the Higher Education Academy in the United Kingdom and before that Director of the Institute for Teaching and Learning in the University of Sydney in Australia. Michael's academic development and research has focused on how students learn in higher education, how teachers teach in higher education and the relationship between the two. He has extensive experience in developing and using student evaluation surveys for both quality assurance and quality enhancement. In 2005 he was elected as a life member of the Higher Education Research and Development Society of Australasia for distinguished contributions to teaching and research in higher education.

Christoph Rosenbusch Since 2007 Christoph Rosenbusch has worked as a research associate at the Centre for Quality Assurance and Development (ZQ) at Johannes Gutenberg-University in Mainz. He holds a Master's degree in social and communication science. In recent years he has been working on a range of evaluation and consulting projects for federal and regional ministries, foundations and higher education institutions. At the same time he is pursuing a PhD at the Department of Organizational Studies at Johannes Gutenberg-University, dealing with the evolution of organizational self-regulation and strategic management within German universities. His scientific interests currently lie in the fields of educational and organizational studies in general, especially focusing on organisational development within educational institutions.

Murray Saunders is the Director of the Centre for the Study of Education and Training, in the Department of Education at Lancaster University, UK. He holds a chair in the evaluation of education and work and had directed some 40 evaluations over a career of 30 years. He has been president of the European Evaluation Society and the UK Evaluation Society and was a founder member of the International Organisation for Cooperation in Evaluation. His interests are in the development of the theory and practice of evaluation and the evaluative research of policy and change.

Uwe Schmidt is a trained sociologist and Director of the Centre for Quality Assurance and Development (ZQ) at Johannes Gutenberg-University, Mainz. Today ZQ is one of the leading institutes in the field of quality assurance and development in educational institutions and programs in Germany. Most ZQ members work on a broad range of third-party funded projects for different clients and research funding institutions. Furthermore, ZQ functions as headquarters of the 'Hochschulevaluierungsverbund Südwest', a co-operation of 15 German higher education institutions. Among other things, Uwe Schmidt is deputy chairman of the German Society for Evaluation (DeGEval), member of the scientific steering committee of the Austrian Quality Agency (AQA) and vice-speaker of the interdisciplinary centre for educational research (ZBH) at Johannes Gutenberg-University. His main areas of interest lie in the fields of higher education research, evaluation studies, family sociology and sociological theory.

Alison Shreeve is currently Head of the School of Design, Craft and Visual Arts at Buckinghamshire New University. Between 2005 and 2010 she was the Director of Creative Learning in Practice at the Centre for Excellence in Teaching and Learning (CLIP CETL) at the University of the Arts London. The centre was one of 74 CETLs which were designed to raise the profile of teaching and learning in higher education. CLIP CETL developed knowledge and understanding of innovative and effective teaching in the creative arts and developed a wider awareness of these through development activities. A teacher in embroidered textiles for over 20 years, Alison has a Masters in Art Education and a PhD in Educational Research from Lancaster University. Research interests include the student and tutor experience in creative arts higher education. She is associate editor of the journal *Art, Design and Communication in Higher Education.*

Paul Trowler is Professor of Higher Education in the Department of Educational Research at Lancaster University, UK. His research interests include: planning and managing change in universities; the implementation of planned change particularly related to the enhancement of the curriculum, teaching, learning and assessment; higher education policy-making and environmental change; cultures in universities; academic 'tribes' and their disciplinary territories, and approaches to evaluation. Paul's most recent books are *Cultures and Change in Higher Education* (PalgraveMacmillan, 2008) and (edited, with Murray Saunders and Roni Bamber) *Enhancing Learning and Teaching in Higher Education: Theory, Cases, Practices* (Open University Press/SRHE, 2009). More details on Paul's work can be found at: http://www.lancs.ac.uk/staff/trowler/cv.html

Massimiliano Vaira is a researcher at University of Pavia where he teaches Sociology of Culture and Sociology of Education. He is a member of the Interdepartmental Centre of Studies and Researches on Higher Education Systems (CIRSIS) at the same university, which is part of the Italian Centre for Research on Universities and Higher Education Systems (UNIRES). He is a member of the Consortium of Higher Education Researchers (CHER) and of the scientific committee of the Italian Sociology Association –

Education section. Currently he is acting as a reviewer for a higher education journal. His main research interests are in higher education comparative analysis, reform policies and organisational change processes of systems and institutions.

Christine Winberg Professor is head of the Department of Academic Staff Development in the Fundani Centre for Higher Education Development at the Cape Peninsula University of Technology in Cape Town, South Africa. The Fundani Centre is responsible for enhancing teaching, learning, and educational research at the institution. Chris's work involves academic development and programme evaluation. She is also director of the Work-integrated Learning Research Unit, which is supported by the South African National Research Foundation. Her research focus is professional and vocational education and technical communication. Previously she lectured in applied linguistics and language education in South Africa and in Sweden. She is chairperson of the South African Association for Applied Linguistics.

1

Setting the scene: the four domains of evaluative practice in higher education

Murray Saunders

Introduction and approach

This book marks a departure from convention in that it seeks to dismantle traditional boundaries in approaches to evaluation. It does so in a sector that, ironically, is replete with many forms of evaluation, but has yet to become a focus for research into evaluative practices. This book is about how value and worth is attributed to what goes on in Higher Education (HE). It is about how society, through its governance structures, decides on what is worthwhile, how its agencies attribute value to its policy and programme interventions, how institutions decide on the quality and merit of its internal practices and how groups of stakeholders (teachers, researchers, students, external collaborators) decide on the value of what they are doing. It is not a book on the *evaluation of* HE but on *evaluative practice in* HE.

We have many single accounts of evaluations of HE policy, programme interventions, inspectorial and quality practices, but this book's focus is the range of practices involved in the attribution of value wherever it may occur. It conceptualises, theorises, and gives empirical examples of evaluative practices across the HE sector in both the UK and, comparatively, in diverse international contexts. The book argues for a specific position on evaluative practice as embedded in particular academic contexts.

The position taken here is that the idea of evaluation needs to be recast. Evaluation theory has a history of introspection (common in areas of social activity striving to position themselves with a distinctive disciplinary identity or professional status) that has resulted in a preoccupation with 'approach' and a plethora of evaluative 'studies' i.e. of programmes, policies and interventions. It is unusual to focus on evaluation practice as an object of study outside the painstaking exposition of approach in the context of a report on an evaluation or a theoretical, ethical or procedural justification for a particular stance. The preoccupation with demarcations and identity can be a distraction. What we are interested in is constructing a representation of evaluation as a type of social behaviour using a generic model of evaluative practice. This requires two steps. The first is to be clear about what we mean by 'practice'; the second is to be clear about what we mean by 'evaluative'.

What we mean by 'practice'

We have adopted the perspective that depicting and understanding what goes on in social domains like HE requires an operational definition of social practice. This perspective denotes a concern with activity, with behaviour, with what people do, what they value and what meanings they ascribe either singly, in groups, in institutions through their systems, or nationally through national managing structures. We are not interested in abstract or a priori discussions about theoretical prescription or turf wars on epistemology. To that extent our approach is grounded in whatever it is that people do in the name of value attribution or evaluation. So, how do we depict or understand 'what people do'? At its core, what people do is a social phenomenon, multi-hued of course, but we consider it to have discernable characteristics. What people do then can be termed 'practice', and all social life can be interpreted as consisting of a series or clusters of practices in different fields of activity, within families, friendships groups, at work and so on.

The idea of practice is a key aspect of sociocultural theory, and it takes as its unit of analysis social practice, instead of (for example) individual agency, individual cognition, or social structures. By social practice we mean the recurrent, usually unconsidered, sets of practices or 'constellations' that together constitute daily life (Huberman, 1993, talks about 'engrooved' practices). Individuals participate in practices, as 'carriers' of 'routinized ways of understanding, knowing how and desiring' (Reckwitz, 2002: 249–250). So, a social practice perspective leads us to direct our interest towards how a nexus of practices affects, for example, the way that evaluation is undertaken in a particular locale (Reckwitz, 2002: 258). Moreover, a social practice viewpoint alerts us to the danger of a rational-purposive understanding of change, one which assumes that people on the ground will act in 'logical' ways to achieve well-understood goals, or that managers and policy-makers will have clear and stable goals in mind and be able to identify steps towards achieving them. This 'hyperrationalised and intellectualised' (Reckwitz, 2002: 259) view of behaviour just does not stand up to scrutiny in university contexts. In this book then, practices can be usefully conceptualised as sets or clusters of behaviours forming ways of 'thinking and doing' associated with undertaking evaluative activity, this includes the rooted identities and patterns of behaviour that characterise shape and constrain understanding of evaluative practice. As cultural phenomena, practices can be defined as:

> a routinized type of behaviour which consists of several elements, interconnected to one another: forms of bodily activities, forms of mental activities, 'things' and their use, a background knowledge in the form of

> understanding, know-how, states of emotion and motivational knowledge ... [A] practice represents a pattern which can be filled out with a multitude of single and often unique actions reproducing the practice ... The single individual – as a bodily and mental agent – then acts as the 'carrier' of a practice – and, in fact, of many different practices which need not be coordinated with one another.
>
> (Reckwitz, 2002: 249–250)

So, the social practice perspective of sociocultural theory sets into the foreground social practices and focuses on the way practice itself, in whatever domain, becomes an object of scrutiny. This perspective integrates a number of theories: those that explore professional learning processes (see Eraut, 2000; Schön, 1991), those that develop the idea of practice itself (Giddens, 1976; Lave and Wenger, 1991; Wenger, 1998 and 2000), along with the concept of the knowledge resources (formal, explicit and technical, on the one hand, informal, tacit, social, cultural and discursive on the other) that are produced and accessed, metaphorically as 'rules' (Blackler, 1995; Bereiter and Scardamalia, 1993).

Practices are inherently social and evolving. They are nested in cultures that form a major part of the intellectual, moral and material resources on which the practices themselves depend: cultures and practices constitute one another – they are not separable. Constellations and clusters of practices are bound together by social groupings, which are sometimes called communities of practice, sometimes called activity systems. We are able, however, to depict social life as constellations of practices within particular domains and at the same time, cross cut by horizontal and vertical considerations associated with distributions of power and resources, gender, ethnicity, identity/biography and place. The focus of this book is the constellation of practices associated with HE and further, the constellations of practices which are evaluative in nature.

What we mean by 'evaluative'

Working within this approach, we can see that evaluation is essentially a social practice. It is undertaken by people, within structures of power and resource allocation. We can say that evaluative practice is social practice bounded by the purpose, intention or function of attributing value or worth to individual, group, institutional or sectoral activity. In order to depict evaluative practice within a sector of activity like HE, we can discern four domains of practice:

- National/systemic
- Programmatic
- Institutional
- Self.

These domains are not definitive but will form the basis of the structure of this book, and are described below. But first, we will summarise what social practice theory means when linked to evaluation. Stern (2006: 293) has outlined the complexities of the widely shared view that evaluation is a 'practical craft' by identifying at least seven taken for granted assumptions about where the emphasis should be. These range from evaluation as technical practice, as judgement, as management, as polemical and as social practice. We are defining evaluation as clusters, or 'constellations', of practices which form a 'first order' definition of which the various manifestations in his formulation are expressions. As Stern points out, these expressions may well be very different in focus and not particularly consistent; it is these differences this book sets out to explore.

Social practice and evaluative practices within HE

The application of social practice theory to evaluation leads us to take a perspective which emphasises the way evaluative practices are embedded in specific HE contexts. Without this appreciation of the contextual factors which affect outcomes, then evaluative practices will be ineffective (Pawson and Tilley, 1997: 114). This means that in our perspective, evaluation,

- is characteristic of all social policy areas.
- involves dimensions of evaluative practice consisting of symbolic structures, particular orders of meaning in particular places, and has unintended effects.
- consists of practices which use implicit, tacit or unconscious knowledge as well as explicit knowledge.
- can have progressive enabling characteristics but are also perceived and experienced as controlling, as part of a 'surveillance' culture.

The approach depicts the growth in externally derived requirements for judgements about value in a domain (HE) that has traditionally been self-policing. This can be understood as a form of 'breakdown' of the tacit contract between professional groups and society (through its governance structures) that enabled them to police themselves through self-regulatory, internalised ethics, standards and frameworks for action. The way we 'value what we do' therefore has changed. We depict the growth of a complex set of evaluative practices that are embedded within the sector and are occupying an increasing amount of time, energy and new expertise. This book will examine these practices which are located within four domains.

How to describe the 'object' of this book in this way is not straightforward. The four domains constitute an analytical frame which could be used to represent evaluative practice in any social policy sector (health, criminal justice, social services etc.). We will present these four domains as a way of organising the focus for our contributors. It will show that depicting evaluative practice within HE in this way foregrounds the situated nature of the purposes and uses of evaluation highlighting strong differences in emphasis. The next section explains what these four domains are.

National systemic evaluative practice

This domain concerns the embedded practices associated with the way a national sector is regulated, controlled or managed within what has been called 'the evaluative State' (Neave, 1998). In many cases the practices that are associated with the way in which value is attributed across HE institutions within a nation state are inspectorial, standardised, associated with audit, externally imposed and used for comparative purposes or ranking. Within the UK, the Research Assessment Exercises (RAE, now called REF (Research Excellence Framework)), the Quality Assurance Agency (QAA) institutional reviews, the periodic reviews of departments, are all examples of this kind of systemic evaluative practice. For example, HEFCE (The Higher Education Funding Council for England) sanctions the QAA to coordinate the institutional audit processes of teaching quality which have a regulatory function:

> The mid-cycle follow up is an integral part of the overall institutional audit process and will support the same aims. It will serve as a short health check, for the institution and for QAA, on the institution's continuing management of academic standards and quality of provision, normally some three years after an institutional audit. It will be an opportunity to reflect upon developments made in the management of standards and quality within the institution since the previous institutional audit, and, in the context of the findings of that audit, for QAA to advise the institution of any matters that have the potential to be of particular interest to the team that conducts the institution's next audit.
> (QAA, 2009: 1)

Often, such audit processes will have unintended effects that create a backwash of influence on routine practice within institutions. All of the countries within the UK undertake equivalent processes, and all sectors within the UK have their equivalent systemic evaluative practices. In the UK school system, for example, all schools are subject to review and inspection by the Office for Standards in Education (OFSTED), while social work is reviewed by the Social Work Inspection Agency. Interestingly, these processes within the UK system operate within a structure which in many ways celebrates the semi-autonomous governance of UK HE institutions. Their power lies in the effect such processes have on the procurement of resources and the reputation on which institutions thrive. The example from the UK of the Research Assessment Exercise (RAE) has as its primary purpose the following:

> to produce quality profiles (see paragraph 30 and Annex A) for each submission of research activity made by institutions. The four higher education funding bodies intend to use the quality profiles to determine their grant for research to the institutions which they fund with effect

from 2009–10. Any HEI in the UK that is eligible to receive research funding from one of these bodies is eligible to participate.

Critiques of this orientation within the UK HE sector have centred, in particular, on the way in which assessments of research outputs distort the quality and nature of the research process as Walford (2000), for example, has suggested. He argues in the context of research in the Maths discipline that an RAE usually involves a double use of peer review in that a researcher has to submit publications, and these will in general have been peer reviewed. He notes that the review by the RAE panels is itself a peer review and argues that this exclusive reliance on peer review is a major defect of an RAE, for it is likely to lead to a systematic failure to recognise ground-breaking research. He reminds us that the study of the history of science shows that peer review can give results which are conservative and it often happens that researchers produce work which is judged at the time by their fellow researchers to be worthless, but which is later (sometimes much later) recognised to have been a major advance.

The RAE is one example of a systemic evaluation which is located, in this case, within UK HE. However, the book is not limited to the UK experience. It compares practice across cultures and experiences, to scan the range of practice at this domain. Cross-cutting themes involve degrees of control, regulation, autonomy and consensus within specific country systems.

Internationally most systemic domain evaluative practice functions in this way. In Australia, the THES reports a debate which is currently in full flood which is arguing over the pros and cons of peer versus metric-based systems of assessment of research quality. Peer review will continue to form a 'fundamental' element of Australia's national system for assessing the quality of university research. Kim Carr, the Innovation, Industry, Science and Research Minister, has launched a consultation on how to replace the now-defunct research quality framework. The new system will use metrics – measurements of research outputs, such as the number of times an academic's published research is cited by other scholars – but it will continue to incorporate an element of peer review. The move comes as the UK consults on plans to replace a peer review-based research assessment exercise with a system based largely on metrics for science subjects. Australia's new system, to be called Excellence in Research for Australia (ERA), will use 'metrics, including citation data, to help keep costs down'. In the USA, in contrast, sector wide systemic evaluative practice does not exist. Evaluative practices are solely undertaken at institutional levels and tend to be driven by issues associated with the HE market place, recruitment and fund raising.

Programmatic evaluative practice

This domain of evaluative practice is concerned with more familiar territory for most individuals in HE, in that it covers evaluative practices associated with policy or programme interventions of various kinds. Evaluative practices in the programmatic domain deal with policy and project interventions designed to change the emphasis of national processes and practice. An example is the evaluation of the Institute for Learning and Teaching in Higher Education (ILTHE) in the UK undertaken by the Teaching Quality Enhancement Committee (TQEC), chaired by Sir Ron Cooke (2003), or evaluation of the Enterprise in Higher Education initiative in the early 1990s.

More recent examples are the evaluation of the Scottish Enhancement Themes, undertaken by two of the editors of this book, or the Centres for Excellence in Teaching and Learning in England and Wales. What is clear is that evaluations in the programmatic domain are often used as policy tools (Bleiklie, 2002: 30), since the evaluation is normally trying to ascertain whether investment in the programme has been worthwhile. Evaluations of interventions, programmes or policies within HE are not uncommon, and the evaluation is normally justified by various types of theoretical position. An example of the approach adopted for a policy evaluation concerning the Scottish Enhancement strategy is embedded in the following extract:

> The overall approach to be taken and a provisional schedule of work are outlined below. It builds upon that taken in our previous evaluation of the SHEFC's (now SFC) Strategy for Quality Enhancement (2003–2006). In brief, it combines two powerful traditions of evaluation – Utilisation Focussed Evaluation and Theory Based Evaluation.
>
> Utilisation Focussed Evaluation takes seriously the needs of commissioners of evaluations and has a strong sense of the need for evaluations to have usability. It is responsive to needs that evolve and opens up multiple layers of communication. Its style is communicative yet independent. Theory Based Evaluation focuses on the connections between strategies and intentions. It has a firm basis in evidence but is open to unintended and unanticipated processes and outcomes. It helps to articulate the informal theories of change embedded in policy strategies and the adaptations and modifications which occur as a policy is created in practice. Theory based approaches also recognise the importance of a strong theoretical framework within which, in this case, change might be understood. Often such theories are derived from the social sciences and act as a way of proposal to evaluate an aspect of the Scottish Funding Council's programme of themed support in which changes in practice formed the core focus:
>
> We have built the evaluation on the idea of 'practice' as a key indicator of cultural change but we include in this idea, ways of thinking and writing about quality (we see this as a form of rhetorical practice) as well as day to day practices by stakeholders at different levels in the sector and systemic practices undertaken by institutions, departments or schools and course teams along with sector wide systems associated with the overall strategy.
>
> (Saunders et al., 2008)

It is interesting to note that programmatic evaluative practice, typified in the case above, can be informed by theory in different ways. It is a cliché to write there is 'nothing so practical as a good theory'. We suggest that theory can enter consideration at a very early moment in evaluation design. In other words, theories orientate evaluative practice in this programmatic domain and determine the kinds of claims that might be made on the basis of the evaluation.

A starting point concerns the theories of evaluation as inquiry embedded in an evaluation either explicitly or implicitly. This is usually connected to a theory of social science. There are some obvious parallels, for example, between the uses of random controlled trials or their variants in evaluation, for example, and a view of the social world that assumes there are social facts out there to be discovered and tabulated, i.e., a form of positivism. This is a method supported and practised by Carol Fitzgibbon (1998) in the UK. This can be contrasted to an approach developed by Saville Kushner (2000) who suggests that constructing the stories or narratives of key participants and personalising evaluation is an important approach in the evaluation process. Whatever our predilection, we have to make some choices about how we connect to the social and technical world in order to identify what counts as evidence of what.

A second, rather more methodologically neutral issue (in the sense of the form evidence or data might take) concerns theories of evaluation as a process, i.e., the way evaluations should be carried out (mainly theories about how evaluations connect with elements or stakeholders in an evaluation process). Examples of this might be evaluation theory that espouses the advantages of a goal free approach, in which according to Scriven (1991), programme intentions are not relevant but the experience of a programme is. Michael Patton's utilisation focused approach (1997) to evaluation is another, in which key elements of a design explicitly express the interests and intentions of the evaluation commissioners and programme designers. This is the approach adopted in the Scottish Enhancement strategy example offered above.

Third, Carol Weiss (1997) and Connell and Kubisch (1999) discuss the way we should be looking for the underlying theories about change that guide programme designs and it is this that should form the focus of our designs. This can be understood as programme logic. The idea of a bad change theory is an interesting one. There is a debate in the UK at the moment on whether or not a pilot project approach embodies a good or bad theory of change. On what basis should a good example of practice, embedded in the special circumstances of a pilot, create wider changes? We have heard it rather pithily expressed that 'the reality of a roll out from a pilot involves the application of fewer and fewer resources to more and more resistance'. The challenges associated with scaling up are many.

The fourth way in which theory has a presence in evaluation, especially programmatic evaluation, is through social theory of a more general kind. These are theories which provide explanatory frameworks for evaluation that can structure our effort, suggest what kind of data is useful and, in our view, enhance the chance of the evaluation making a contribution to positive developments.

Evaluative work based in the Centre for the Study of Education and Training (CSET) in the Department of Educational Research at Lancaster University over the last 15 years for example, and continued in HERE@ LANCASTER, in the same department, is influenced by social practice theory and is consistent with the approach advocated in this book. As we note above, it is an approach that emphasises the situated activities and experiences of the stakeholders who are involved in or affected by the programme.

These stakeholder activities and experiences should form the centre of an evaluation and will yield the resources for judgement about value and worth. It also does justice to the diversity of experience and the voices of all those in the programme's orbit. We can illustrate this by reference to a metaphor embodying implementation theory called the 'implementation staircase'. The staircase metaphor is intended to capture the idea that the programme's messages are understood and acted upon divergently by stakeholders as the programme's message goes down and up the staircase of implementation. We understand the project implementation process as highly adaptive and practice-based. This conceptual framework emphasises the way in which policy messages are adapted and modified through the process of enactment. It is also important to understand the way in which policy messages are transmitted through a system and are modified and adapted as they move from one group of participating stakeholders to another (see Saunders et al., 2004).

Stakeholders occupying steps on the implementation staircase are both recipients and agents of policy and through this process the project message will undergo adaptation and be understood very differently according to the unique and situated experience of each stakeholding group. Crucially, it is their interpretation of policy priorities, emphases and embodiments that are passed on to other stakeholders. There are two implications for evaluation here. First, policy should be depicted as multiple policies in action through the experiences of different stakeholders and second, policies and programmes are shifting and evolving entities depending on stakeholder experience of them. The metaphor of the implementation staircase is used to capture this process of policy implementation in which messages go both down and up the staircase but are modified and adapted as they go. An evaluation approach conceived within this understanding will necessarily evolve and take cognisance of the developing policy situation.

In many programme evaluations there is a preoccupation with impact. There are technical, practical and methodological difficulties in being able to isolate a line of determination between a particular intervention or programme and a change in practice at the level of an individual teacher or the enhanced experience of a student, let alone an increase in learning. However, through tracer studies or trajectory studies it can be possible to provide indicative evidence of the effects/impacts of activities by following up on participants and observing/interviewing/looking at students' work etc.

back in the institutional setting. An important factor to take into account in this process is that impact can also be shaped by the complex and differing culture of departments and disciplines within an HE institution or community. Widely varying departmental structures, ways of communicating, and dominant beliefs about the nature of their core work impede or assist the impact of an intervention.

We would look for evaluative practice at this level, then, that is informed by the trajectory of an intervention or a series of activities which are concerned with charting stakeholders' experiences of change. This involves looking for cases or examples and tracing their evolution from pre-adoption analyses through to adoption strategies and then on to implementation. The Trajectory Study is a common evaluative practice within this programmatic domain. It involves following the progress of an activity/intervention or cluster of activities from conception to end user experience. Trajectory studies can be accumulated over time and can be undertaken on clusters of activities. The technique involves the following process and chronology:

- What was the genesis of the activity? (Where did the idea come from, why was it selected?)
- What was the intervention strategy for the activity, and why was the method chosen? (How was it disseminated and introduced to the target group, e.g. seminar, newsletter, course, individual consultant, workshop, curricular materials etc.?)
- How was it received by the client group? (What was the quality of the intervention activity in terms of participant experience?)
- How was the activity reconstructed by the target group? (How did the target group reproduce ideas, practices, and ways of doing things etc. once back in their normal working environment?)
- What new practices are beginning to emerge which embody the ideas of the original activity and what is their orbit of influence? (Are new practices being routinely used by the target group and are they influencing a wider constituency? Have there been any institutional changes?)
- What is the experience of the end user (students) of these changed practices? (What is the quality of the learning experience, and the quality of assessed work?)

The Trajectory Study would consider the impact of the programme in terms of enabling outcomes (new things in place), process outcomes (new ways of doing things) and changes in student achievements and experience (improvements). We would argue that impact evaluations should identify both desirable and undesirable outcomes differentiated by stakeholders and should include intended, unintended and unanticipated outcomes, and evaluation design should be responsive to each. We stress this because evaluations of impact often underestimate the timescale involved in embedding changes in routine practices and it can be useful to link impact with the underlying theories which connect activities with intended outcomes.

There are of course a variety of practices associated with programme or policy evaluations along with a well established literature in this area. What this book seeks to do, however, is to ground the discussion in case studies of policy or programme evaluations in four different HE systems in order to foreground contemporary practice, identify contrasts and continuities of practice and draw out ways in which evaluative practices might be strengthened and improved.

Institutional evaluative practice

This domain is about the quality, review and reflexive systems in place within institutions, a phenomenon which grew in the UK from the early 1990s, with the onset of an era of formal quality evaluation (Sporn, 1999: 16), and an emphasis on accountability and the responsible use of public money (Tavenas, 2003: 50). These institutional evaluative systems have gained importance over time, as national auditing bodies have increasingly allowed institutional quality assurance processes to inform external audits. The debate about how to balance self-regulation and external evaluation has seen a number of stakeholders taking an interest in how universities evaluate the quality of their provision. Institutions themselves have been keen to show that their internal evaluative practices are effective, to avoid government intervention. While some academics have been 'co-opted' to carry out the evaluative work of quality assurance (Kogan and Hanney, 2000: 104), many others have been sceptical about the ethos and the processes of such evaluation:

> In much of the discussion of quality with respect to universities in recent decades, the external focus has predominantly been on the existence of quality assurance mechanisms, the financial management of the university and its research record. However, inside universities and among academics, there has been a strong scepticism about such a focus on quality assurance mechanisms, which are sometimes seen to be at the expense of a focus on the quality of student learning *per se.*
>
> (Bowden and Marton, 1998: 215)

Given the strong external steer on quality evaluation, institutional evaluative practices have tended to develop in line with external requirements, whilst also reflecting institutional philosophies and priorities. Unsurprisingly, the context of particular institutions and sections of the sector (e.g. their degree of managerialism) can be detected in how light or heavy the institution's review systems are. What is in no doubt, however, is that the quality of academic work is now a matter of public interest, and is open to scrutiny not only within the institution but by a number of external stakeholders. The profound impact of 'the evaluative university', to paraphrase Neave (1998), has been such that the balance of power in the academic community has changed – with more power to the administration and less to academics, and staffing/financial decisions made on the basis of evaluation data (Kogan,

2002: 88). The manner of evaluating that work is, clearly, of paramount importance to all involved.

At best, the evaluative processes used in making these assessments may be said to have at their heart an impulse to strengthen the practice of the institution by making judgements of worth through various types of reflexive practice. However, a set of justifications embedded in the following extract from a quality support office of a UK University is typical. The discourse is regulatory and concerned with standardisation and control (source remains confidential):

> The University is responsible for ensuring that all of its provision (i.e. programmes and contributory modules) is subject to regular and systematic monitoring and review in order to:
>
> - ensure equivalence of academic standards across all programmes offered by the University and compared with the rest of the sector
> - ensure an acceptable quality of student learning experience across all programmes offered by the University and compared with the rest of the sector
> - ensure equality of opportunity for a diverse range of learners
> - ensure that all programmes and contributory modules remain up-to-date and deliver on agreed learning outcomes, relevant in terms of content and pedagogy as referenced by sector standards and benchmarks, and can attract enough students
> - inform departmental, faculty and university priorities and strategies with respect to continued enhancement of the quality of the student learning experience.
>
> The University is responsible for ensuring that its approach to regular and systematic monitoring and review will satisfy regular scrutiny by the QAA through institutional audit.
>
> **Objectives**
>
> **1** be able to demonstrate critical self-reflection on the quality and standards of the programmes and modules for which they are responsible
> **2** take appropriate action to further enhance the quality of the student learning experience
> **3** review the extent to which programmes and modules still meet their intended learning outcomes, and revise either or both as appropriate
> **4** identify factors that are constraining the operation and development of their programmes and modules, and stimulate an appropriate response
> **5** identify effective practice and demonstrate strategies for sustaining and further disseminating this practice within and beyond the faculty.

It is possible to see this type of evaluative practice as using external quality standards while focusing on the individual teacher or teaching and learning experience. But the framework is not individually-led; it is compulsory, external and centrally devised. From the perspective of the staff member, this is received as an external evaluation of their practice and can be contrasted with the thrust of the practices associated with the domain of self-evaluative practice (next section), where bottom-up initiatives prevail. As Filippakou and Tapper (2008) have suggested, the use of top-down systems to improve or control or both is a contested area.

Evaluation within institutions relates to how well they are performing in teaching or research, but has permeated many other aspects of university life, such as in the human resource area. Probationary systems for staff are nothing new: they have been in place for decades, although to greater or lesser extents in different institutions. But other evaluations of staff have been added, such as appraisal, with assessment of whether targets have been met and whether quality of work has been acceptable. Such systems are now becoming a ubiquitous part of university life: pressures on senior management to make their institutions more accountable have fed down through the system to individual academics (Thorley, 1995: 59). In some senses this has happened organically, as systems have adapted to external expectations and demands, but there has also been a conscious attempt to challenge 'the culture of individualism' and increase 'professionalism', as expressed by Newby (1999: 269).

There is no shortage of topics which could be covered in this domain. Evaluations are being carried out on how well the institution is doing on diversity, disability and equality; on whether resources are well deployed, giving 'good value for money'; on how the university compares with its benchmark institutions; on whether staff roles reflect the appropriate salary grade; on the impact of staff training and development; on whether academic courses meet professional body accreditation criteria; on whether PhD students are being supported appropriately; on whether students are satisfied with learning technologies; on whether staff feel bullied at work etc. In this book we will focus on case examples which are central to the work of most academics: institutional and departmental quality review, course validation, and staff appraisal. We will explore the extent to which there are cross-cultural differences in practice with respect to the control, management and use of evaluations.

Self-evaluative practice

This domain offers examples of participatory or bottom-up developmental approaches to evaluation. These evaluations take place when practitioners, either individually or in groups, undertake evaluation to inform their own practice – although the evaluation may have sub-agendas, such as the wish to demonstrate that the individual merits reward and recognition. Such evaluations are sometimes mirrored in higher level systems. For example, individuals self-evaluate as reflective practitioners; this process has been recognised and adopted by HE accrediting bodies such as the UK Higher Educational Academy (HEA) or the Staff and Educational Development Association (SEDA), to whom individuals can submit their reflections in a specified format in order to gain professional accreditation. Practitioners also evaluate their practice in order to gather data on and improve their professional activities. Action research is commonly used in this way, when practitioners investigate a problem, plan and implement an innovation, and then evaluate its impact before restarting the cycle.

These are a range of activities that closely resemble evaluation and might legitimately be called a form of informal evaluation, remembering of course that informality does not preclude 'systematisation'. The position adopted in this book is that evaluation can take place within a set of social practices or within an organisation as part of a cultural orientation rather than an over-evaluated or performance ridden raft of controlling measures and systems. An interesting aspect of individually driven evaluation is that it is, by its nature, more likely to be rooted in academic values and norms than other, more top-down evaluative practices. The implication is that the results of such evaluations may be more readily accepted and taken on board by academics. Self-evaluation is perhaps seen at its best when individuals or groups work to build an evaluative culture that has as a central tenet a series of reflective practices. New knowledge is developed as people engage in a process of reflection related to real problems and issues in their own context. As Barab and Plucker (2002: 173) note, there may be little observable teaching in work situations, but a great deal of learning goes on. This learning, increase in knowledge, can be tacit and, therefore, difficult to evaluate. This does not mean that evaluation should be avoided, only that evaluative practices need to be sensitive to the complexity of all the factors involved. In fact, evaluating individual development is a challenge that, in our view, has not yet been met. For example, the efforts of the 'Rugby Team' in the UK[1] to work out how to assess the impact of training and development for researchers in universities have confirmed that it is simple to evaluate levels of satisfaction with courses (output) but extremely difficult to evaluate the extent to which such courses affect the way people think and work, and their contributions to the institution (outcomes). Nevertheless, the investigation is a valuable one for our growing understanding of the nature of reflective cultures and 'what works'.

The use of reflective practice as an evaluative tool is not new in educational and professional development circles in which Schön (1991) and Eraut (2000), for example, have identified the value of developing these processes in terms of organisational health, the adaptive capacity of organisations and in the development of professional identities that understand and are

[1] A UK-wide working group on how to assess the impact of efforts to develop researchers in universities.

sympathetic to collaborative and creative responses to change. That tacit learning is continuous within social practice is axiomatic. The attribution of value and worth through judgements on what is professionally useful, rewarding or what works is part of social practice that can form the basis of such a reflective culture. In our view these processes of judgement are profoundly evaluative – although we do not underestimate the problems associated with using fuzzy concepts. As Brookfield says (1995: 29–30) the reflective practitioner concept seems to mean 'all things to all people . . . a premature ultimate . . . [which] stops any critical debate dead in its tracks'. For this reason, our focus on evaluative practices is a useful one: we bring our theoretical perspective to bear on observable, practical situations, while keeping in mind these complex contextual considerations.

An interesting and evocative way of depicting such embedded evaluative practices is offered by the work of McCluskey et al. (2008) in which they are described as 'evaluative moments'. The phrase was coined to cover a set of widely found practices that retained some of the characteristics of evaluative practices as recognised by experts in evaluation, without necessarily being seen as evaluation by those carrying them out (or by those people who are professional evaluators) within a project environment. One of the essential characteristics of evaluation is that it generates new knowledge (or reveals or makes apparent existing or 'hidden' knowledge) that can be used by participants or others. In evaluative moments, this generation of knowledge may well not be seen explicitly as knowledge or learning by those undertaking it, just as they may not see it as evaluation. But it serves an evaluative purpose in a working situation and uses some of the tools and processes also used by evaluation. Evaluative moments generally entail a number of related phases that might include the negotiation of work to be done with colleagues concerned, the process design and the creation of tools, the collection or generation of data, the analysis and/or reorganisation of that data and the integration of this (new) knowledge in a process.

This territory is one in which there are unclear boundaries between institutional learning and evaluation, where evaluation can be embedded as a culture of reflection. This can be translated into some highly practical approaches, from relatively informal embedded evaluation through review meetings and reflection, to responsive approaches to quality enhancement and assurance, as well as ideas such as the learning organisation (see Easterby-Smith, Aráujo and Burgoyne, 1999; Senge, 1990). From the point of view of the individual academic, this could involve action research into a particular teaching issue. It could involve the preparation of a portfolio to evaluate and demonstrate their achievements, when they are seeking promotion. It could also relate to how they evaluate their own research project. For groups of academics, evaluative moments tend to occur when the work group (e.g. a course team) decides to review their curriculum, or one aspect of it, such as how they prepare Masters students for research projects, or how they run laboratories or studio teaching. The pressures on course teams and other work groups to be more 'efficient and effective' puts constant pressure on them to review and evaluate what they do, how they do it, and how they could do it better. This book will contribute to their understanding of helpful evaluative practices in these situations.

The structure and approach of this book

The book is divided into four sections, corresponding to the four domains described above:

- National/systemic evaluative practice
- Programmatic evaluative practice
- Institutional evaluative practice
- Self-evaluative practice.

Each section introduces the evaluative practice under consideration and contains cases of evaluative practice both in the UK and other countries. Each section is concluded by a synthesis of what the case studies can tell us about the nature, scope and significance of evaluative practice within that domain. In the final chapter of the book we provide an overview of what seems to us to be the particularly interesting differences and commonalities in the evaluative practices within the four domains. These analytical observations aim to help people across the sector, in different roles (such as managers, educational developers, academics and researchers) to see evaluative practice in a new light and manage their evaluative practices in a more informed way. Our hope is that they will find that, whatever the discipline and locus of their work, the combination of theory and empirical examples we offer will enlighten their evaluative efforts.

In order to help orientate and cohere the book, we will borrow the categories in the RUFDATA framework. RUFDATA (Saunders, 2000) was originally an acronym for the procedural decisions in evaluation planning. We use it here to enable a depiction of a domain of evaluative practice within HE. They stand for the following elements:

- Reasons and purposes
- Uses
- Focus
- Data and evidence
- Audience
- Timing
- Agency.

RUFDATA captures evaluation as a series of knowledge-based practices. These knowledge-based practices form the resources of 'communities of practice', i.e. groups of practising evaluators. In essence, it involves a process of reflexive questioning during which key procedural dimensions of an evaluation are addressed leading to an accelerated induction to key aspects of evaluation design. It was initially designed to enable initial planning of an evaluation to help it 'get off the ground'. RUFDATA is the acronym given to questions that consolidate this reflexive process. To that extent, the approach is a 'meta-evaluative' tool.

In order to provide a practical framework to structure this book, we focus on aspects of evaluative practice that consists of problem solving, procedural characteristics and routine behaviour which might use a community of practice of evaluators as a resource. But, in what sense might an evaluation framework be 'practical', i.e. based on practices? In day-to-day usage, the idea of the 'practical' has a cluster of meanings: solving everyday problems, having an obvious utility or relevance, emphasis on the procedural rather than the theoretical and uses of a straightforward and accessible kind are all immediately recognisable. Giddens (1984) refers to practical consciousness; that is what someone might know about their work practices including the conditions of their own action, but cannot express 'discursively'. If Giddens is right, most work-based problem solving will involve practical consciousness. We should be trying to find ways of 'freeing' this resource for use by our contributors. However, knowledge, whether it is practical in the way we describe above, discursive or 'technical', has been described in different ways.

Reification is of particular interest in the context of this book in that it refers to the way in which processes and practices are consolidated into 'artefacts' or things. Wenger talks about experience becoming 'congealed' into 'points of focus around which the negotiation of meaning becomes organised' [Wenger 1998: 58]. A community of practice produces

> abstractions, tools, symbols, stories, terms and concepts that reify something of that practice in a congealed form. . . . with the term reification I mean to cover a wide range of processes that include making, designing, representing, naming, encoding and describing . . .
>
> [Wenger 1998: 59]

In this sense, RUFDATA is an example of reification derived from the consolidated practices of a group of evaluators providing an interrogatory 'tool' for use. In our adaptation of RUFDATA, each domain of evaluative practice can be analysed or presented by a consideration of categories within this frame. However, the RUFDATA framework is used loosely in this book. It is not applied as a structure for the individual contributions although some have used it. Its use has been more in the synthesising sections that bring together some key analytical points from the contributions within a particular domain. However, the lead editors for each section have been selective in their use of the RUFDATA categories, using those that appear to be particularly apt or thought provoking.

The book will use 16 case studies, organised into the analytical domains we have presented. They are authored so that they do not comply rigidly with a particular format. However, they all have a preoccupation with and focus on the depiction of recurrent practices which draw out the limits, possibilities and challenges of the evaluative practices embedded in HE.

2

The Higher Education policy context of evaluative practices

Paul Trowler

> . . . 1964 marked the end of the hands-off approach to university finance. The era of pushing a cheque through the letter-box and walking away was over. Governments and their funding agencies wanted increasingly first to knock on the door, then to open the door, then to peek inside, then to walk inside, then to observe what they saw, then to ask questions, then to expect answers, then to suggest changes and then to change the size of their cheques if the changes did not occur.
>
> (Wagner, 1995: 16)

Introduction

This chapter examines the policy context around the world in which Higher Education (HE) evaluations are framed. Clearly there are considerable differences country-by-country, nonetheless global policy trends can be identified, with local variations. The purpose here is to situate evaluation practices in the context of application, and to help illuminate the provenance, shape and purposes of these evaluations. In doing this the chapter will focus predominantly on system-level, or systemic, HE evaluations. We define this as follows (after Patton, 1997: 23):

> Systemic HE evaluation refers to the organised collection of information about the activities, characteristics, and outcomes of a specified field of practice (such as research or teaching) across a country's higher education institutions to make judgments about value, effectiveness or efficiency and to inform decisions.

The chapter begins by situating the discussion within the social practice theoretical lens discussed in Chapter 1. It then elaborates on a dominant sets of *ideas and practices* around HE and its role in society which serve to frame the policy-making context (the 'policy framework'). The chapter goes on to look at broad trends in the *content* of policy that can be identified around the world (the 'global policy ensemble') and moves from there to look at the range of *techniques* commonly used to actuate those pol-icies ('policy instruments'). The chapter then identifies the links to contemporary HE evaluative practices from this analysis of policy framework, ensemble and instruments, and considers what alternative practices are excluded or bracketed out. Finally the ways in which social practice theory can offer illumination on all this are considered, and the related underlying rationale for providing the case studies within different domains in the next four sections is explained.

The policy framework: new managerialism, new relationships, new subjectivities

Social practices are not simply behaviours, rather they include a constellation of features involving recurrent practices, emotions and sets of values, and so a policy framework represents a form of social practice. Reckwitz (2002: 249) defines practices as routinised types of behaviour which consist of several interconnected elements:

> forms of bodily activities, forms of mental activities, 'things' and their use, a background knowledge in the form of understanding, know-how, states of emotion and motivational knowledge. A practice – a way of cooking, of consuming, of working, of investigating, of taking care of oneself or of others, etc. – forms so to speak a 'block' whose existence necessarily depends on the existence and specific interconnectedness of these elements, and which cannot be reduced to any one of these single elements. . . .

Education policy and the processes involved in its creation, reception and implementation, represent a site of social practice. Mazzeo's (2001) useful article develops the concept of *policy frameworks* which are, in effect, shorthand for a specific configuration of social practices in the policy area. By that concept he means:

> institutionalized clusters of normative and causal ideas . . . in educational policy making. These idea structures . . . define the core principle or principles that animate state action, the legitimate aims served by intervention and the manner in which these ends are to be achieved.
>
> (Mazzeo, 2001: 367)

By the word 'institutionalized' Mazzeo appears to be saying that these 'more or less coherent' (p 374) clusters of ideas are hegemonic and embedded in the fabric of principles and practices in government and elsewhere. Social practices in general certainly do become reified into systems, ossified, and of course this also applies to practices associated with policy-making and implementation. Examples are easily seen in individual organisations, in national systems and even internationally. They become set in stone in organizational architectures – documentation, processes committee structures. More importantly however, the attribution of meaning, the knowledge resources particular practices depend upon and the sense made of such practices are part of a cultural field that can likewise become ossified. So, symbolic structures, particular orders of meaning in particular places, are very significant in conditioning practices.

Mazzeo suggests that policy frameworks are very broad in their influence. They both reflect and influence the way in which 'policy makers, professionals, and the public understand and act on a particular policy issue' (Mazzeo, 2001: 374). However, as we shall see below, from a social practice perspective it is quite unlikely that a policy framework would have such 'reach', and unlikely too that it would remain uncontested. So the concept of *policy framework* adopted here is more limited than that advanced by Mazzeo.

As Chapter 16 by Rob Cuthbert shows, the contemporary policy framework in HE (and indeed across public services generally) has been very strongly influenced by 'new managerialism' (or simply 'managerialism' – the 'new' is intended to distinguish it from early, more mechanistic Fordist, versions). This comprises a set of values and relationships which include a focus on outcomes, on high quality service delivery to clients, achieved effectively and efficiently. The roots of new managerialist values and beliefs lie primarily in New Right thinking (Pollitt, 1993: 49), particularly neo-liberalism with its emphasis on markets, competition and consumer choice. But the values and new sets of relationships draw on other sources such as management theorists, politicians of the left and the lived experiences of those in public sector organisations (Fairley and Patterson, 1995). Under new managerialist thinking as applied to universities, education and learning become commodified and the discourse of 'clients' and 'consumers', 'management', 'appraisal', 'accountability' and 'the market' becomes dominant. Relationships become low-trust, so that there is always a perceived need for surveillance and occasional intervention by central agencies such as (in the UK) the Quality Assurance Agency or the Higher Education Funding Councils. This was summed up by an interviewee in Lancaster's New Managerialism research project, a Head of Department who said:

> with it being a very, very, competitive university for survival of departments, for getting research funds, keeping up your [student] FTE's, if the department's not run properly then you're all in serious trouble . . . we are very much governed by league tables, by assessment exercises . . . in research or teaching.
>
> (HoD Science, pre-1992 university, quoted in Deem, 2004: 118)

There is a decline in the authority of professionals, 'de-legitimation' as postmodernist theory would describe it, so that decisions, practices and principles are always contestable. Frequently this process of de-legitimation is accelerated by moral panics over particular events or the unethical, illegal or incompetent actions of specific people or agencies which then inflate into a discourse of derision against a whole profession. This serves to undermine its authority and re-orient the locus of power into the hands of managers.

Operationally, new managerialism involves target-setting and the application of sanctions where targets are missed. There is a shift away from central bureaucracies controlling services to more localised decision-making and delivery, with devolved budgets but with local accountability to clients too, and more scope for feedback from them. While there is devolution of decision-making and budgets, accountability to the centre is also key, so the point of delivery becomes a point of pressure for those who work there as they attempt to meet the demands of those above them and the increasingly strident voice of their clients. Wagner's description at the head of this chapter is both entertaining and accurate as a description of the new managerialist approach. Government and its agencies do not step inside to re-arrange the furniture themselves. Rather they are the interior designers, deciding what the furniture should be and where it should sit, and who it should be provided for.

Meanwhile *strategic* capacities at the centre are strengthened so that priorities are set and targets aligned with them there. Whatever the current form of 'delivery' of educational services, it becomes provisionalised, with alternatives, such as private delivery or organisational restructuring always a possibility if performance is sub-optimal. Government and its agencies engineer competitiveness within and among providers, so that alternatives and options are created, the rationale being to give clients choice and to encourage efficiency and effectiveness.

Underneath these new managerialist values and relationships and the practices that embody them is an ideological position, a view of society and a very definite stance on priorities for resource allocation. And from that ideology flows a set of discursive repertoires which have the capacity to structure thinking and exclude alternatives. Deem and Brehony provide an example from their research:

> We talk about this as an educational business and we don't talk about courses in a sense, we talk about products which we have to sell to students and to industry. Now, that's a cultural shift . . . the days when you were just delivering to students and they liked it or not have gone. You're delivering to clients now. And you've got to deliver on time, to quality or walk away. And if they walk away there's no income and if there's no income there's no business. If there's no business, there's no job.
>
> (HoD, Applied Science, post-1992 university, quoted in Deem and Brehony, 2005: 229)

But, as I indicated above, we should not over-emphasise the taken-for-granted dominance of a single set of ideas, structures, practices or discourses. There are internal divisions, different understandings, competing ideologies and political positions as well as alternative sets of interests within government and between its agencies. So policy is the outcome of conflict and compromise as well as consensus and is not necessarily oriented to a clear set of coherent goals over time and in different areas. As Engestrom says of activity systems, (among which we can include activities associated with education policy):

> An activity system is not an homogeneous entity. To the contrary, it is composed of a multitude of often disparate elements, voices and viewpoints. This multiplicity can be understood in terms of historical layers. An activity system always contains sediments of earlier historical modes, as well as buds or shoots of its possible future. These sediments and buds – historically meaningful differences – are found in different components of the activity system, including the physical tools and mental models of the subjects. They are also found in the actions and object units of the activity.
>
> (Engestrom, 1993: 68)

This focus on disparate elements, on heterogeneity, contrasts markedly with the position of Lave and Wenger on the nature of social practices. They 'do not make conflicts of interests, ideology or power into central elements of their theory' (Arnseth, 2008: 299). Engestrom's description is closer to what we observe in educational policy: at both the national level and the levels below that what we see is a series of embedded layers and sets of meanings, sometimes consensual, but often competing and incommensurable, rather than one homogeneous set of understandings and practices.

This heterogeneity and the complexity of the picture is augmented by a nuanced understanding of individual subjectivities when considering the degree of consensus or conflict around specific policy frameworks. Patton (1997: 43) makes the point that 'people, not organisations, use evaluation information'. And people exist in socio-cultural contexts, though they also have particular personalities, proclivities and goals. The two are intertwined, as Lave and Wenger identify:

> the production, transformation, and change in the identities of persons, knowledgeable skill in practice, and communities of practice are realized in the lived-in world of engagement of everyday practice.
>
> (Lave and Wenger, 1991: 47)

For Lave and Wenger then, the lived-in-world of everyday activity is the key site for identity production for the enactment and re-creation of skill and knowing. In this 'the personal factor', as Patton calls it, is important, as is the network of practices that people exist in. Discourses and sets of ideas can and do structure thinking and rule out alternative ways of thinking about a policy area, but people are not necessarily 'captured by the discourse' (Trowler, 2001). Rather they can mobilise their own sets of interests, viewpoints and values into alternative discourses and responses. Policy located in a particular policy framework is not just accepted, but 'read' in an active, perhaps critical way, or at least can be. Rosemary Deem and her co-researchers in the New Managerialism project referred to above have shown how academic staff can be 'bi-lingual', moving in and out of dominant discourses according to context and need. That project found most university heads of department interviewed are able to draw on discursive resources rooted not only in new managerialist thinking but also those which flow from their disciplinary background as well as from an earlier humanist, collegial set of understandings of HE. These managers were largely unpersuaded by new managerialist thinking, yet were forced to operate its technologies: devolved budgets, sometimes robust staffing and other strategies, and the rest (Deem, 2004).

So, the policy picture is a complex one, and try as they might, governments find it hard to achieve 'joined up' policies because the 'coherence' that Mazzeo refers to is often rather limited. Despite this, taking a helicopter perspective, it is possible to identify a dominant policy framework in HE across large parts of the globe. And this framework has led to an identifiable set of policies in HE. Stephen Ball (2008) refers to this as 'the global policy ensemble'.

The global policy ensemble

Ball identifies a number of common educational policy directions across the world; a collection of generic policies which, he claims, have global currency. There has been a 'policy epidemic' (Levin, 1998) which has brought about 'new values, new relationships and new subjectivities' (Ball, 2008: 40) in education practices. Above, we identified these in terms of new managerialist ideology and practices. The HE policy ensemble which flows from that has the following broad features:

- A push from governments towards universities' 'third mission' activities, income-generating projects and research with and for industry, commerce and the public sector: what Slaughter and Rhoades (2004) refer to as 'academic capitalism'. There has been a parallel reduction in government funding for HE as the balance shifts in the direction of income generation from these activities.
- A policy emphasis on the purposes of HE oriented to business and commerce (sometimes referred to as 'the new vocationalism', Symes and Mcintyre, 2002), and the parallel displacement of their more 'liberal' missions of cultural development and student growth (Trow, 1992). Barnett (1997, 2000) refers to the 'slide to performativity' which involves not just a shift in the university curriculum towards operational competence but a fundamental change in what counts as useful knowledge, with consequent changes in discursive repertoires inside and outside universities.
- An increased emphasis on HE as a private good rather than a public good, and so a move towards making students pay more for it, as they are the prime beneficiaries.
- A push towards higher participation rates in HE with, at the same time, a reduction in the unit of resource to teach the increased numbers. The

rationale mobilised for this policy is the demands of the 'knowledge economy' for a highly skilled, flexible workforce.
- A move to equip the HE policy machine with more sensors to monitor processes and outcomes in universities, and so the growth of an 'audit culture'. Universities now exist in an environment where government and its machinery comprise the 'evaluative state' (Neave, 1998).
- A push for greater openness and accountability in HE so that clients have more information with which to make choices and to encourage greater competitiveness which will lead, in theory, to raised standards throughout the system.

Mandated provision of data to central agencies for the compilation of league tables and evaluative purposes has become the norm. This was summarised by the Quality Assurance Agency in 2006 in the UK when talking about institutional audit, their evaluation of institutional performance, which, they claim:

> balances the need for publicly credible, independent and rigorous scrutiny of institutions with the recognition that the institutions themselves are best placed to provide stakeholders with valid, reliable and up-to-date information about the academic standards of their awards and the quality of their educational provision. Institutional audit encourages institutions to be self-evaluative, and is therefore a process that, in itself, offers opportunities for enhancement of institutional management standards and quality.
>
> (QAA, 2006: 1)

However the costs of compliance to these requirements for audit data for universities are enormous, and there are frequent questions about the cost/benefit ratio in terms of their real versus claimed improvements in quality.

In the next section I give a few examples from the UK to illustrate each of these 6 characteristics. The sections that follow provide further case studies and examples from around the world, as well as describing situations where the global policy ensemble does not (yet) apply.

Characteristic 1: *the push to 'third mission' activities.* Here the push has been through a continual reduction in the unit of resource provided by the state. All UK universities have seen their pie charts showing sources of income change shape over the past decades, with more slices and a shrinking slice of pie representing government income. The 1997 Dearing Report (NCIHE, 1997) estimated that there had been a 40% reduction in state expenditure per student over the 20 year period 1976–1996, forcing universities to look elsewhere for income. Meanwhile criteria for success in the Research Assessment Exercise (see below) began to emphasise success in winning funding externally as well as the impact of research for users outside the traditional research community.

Characteristic 2: *the new vocationalism in HE.* In Scotland a number of the 'enhancement themes' which universities have been required by their funding council to address have been related to the 'world of work'. Some are very explicitly related to this, such as *employability*, but all of the themes have a significant dimension which relates to employment, skills or orientation of the curriculum to employers' needs. The account given under each of the four categories 'getting there', 'staying there', 'being there', 'moving on from there' illustrates this nicely (see http://www.enhancementthemes.ac.uk/themes/Guide/default.asp). In England there was initially encouragement and reward for introducing 'enterprise' into the curriculum with, for example, the well-funded 1987 Enterprise in Higher Education initiative. More recently though the Quality Assurance Agency has included criteria for industrial and commercial relevance in all aspects of its regulatory requirements.

Characteristic 3: *HE as a private good.* In the UK this is most clearly seen in the switch from provision of means-tested grants for HE for all students to their paying fees for study and being responsible for their own living expenses. University entrants in 1999 were the first to be unable to claim grants to cover some of their living costs but had to take out a student loan instead and pay up to £1,000 in fees in addition. Provision is different in each of the four countries of the UK, with England adopting the most clearly-defined version of this policy.

Characteristic 4: *increased participation rates.* The prime minister Tony Blair set a target in a speech to the 1999 Labour Party conference of 50% participation for 18–30 year olds by 2010. In fact by 2008 the figure in England had increased from 39.2% in 2000 to 39.8% (Gill, 2008), a less than impressive increase of 0.6% of that age group deciding to undertake university education. This failure illustrates the fact that policies are not self-contained but rather interact with each other. It is not surprising, given the introduction of university fees for students and the shifting of responsibility of living expenses onto them, described above, that HE became less attractive, particularly for those in older age groups than the 18-year-old entrant.

Characteristic 5: *evaluative 'sensors' for central control.* In the UK the Research Assessment Exercise (RAE) has evaluated the research in UK universities since 1986, with four assessment points since then (the last in 2008). As we write a new system, the Research Excellence Framework (REF), is proposed to replace it, the differences largely being in relation to the method of assessment with the REF more based on bibliometrics, at least in some disciplines. The outcomes of the RAE have very serious, direct and immediate consequences in relation to research funding for institutions. This is not true of the outcomes of Institutional Audit (of universities), which has been in place in England since 2002. Scotland diverged from the audit model at that point and set up its Enhancement-Led Institutional Review (ELIR), with at least rhetorically a different focus. Nonetheless universities take is seriously, as they do their position on league tables which come out of such exercises.

Characteristic 6: *openness and accountability.* This is most explicitly seen in the Scottish Quality Enhancement Framework (QEF), discussed in Chapter 13, which consists of a number of strands of which one is 'new approaches to public information'. This involves providing information appropriate to 'addressing the different needs of a range of stakeholders including students and employers' (QAA Scotland, 2009). The guidance, elaborated by the Scottish Funding Council (2004) requires universities to publish reports from institutional reviews, data on first destination and employment of its graduates, as well as information on the use made by institutions of external examiners' reports, as well as other data. With this greater access to information about the inner workings of universities and their performance has come the development of league tables by newspapers such as *The Times Higher* and *Guardian* as well as international tables of performance such as the Shanghai Jiao Tong University ranking. These have had very significant effects in 'disciplining' universities and altering social practices within them (Sauder and Espeland, 2009).

Describing these few examples of the global policy ensemble has involved also talking about how and by whom they have been implemented. The next section moves on to discuss in more detail the ways in which HE policies are put into practice, and how this relates to evaluative practices.

Policy instruments and evaluative practices

'Policy instruments' are mechanisms of change, the strategies by which policies and principles are realised in the form of changed practices and relationships. These have been categorised in a number of ways. Vedung (1998) famously talks about 'carrots', 'sticks' and 'sermons', by which he means instruments that employ the use of remuneration, deprivation of resources, coercion and intellectual and moral appeals. The RAE, described above, provides a clear example of the carrot and stick instruments, whereas the assessment of teaching quality within institutional audit has no resource implications and belongs in the 'sermons' category. Bleiklie (2002) develops a similar typology: *authority tools* (statements enabling, prohibiting or requiring actions, backed by the legitimate authority of government); *incentive tools* (which give tangible rewards or sanctions for compliance or non-compliance); *capacity tools* (providing resources for increased capacity among different groups); *symbolic or hortatory tools* (the equivalent of 'sermons', which seek to motivate actions through appeal to values); and *learning tools* (those which facilitate learning by target groups to guide and motivate their future actions).

All of these are applied in various ways but with different emphases to try to ensure outcomes consistent with the policies described above. But underpinning the policy ensemble is a particular stress on a set of evaluative practices and associated tools which are well suited to new managerialism. There is, says Ball, 'a new architecture of regulation' (2008: 41) underpinning the policy ensemble. As one might expect from the account above of new managerialism, this involves:

> a new mode of state control – a controlled decontrol, the use of contracts, targets and performance monitoring to 'steer' from a distance, rather

> than the use of traditional bureaucracies and administrative systems to deliver or micro-manage policy systems, such as education.
>
> (Ball, 2008: 41)

It is possible to identify a range of forces which have foregrounded *evaluation* as a policy instrument of the global policy ensemble described above. First, the enlargement of HE ('massification') has led to increasing public expenditure on the sector, despite the declining unit of resource, and so governments and their agencies have been keen to ensure value for money and the proper expenditure of tax-payers' money:

> When the HE system was small and largely uniform, and made a relatively small claim on public funds, reliance upon implicit, shared assumptions and informal networks and procedures [for quality assurance] may have been possible, and sufficient. But with the rapid expansion of numbers of students and institutions, the associated broadening of the purposes of HE, and the considerable increase in the amount of public money required, more methodical approaches have had to be employed.
>
> (QAA, 1998: 6–7)

The spread of new managerialist ideology and techniques has meant that evaluation of performance against *targets* has become ubiquitous in HE and other public sectors. The dominance of new right political thinking has foregrounded the purported interests of 'the informed consumer'. The provision of information to the public, usually in the form of comparative data and league tables has been one dimension of this and so evaluative practices have been employed to provide this type of information.

DuGay's (1996) description of new managerialism as operating 'controlled decontrol' explains the importance of evaluation as a policy instrument: it is used to monitor processes and outcomes at the periphery so that the centre can steer from a distance.

The following characteristics are notable about the specific evaluative practices employed as policy instruments in the new managerialist policy framework:

- they evaluate outcomes against explicit targets
- outcomes can be easily reducible to numbers, accessible to 'consumers' and incorporated into league tables
- they have a primary intended audience which is external to the institution being evaluated: *accountability* is a watchword
- they employ a discourse of ranking
- they result in reports that are normally in the form of long, written, 'deliverables' to funders
- they produce evaluation outcomes that have significant effects on practices, though these are sometimes not those intended by evaluation funders.

The British Research Assessment Exercise is an example of this type of practice. This is in marked contrast to many other areas of evaluation where there is sometimes little discernible change after the evaluation has taken place (Patton, 1997: 8). Though Hood (1986: 3) distinguishes between *detectors* and *effectors* (instruments governments use to acquire information and those through which they change practices and relationships), this distinction is unhelpful in the case of the RAE because the detectors are simultaneously effectors – that is, the act of acquiring information for evaluative purposes itself has an effect, intended or not.

These characteristics are most clearly seen when they are viewed in the sharp light and shadow cast by alternative ways of doing things. Doing this throws into relief the following questions about the evaluative process of information collection, analysis and reporting, which otherwise might be taken for granted (these questions draw on the RUFDATA framework of evaluation issues discussed in Chapter 1):

- what are the expressed purposes of the evaluation, and are there any latent purposes?
- who is empowered to conduct the evaluation?
- what kind of information is sought and then produced, and about what?
- who is the information for?
- how and to whom is the information presented?
- and underpinning all of the above – whose and what values are being expressed in the framing of the evaluation?

In a different kind of policy framework to the one described above, the answers to these questions would look quite different. For example in *appreciative inquiry* (Cooperrider and Srivastva, 1987) there is a stress on articulating positive images of future possibilities: the appreciative eye sees 'what is' rather than 'what is not', and looks for its value, not negative aspects. Adopting an appreciative approach to enquiry, be it action research or evaluation, is claimed to excite curiosity, stir feelings and provide inspiration, both for the enquirer and the subjects of enquiry. Though written in a somewhat mystical language, the point being made is pertinent to the effort to cast new managerialist evaluative practices in a sharp light:

> Appreciative inquiry is presented here as a mode of action-research that meets the criteria of science as spelled out in generative-theoretical terms. Going beyond questions of epistemology, appreciative inquiry has as its basis a metaphysical concern: it posits that social existence as such is a miracle that can never be fully comprehended. . . . Proceeding from this level of understanding we begin to explore the uniqueness of the appreciative mode. More than a method or technique, the appreciative mode of inquiry is a way of living with, being with, and directly participating in the varieties of social organization we are compelled to study. Serious consideration and reflection on the ultimate mystery of being engenders a reverence for life that draws the researcher to inquire

> beyond superficial appearances to deeper levels of the life-generating essentials and potentials of social existence. That is, the action-researcher is drawn to affirm, and thereby illuminate, the factors and forces involved in organizing that serve to nourish the human spirit. Thus [we seek to use appreciative inquiry] to enrich our conception of administrative behaviour by introducing a 'second dimension' of action-research that goes beyond merely a secularized problem-solving frame.
>
> (Cooperrider and Srivastva, 1987: 131)

Val Chapman discusses appreciative inquiry in more detail in Chapter 22. By contrast utilisation-focused evaluation, introduced in Chapter 1, is 'evaluation done for and with specific, intended primary users for specific, intended uses' (Patton, 1997: 23) and is somewhat less radical in its assumptions and intentions. Again however it offers a sharp contrast to new managerialist evaluative practices. Here the evaluative process is participative, engaging with communities, and evaluation is interactive, not just one-way, while the design of evaluations is adaptive to the situation of engagement. The notion of 'use' employed here is not just about identifying what is valuable and what is not, it is also potentially about changing notions of 'value' in fundamental ways.

Pawson and Tilley (1997) provide another alternative with their 'realistic evaluation', based on critical realism. They argue that positivist evaluation (of the sort usually seen in new managerialist systemic evaluations) cannot take into account the rich variety of contextual differences, and so they are very critical of it. Their mantra is that 'causal outcomes follow from mechanisms acting in contexts', and so they believe that the flow of causality and the effect of mechanisms (such as policy instruments) will be conditioned by contextual differences. In terms of evaluation the corollary of this is that evaluative methods also need to be responsive to context and that in determining appropriate methods the realist evaluator needs first to formulate hypotheses about potential configurations of context, mechanisms and outcomes in the area they are evaluating. A practical example of this is provided by Luckett's (2007) analysis of how the South African Higher Education Quality Committee's evaluative mechanisms were incommensurable with the post-apartheid transformation agenda, limiting the possibilities for effective change.

These alternative sets of evaluative practices point up several regular *absences* in new managerialist ones:

- any openness to unintended consequences of policies being evaluated, and to alternative viewpoints on them
- any active involvement of primary intended users in focusing evaluation questions
- any responsiveness in evaluation, in the planning stages and later, to the uses it is/will be put to, and evaluation design changes as feedback is received
- any mobilisation of an explicit theory of action in the conduct of evaluation or any developed understanding of the effects of the evaluation itself

- any joint planning of methods with intended users or responsiveness to changing circumstances
- any communication of initial conclusions with intended users, and feedback from them, as data analysis is conducted alongside, not after, data gathering
- any active engagement by evaluators with multiple users or accountability to audiences when their report is finalised
- any bias towards appreciation rather than deficit.

Conclusion: the policy context and the level of analysis

Seen from a social practice perspective it is relatively easy to identify a chain of linkage between the policy framework, the global policy ensemble and its associated policy instruments, including evaluative ones, through to changing social practices on the ground in universities. Practices in relation to both research and teaching have changed as a result of the changing sets of values, relationships and the characteristics described above. Motivational know-ledge, emotional responses, meanings, values, attitudes and ways of working in general have altered in quite fundamental ways, but not without opposition and not everywhere. Because individuals participate in practices, as *carriers* of 'routinized ways of understanding, knowing how and desiring' (Reckwitz, 2002: 249–250), academic identities have been challenged and changed, though again not without resistance and counter-tendencies. With regard to evaluative practices and evaluation tools in particular, these have both shaped and been shaped by the policy context, as social practice theory predicts would happen:

> the transparency of any technology always exists with respect to some purpose and is intricately tied to the cultural practice and social organization within which the technology is meant to function: It cannot be viewed as a feature of an artefact in itself but as a process that involves specific forms of participation, in which the technology fulfils a mediating function.
>
> (Lave and Wenger, 1991: 102)

Simply applying these tools has led to changed practices in research as, for example, the many studies of the effects of the Research Assessment Exercise in the UK have shown (McNay, 2003; Elton, 2002). But working through the details of these changed practices, the causal mechanisms and the exact nature of the linkages between national and even global policy frameworks and ensembles on the one hand and practices in universities is not easy, nor is it the same in every location. We recognise that *where* one looks for these has a strong influence on what one finds. As Sibeon notes (1988: 127) in his understated way, making the links between small-scale and large-scale processes, between micro-social and macro-social processes, 'is not the easiest of tasks'. Using an analytical lens which spans the micro, meso and macro levels of social life is one way to do this. In the next four sections we move from a focus first within the national systemic domain, and then on to the programmatic, institutional and self-evaluative domains of analysis. The case studies offered within each section illuminate the connections between practices within the different domains sketched in broad terms in these opening chapters.

Part One

National systemic evaluative practice: power and regulation

3

National systemic evaluative practice: power and regulation

Paul Trowler

> Practice theory . . . encourages a shifted self-understanding. It invites us to regard agents as carriers of routinized . . . complexes of bodily movements, of forms of interpreting, knowing how and wanting and of the usage of things. [It] does not seem out of place to assume that practice theory encourages us to regard the ethical problem as the question of creating and taking care of social routines, not as a question of the just, but of the 'good' life as it is expressed in certain body/understanding/things complexes.
>
> (Reckwitz, 2002: 259)

The case studies which follow in this section each examine practices of evaluation of Higher Education (HE) at the national level. Most of these are unproblematically 'systemic' in character, i.e. embedded in the HE system itself and part of the way the system is managed and regulated over time (for instance, national quality review systems). One example, though, Winberg's, presents a fascinating instance of the kind of one-off targeted national systemic evaluations of existing practice which sometimes happen. These tend to review HE practices which are seen as problematic, important or otherwise strategically necessary at the national level. They represent a kind of selective regulatory or 'assurance-inspired' approach to key areas of HE practice. So in this section we have case studies of evaluations which are systemic and embedded, an integrated part of the HE framework in a particular country, and one which is systemic, at the national level, but highly focused and time-delimited.

Evaluation at this level could be defined and described simply in terms of the rules in place for universities to be evaluated, and so the section would involve a description of different national systems of rules and procedures: 'canonical practice' (Brown and Duguid, 1991).

But from a social practice point of view, the more significant issue is not so much the level of prescription and regulation at the national level, the formal rules in place (though these of course set the scene) but rather the actual practices that occur at different levels of the system. These may be non-canonical in character, i.e. sets of practices which are situated in their context and developed at variance from formal procedures.

Within a national HE system there are numerous locales for such social practices to happen, and so there are many different social spaces in which recurrent practices with associated orders of meaning, sense-making and knowledge creation and use occur.

These socially constructive processes do happen in a confining context however, and not only in terms of formal regulation. Agency certainly is not supreme, individuals and groups are not free to decide their own futures and to 'construct' the world around them through the meanings they place on it. Clearly there are constraining forces, resource issues and forces which channel practices and meaning in particular directions while closing off other possibilities. For example, as I noted in the previous chapter, in many countries nowadays there is often a context of new managerialism and an associated 'new architecture of regulation' (Ball, 2008: 41) in circumstances where the state is undergoing a fiscal crisis. Increasing accountability is demanded from and performance indicators are identified for universities and lecturers in return for the public money that they are spending. Targets are set and sanctions are applied when they are not met. What is attributed value, at least formally, becomes increasingly linked to the measurable, and league tables set out the relative merits of institutions and courses according to these.

Meanwhile new managerialist ideology constructs particular understandings of 'value' in HE work, and so of the nature of evaluation. These understandings tend to be associated with performativity and with use value. They operate as structural conditions which constrain and direct practices on the ground, and evaluative practices too.

Despite such broad trends occurring widely, according to a social practice theoretical perspective there is nonetheless the local development and interpretation of meaning. And in a situation of 'supercomplexity' (Barnett, 2000) the attribution of value remains contested.

This is true too at the level of top policy-makers and funders. While there may be the appearance of a clear set of intentions in setting the regulatory and evaluative framework, we noted in Chapter 1 that social practice theory tells us to be wary of adopting a rational-purposive understanding of behaviour. As Reckwitz (2002) suggests, such assumptions involve 'hyperrationalised and intellectualised thinking'. We need to beware reification of policy and policy-makers: the policy process at the top level is a human one too, enacted by real people engaged in political process and subject to the same fallibilities, confusion and fuzzy thinking as everyone else. So, at upper levels there will be fuzziness, conflict, negotiation and the attempt to accommodate competing or alternative sets of understandings and intentions as regulatory and evaluative frameworks are developed.

A significant set of questions, then, for the top level of national evaluation concerns policy-makers' practices, intentions and understandings, and the processes involved in the development and change of regulatory and evaluative frameworks. These questions are about the degree to which there is consensus among policy-makers, what ideological and political differences there are between them which will impact on the policy-making process, and how the policy formulation process itself works.

At a slightly lower level, that of the top team of universities themselves, the adoption of a social practice lens leads to questions about the reception and implementation of the systemic evaluation framework: how is it received and understood; how is it put into practice in different university settings. Context is very significant in this and even in a tightly regulated national system, social practice theory would lead us to the view that responses and actions will be contextually contingent, because of the different practice frameworks that are already in place.

We know, too, that the insertion of new tools into sites of social practice almost always results in contextually-specific ways of using those tools (because of the pre-existing practices there). But at the same time the tools bring about changes to those practices – both the tool itself and the way it is used as well as the broader range of practices around it are affected. So, the insertion of new regulatory and evaluative regimes will affect social practices locally in ways that were not necessarily foreseen. There will be unintended consequences, or 'backwash'.

To concretise this with an example: in the UK there is a considerable literature demonstrating that the development of the Research Assessment Exercise (RAE) and the evaluative tools it used had multiple effects on research and publication practices, on employment practices in universities and on less palpable areas such as the attribution of value to different types of research and research practices. Not all of these, by any means, were foreseen or wanted by policy-makers or those on the ground. Pressing the 'quality button' almost always leads to a series of unintended consequences as well as (in the best cases) those which were intended. Evaluative practices themselves become one of the practice clusters which exist at the systemic level, and engage with other clusters. They become a very significant element in the system of practices as a whole.

Finally, at the ground level of academics and their students, the social practices in place both affect and are affected by systemic evaluative practices. So, for example, in Scotland the 'Enhancement-Led Institutional Review' (ELIR) system was part of the new (in 2002) Quality Enhancement Framework there. This was designed to shift the regulation and evaluative regime to give institutions more autonomy in defining and measuring 'quality' as well as marking a shift from assurance to enhancement. Yet the signs and symbols of the ELIR system, with a team in suits descending on the university for their evaluative visit, had the look and feel of the previous audit regime. To those on the ground, the social practices they experienced were simply 'same old, same old'. And they often responded with cynicism to what they saw as the rhetoric of 'autonomy', 'enhancement' and the 'light touch'. For the teams themselves there remained the difficulty of breaking out of the engrooved social practices in relation to the institutional visits. These difficulties were compounded by the diversity of interpretation on what exactly the criteria of 'value' were that were being tested. Was the visit about the identification of waste, perhaps fraud, inefficient or wrong-headed practices? Or was it about offering assistance, identifying and spreading good practice? Indeed, behind all this was the charged, and highly interpretable, notion of 'The Scottish Way': a distinctively different approach to regulation and evaluation than that adopted in England. But of course this idea itself was not fixed or agreed. It had different and unpredicted interpretations and outcomes in different locales.

The four chapters in this section offer quite different but illuminative accounts of evaluative practices at the national level in different countries. Max Vaira's chapter shows how the Italian system has followed the global trend towards imposing evaluative frameworks on HE: before 1993 there had been no such framework. Yet in this account these evaluative practices have little or no effect on practices on the ground: their function is ceremonial, ritualistic. Mike Prosser, discussing national evaluations based on student surveys in Australia and the United States, offers a warning note about the interpretation of survey results and any initiatives to change practices on the ground based upon a simplistic understanding of what they have to tell us. We should read the data with care, he suggests: a facile reading 'may actually be counterproductive to improving student learning experiences'. Perhaps Italy is fortunate, then, to have not jumped to using evaluation results to change practices and could learn from these early adopters. Ian McNay meanwhile discusses another set of problems around the conversion of evaluation results into changed practices as it has emerged in the UK. Here there was 'struggle' in a number of senses, but primarily a Hobbesian struggle of each against all to reap the most rewards from the evaluative and resource distribution environment constructed through the Research Assessment Exercise. This led to the kinds of unintended and often deleterious outcomes that I alluded to above. Again, Italy may be wise to wait, look and learn from primary adopters in this field too. Finally, Chris Winberg's account of the evaluation of postgraduate studies in South Africa illustrates well the health warning sounded above about not reifying policy-makers' intentions: she identifies the 'conceptual confusion in policies and programmes that link the creation of a high skills economy to the production of postgraduate outputs'. This is the big elephant in the room: the lack of alignment across relevant social institutions. Without greater clarity about concepts and intentions, and alignment of practices to address them, the value of evaluative practices in terms of improving practices at ground level is always going to be limited. Winberg identifies in her detailed analysis the kind of policy paradox that, sadly, is found in many countries – this is not just an *African* elephant.

The following four chapters, then, raise some broad questions at the national systemic level:

- How do evaluative practices in a national context interact with the practices found on the ground in universities and classrooms, and what are the drivers for engagement between the two? How are evaluative data received, understood and interpreted in different contexts? How well do discursive repertoires and sets of meanings travel between different groups involved, in one way or another, in evaluation?

- Where does power lie and how does it condition the different aspects of evaluative practices? For example how are the choices about the focus of evaluations made?
- To what extent is there really an 'HE system': are there in reality more often multiple systems in place in individual countries?

In Chapter 8 I will analyse the detail of the case studies to address the issues these questions raise.

4

Evaluation as ceremony in the Italian university system

Massimiliano Vaira

Evaluation policies, structures and practices in the Italian university system have been in place since early '90s as part of HE system's reform policies in line with the general trend toward the so-called 'evaluative state' (Neave, 1998). After a brief historical account of how evaluation policy and infrastructure developed in Italy, the chapter deals with how the evaluation of universities' performance works, in particular regarding research and teaching and their links with funding. This discussion highlights the largely ceremonial nature of evaluation practices in that country. By this I mean that while the evaluation infrastructure and activities are instituted and operate at the formal level, at the operational one they have almost no real consequences, creating a structural decoupling between the two levels (Meyer and Rowan, 1977). Evaluation practice and activities are thus reduced to the status of ritual and ceremony that is a formalistic accomplishment of formal rules with few concrete effects on the evaluated objects.

A brief history of university system evaluation in Italy

University system evaluation policies, structures and practices are quite a novelty in the Italian system. Until 1993 the question of the evaluation of Higher Education (HE) was completely absent in political debate. The issue came onto the agenda only after a major structural reform between 1989 and 1991 which introduced university autonomy and so led people to ask questions about quality and effectiveness.

This doesn't mean that there was no evaluation infrastructure prior to that time. It did exist but it was structured on two traditional pillars, namely the professional-based and the bureaucratic-based models (Vaira, 2007; 2008). The first was characterised by the strong control of evaluation and assessment criteria, practices and judgements by the professional community of academics which set the standards to evaluate activities and products. The second concerned the role of central administration in assessing the formal and procedural conformity of activities to a set of formally defined and mandatory bureaucratic standards. These two kinds of evaluation cohabited almost without conflict, since the formal and procedural evaluations of the centre didn't interfere with the professional-based one with a more local focus. This cohabitation reflected the double balkanization of Italian university system governance highlighted by Clark (1977: 67–74).

In 1993 a new financial law introduced a lump-sum budget for universities' funding, which meant they became more autonomous and responsible for the way they spent the allocated money. This, in turn, entailed a call for the evaluation of universities' activities aimed at assessing how institutions used their budgets. For this purpose in 1996 the Observatory for the Evaluation of the University System was instituted. This evaluative body was paralleled at the institutional level by Internal Evaluation Units whose task was – and still is – to gather the same, but more fine-grained, data at the local level and to provide them annually to the Observatory for further analysis.

From the second half of the 1990s a new round of reforms began (Luzzatto and Moscati, 2005; Vaira, 2003). These also concerned the infrastructure of evaluation and in particular led to the establishment of two new bodies: the Guiding Committee for Research Evaluation (CIVR) in 1998 and the National Committee for University System Evaluation (CNVSU), which replaced the Observatory, in 1999. Both bodies' tasks are to produce evaluations, guiding principles and data-based information to help the government in deciding funding allocation for research, teaching and the general functioning of the whole system and for individual institutions.

More recently, since 2006, a debate has been taking place at the national level on the HE evaluation system. A new policy and a new body for evaluation is now deemed to be needed in order to create a more comprehensive evaluative system. For this purpose the institution of a new national body has been proposed, to be called the National Agency for University and Research Evaluation (ANVUR). The new agency's tasks are expected to provide evaluation not only for universities' research, teaching and general functioning, but also to engage in academics' recruitment and career advancement issues. At the moment though the agency is still a project and it is not clear when it will be instituted or what its precise role will be.

In general these changes to and developments in evaluation have been not welcomed by the academic world, since they are seen as a threat both to academic freedom and to the formal equality of universities and of education they provide. Thus, evaluation in the Italian university system has been and is a highly contested issue in terms of principles, methods and goals, and these disputes have led to an evaluation system and set of outcomes which are only partially developed.

Evaluation as ceremony

So in formal terms, while the Italian university system shares with other developed countries the presence of evaluation infrastructures and activities, this doesn't mean that evaluative agencies and their activities produce the expected outcomes for which they were designed. Indeed, I argue that evaluation is working more on a formal and ceremonial level than on a concretely operational one. In other words, there is a structural decoupling between the formal structure of evaluation and its operational and practical implications (Meyer and Rowan, 1977). Let me go into a little more detail about the current system to substantiate this assertion.

As mentioned above, the 1993 law introduced the evaluation of both university system and individual institutions' performance. Currently the central body charged with this task is the CNVSU. Institutions' funding should be determined on the basis of the evaluation of seven quantitative indicators:

1 institutions' vital statistics;
2 the number of enrolled students;
3 academic and non-academic staff employed;
4 teachers/students ratio;
5 teaching performance measured by the number of exams passed annually by regular students;
6 the number of graduates in each academic year;
7 research potential (in terms of number of researchers) and funding attraction (Research Projects of National Interest and private sources).

The first four indicators are structural and not dependent on institutional performance (with the partial exception of indicator 2 concerning institutional attractiveness and students' mobility[1]) and thus they are linked to fixed costs. However the other three are performance-based. It is clear that the first two of these performance indicators (5 and 6, above) are rather weak, because institutions and in particular their teaching functions can be manipulated by making exams easier to pass and by grade inflation. There will naturally be a temptation to do this in order to maintain or increase the funding stream linked to these indicators. Apart from this critical aspect,

[1] It must be noted that the students' mobility in Italy is very limited, since families and students generally choose the close-to-home university. Mobility is hindered by different factors, the most important of them are: a) a familistic culture that entails that students prefer to stay at home (and parents too do prefer that they stay) instead of going to study in another town or region; b) the lack of accommodation offered by institutions to students (such accommodation is available for only 2% of enrolled students) and the high cost of private flats and room rental; c) a rather high uniformity in the programmes offered by institutions, limiting effective choice; d) the lack of any kind of formal or informal diversification, differentiation or stratification among institutions.

what is more important is that the portion of funding allocated on the basis of these indicators amounts to less than 5% of the total budget, while 75% is based on the structural indicators (numbers 1–4 above). This means that evaluation-based funding is playing an almost irrelevant role: for all practical purposes the evaluation of performance has no effects. Further, although CNVSU produces annual reports on several aspects and indicators of university system performance and functioning, none of them are used to guide the budget allocation, so that evaluation activities and information become ritualistic and ceremonial in character.

A more recent development in evaluation, or represented as such in the public discourse, took place in the second half of 2008, when the centre-right government decided to impose dramatic funding cuts amounting to 17% over four years (2009–2013) equal to €1500 million[2] (for 2010 the cut amounted to €190 million) without any kind of evaluation on which to base that decision, or decisions about where to make cuts. After strong opposition from the academic world the Higher Education Ministry issued a decree by which the cuts should be graduated by an evaluation of institutions' performance. Now a portion of the total funding, equal to 7% (about €500 million) of it, is allocated as a 'prize' to virtuous universities. This portion is distributed as an increase in their budget. The main indicator used to discern those institutions admitted to this portion is their budget quota used to pay personnel salaries, which should not be over 90%. Institutions over this quota are disqualified. It must be noted that this indicator concerns, at best, institutions' financial quality not performance quality. After this financial quality assessment the qualified institutions are ranked on the basis of research and teaching assessment results. The ranking is generated by a weighted formula considering teaching outcomes weighted for one third, and research productivity weighted for two-thirds. The 7% 'prize' is not spread evenly among qualifying institutions. Those with a lower salary spend receive more of it.

But there are three problems with this. First, indicators and formula have been continuously changed, creating a relevant degree of uncertainty for institutions. Second, and perhaps more importantly, is that research productivity is based on a 2004 assessment exercise which was not repeated (see below). As a result this indicator is time-limited and thus not trustworthy: recent years could have seen either improvement or decline for every institution. Third, the limit of 90% spent for personnel salaries doesn't assess people's work quality: in other words, an institution could be over the 90% threshold but its staff could be also highly productive and effective. In such a case the institution will be penalised despite its good performance. In sum,

[2] This cut has been set in 2008 financial law and is part of a larger strategy of cutbacks in almost all state expenditure. Interestingly enough, the underlying logic of this policy resembles closely the British one during Mrs. Thatcher's government in the early 1980s.

then, these recent developments mark a change in evaluation as it becomes more financially-oriented rather than based on productivity and quality, and it consequently plays a legitimising role by making funding cuts appear to be based on some meritocratic logic.

On the research side, CIVR undertook in 2003–4 the first Triennial Research Assessment exercise (VTR) which evaluated research output produced between 2001 and 2003. The results were published in 2006. The assessment logic closely resembled the pre-2008 English RAE, but unlike the latter the VTR gave more prominence to applied and interdisciplinary research and also to research undertaken by public and private organisations which applied to be assessed. The assessment exercise saw 102 participating organisations (including all 77 Italian universities), including more than 64,000 researchers and 17,000 research outputs assessed by almost 7,000 panellists, a quarter of whom were foreigners. In all it cost €3.5 million and aimed at identifying research quality levels throughout the Italian research system.

CIVR has responsibility for producing guidelines linking the assessment results to funding allocation on the basis of four main indicators: the quality of research; scientific productivity; capabilities in attracting and managing resources; and the research socio-economic benefits. Yet, the goal stated in different policy documents and by CNVSU of linking 30% of funding to the research assessment results has been completely ignored to date. The VTR results have not been used at all to allocate funding.

Further and more importantly, the 2003–4 exercise has been not repeated for the research outputs produced during the 2004–6 period. There are two main reasons for this. The first is political: in 2006 the new evaluation exercise should have been launched but the centre-left government's political weakness and litigiousness, and its subsequent fall in early 2008, made it unable to initiate the process. In addition it must be noted that the ministry at the time wanted to institute the new unified evaluation agency (ANVUR) and so the new exercise was postponed so that it could be managed by the new agency. Even more significant, the VTR results highlighted clear research quality and productivity differentials in the university system in terms of a divide between research-intensive and research-poor institutions. The fear among the disadvantaged academics (a relative majority) was that they and their institutions would get fewer resources as a result. A strong lobbying and opposition movement at political and ministerial levels was undertaken by those academics, backed by those who opposed any innovation in the university system. So, the VTR experience ended up being mere ceremony without any consequences. But, as often happens, the 'victory' of the opposition movement resulted in an unexpected outcome: the VTR 2003–4 results have been used as research quality indicators to redistribute the 7% quota discussed above. Given the time-limited feature mentioned, this is creating many more problems and adverse effects than if those results had been used in a proper way at the time and the new exercise had been launched.

To conclude this part, it must be noted that in March 2009 the ministry issued a decree to launch the new research assessment exercise, covering the period 2004–8. On the whole it follows the same criteria of the previous exercise, but introduces a clear distinction between active researchers (those who present four or more publications or applied research results), partially active researchers (those who present less than four research products) and non-active researchers (those who present no publications). Moreover departments will be ranked in term of their overall research productivity and its quality. The assessment exercise will be carried out by CIVR, since the new unified agency has not yet been instituted. We will see whether this exercise produces real consequences or again ends in a mere ceremony.

Conclusions

If evaluation is designed to ensure that public money is well-spent by universities, as well as to attribute value to what they do and what they could do for society and the economy, one cannot but conclude that in the Italian case it has not yet been able to achieve its goals. The account above demonstrates a growing detachment between the rhetoric and the reality of evaluation. It is largely ritualistic and ceremonial and has left Italian universities standing between a rock and hard place: budget reductions not based on any sound evaluative processes or results.

What Italian universities need is not continuous reform, changes and innovations in evaluation infrastructure and processes, but a set of evaluative practices that take concrete form and produce changed practices and improved results on the ground. The activities of the two evaluation bodies could be improved by learning from other systems' experiences, particularly what works and what doesn't. Many researchers and the institutions in which they work produce high quality teaching and research, but currently their efforts are not recognised or rewarded; on the contrary they are penalised and frustrated by ineffective evaluations and dramatic funding cuts. It is just a matter of responsible political concern, engagement and a decision to institute an evaluation system that values effective work.

5

Student 'satisfaction' or student 'experience': interpreting and acting on evaluation results

Michael Prosser

Introduction

Recent years have seen a growing interest in national surveys of student experiences of teaching and learning at the programme level. In Australia and the United Kingdom these surveys have been developed in response to Government calls for increased accountability: the Course Experience Questionnaire in Australia (Ramsden, 1991) and the National Survey of Students, 2005, in the UK. In the United States of America the National Survey of Student Engagement has been developed by the University of Indiana and used by a large number of universities for benchmarking purposes (Kuh, 2001). For a review of such instruments see Richardson (2005).

Probably the most common way of interpreting the results of such surveys is in terms of student satisfaction. Students make judgements about the quality of the teaching and the courses they receive. But such an interpretation is not particularly helpful in using the results to improve the students' actual experiences of learning. Indeed, interpreting the results as satisfaction ratings, and using them to change the way we teach and how we design our courses to improve the ratings, may actually be counterproductive to improving student learning experiences – and incidentally satisfaction ratings.

In this chapter I propose to outline my perspective, supported by literature and evidence, about productive ways of interpreting the results of such surveys from a student learning perspective (Prosser and Trigwell, 1999). Then I will briefly outline one institution's response to that perspective.

A perspective on interpreting results of student evaluation surveys

Over 30 years of research into the way students learn in Higher Education (HE) have shown that a much more productive way of interpreting such results is as indicators of students' experiences of the context in which their teaching and learning occurs. The way students experience their teaching is a complex interaction between their previous experiences of teaching and learning, their present life experiences, and the way we design and teach our courses (Prosser and Trigwell, 1999). That is, students on a course experience the same teaching and the same course, but they experience that course in different ways. Becoming aware of those differences, and trying to understand them, is the key to improving students' experiences of learning.

More specifically, Figure 5.1 shows a heuristic model in which much of the research from this perspective is summarised (Trigwell and Prosser, 1996).

The model suggests that there is little direct connection between the way teachers teach and design their courses and what students are learning – their learning outcomes. What they learn is a function substantially of how they approach their learning – so-called surface and deep approaches. Obviously student approaches to learning are more complex than what is captured in the surface/deep distinction, but it is a fundamental distinction. The difference between surface and deep learning is between a focus on

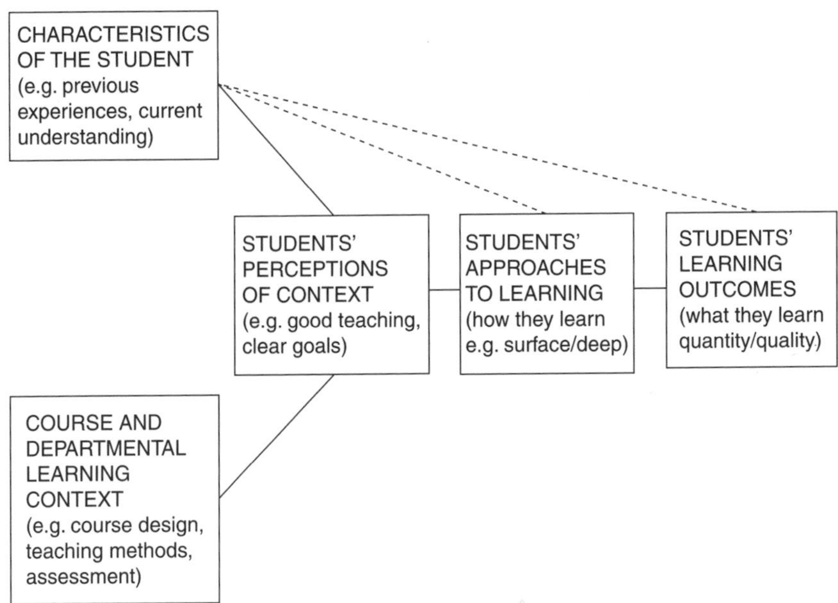

Figure 5.1 Students' experience of learning

short term reproduction (often to meet assessment requirements) and longer term engagement for understanding and application. The approach to learning in turn is not directly related to how teachers teach and design their courses but how their students experience and understand how the teacher teaches and designs their courses. These perceptions are a complex interaction of the students' prior experiences of teaching and learning and the way the course is taught and designed. This is why the focus of evaluation, and the interpretation of evaluation results, needs to be on the variation in the way individual students experience and understand teaching, not so much on the measure of central tendency – the mean.

The fundamental relationship between students' perceptions and approaches is born out in the factor analyses shown in Table 5.1. The table shows the results of some further analyses of a study conducted in Australia and reported in 2003 (Prosser et al., 2003) and another study conducted in Hong Kong and reported in 2009 (Webster et al., 2009). In the Australian study, 8,975 Australian university students responded to the Course Experience Questionnaire (Ramsden, 1991) and the Study Process Questionnaire (Biggs, 1987). The table shows remarkably similar results for both the Australian sample and the Hong Kong sample. It shows that deep approaches to study are associated with perceptions that the teaching is good (including feedback) and that the goals and assessment standards for the course are clear. A surface approach is associated with perceptions of too high a workload and assessment testing reproduction rather than understanding. That is, there is a systematic, coherent and reproducible structure relating perceptions and approaches.

The issue is then to ensure that our teaching and our courses are designed to afford deep approaches and high quality learning outcomes and then to ensure our students understand our teaching and our courses from this perspective. (Ramsden, 2002 and Biggs, 1999 address these issues in detail.)

Table 5.1 Factor analysis of Course Experience Questionnaire and the Study Process Questionnaire

Scale	*Hong Kong Factors*		*Australian Factor*	
	1	*2*	*1*	*2*
Good teaching (feedback)	0.76		0.80	
Clear goals and standards	0.67		0.67	
Appropriate workload		–0.54		–0.69
Appropriate assessment		–0.62		–0.65
Surface approach		0.73		0.81
Deep approach	0.53		0.73	

Note: Hong Kong n=2123; Australia n=8975; loadings less that 0.4 deleted

We can focus on changing our teaching and our courses, we can focus on helping our students to understand the way in which we teach and design our courses, or we can work on both. For example, one of the key outcomes of the National Student Survey was student perceptions of the lack of quality and quantity of feedback. Many students perceived that their feedback on assessment was inadequate. There are many ways to interpret this result. For example, it may be because students are not getting sufficient feedback or because they do not appreciate the feedback they are getting. We need to better understand why students have responded the way they have. To illustrate this; in science tutorials, they receive feedback in class on problem-solving strategies; in the humanities, feedback on how to present and structure arguments. Helping students to see this as feedback will be one way of addressing this problem. But in any event, interpreting the results as satisfaction ratings is not appropriate.

Nor should we use the results of such surveys to form league tables. We should focus more on the distribution of results – the proportions of respondents who agree and disagree with the survey statements – than on the mean scores, which may be totally meaningless in terms of improving student learning. We may need to better understand why some students are experiencing the teaching and the course more positively than other students.

We also need to read the open-ended comments carefully and perhaps conduct further focus group discussions to help us understand why our students have experienced their teaching and courses the way they have.

A further complication arises when the questionnaires survey student experiences of whole programmes of study rather than single units. Past surveys suggest that students' experiences of the whole may be less than the sum of its parts. Attempts to improve student experiences in their programmes as a whole often require broad cultural change at the department or faculty level, and the research on broad cultural change suggests that we should not be surprised if careful attempts to improve student learning experiences result in only small changes in indicators of those experiences. It is much easier to address student learning experiences in a single unit of study than in the programme as a whole.

So, interpreting the results of student evaluation questionnaires as ratings of satisfaction are unlikely to result in major improvements for the students. Instead we should use the results to help us better understand how our students are experiencing what we teach, and follow up particularly problematic aspects of their experience with focus groups and other forms of investigations. That is likely to be much more productive in improving those experiences – as well as students' overall satisfaction rating.

Practice

Having outlined my perspective, I wish to outline how one institution has used it at an institutional level to address the results of their National Student

Survey (Flint et al., 2009). The authors had drawn upon an earlier presentation of the arguments in this chapter (Prosser, 2005) to develop an institutional response to the Institution's NSS results. In outline:

> For quality enhancement purposes and following the Prosser (2005) analysis we wanted to go beyond the mean scores to a deeper, contextual understanding of why the institution had received the spread of scores it did. . . . **Our starting position acknowledged the necessity of placing the student voice at the centre of this analysis so that we could be sure that all actions we developed in response to the NSS results were the right actions: that they accurately addressed the real issues underpinning** [my emphasis] the responses students gave.
>
> (Flint et al., 2009: 608)

That is, they proposed not to take the results on face value but to try to understand why the students responded as they did.

Flint and her colleagues then set out to systematically investigate why students responded the way they had. They established a dialogue with the Students Union. They conducted extra surveys and focus groups discussion with students, further analysed the open ended response from the students on the NSS and surveyed subject and course leaders. Having collected all this evidence they then organised an institution-wide event bringing together 70 people from different areas of the institution and the Students Union to better understand the students' experiences and why they had responded the way they had to the NSS survey. The outcomes of the day were a series of institutional actions.

In conclusion, the authors state that 'the challenge ahead is to reconcile the articulated dual purpose of the survey – public accountability and informing future students' choices – with the third implicit aim that the survey be used with QE [quality enhancement] (Prosser, 2005). The focus needs to shift from simply improving scores to getting to the root of the issues raised.' (Flint et al., 2009: 617)

Conclusion

In this chapter I have tried to argue for a practice approach to addressing the results of evaluative surveys such as the Course Experience Questionnaire, the National Student Survey and National Survey of Student Engagement by better understanding the students experience underlying the results. The focus should be on the understanding of the experience, not on the results themselves. Such surveys provide indicators of students experience; they do not provide an understanding of those experiences. If we wish to use the results of such surveys to enhance students' learning experiences and outcomes, we should not use the results as indicators of satisfaction but of experience, and work towards understanding why students respond the way they do.

6

Research assessment: work in progress, or 'la lutta continua'

Ian McNay

National arrangements for research assessment have been subject to disputation and contestation almost since their inception (Taylor, 1989). The diversity of approaches adopted internationally suggests there is no common view on its purposes, nor agreement on processes or criteria (McNay, 2009). This case study deals mainly with the UK arrangements and the experiences and perceptions of a participant observer over nearly 20 years as an academic manager, a researcher, an assessor and an advisor.

The stated purpose of the early assessment exercises was simply 'to inform the allocation of research funds' administered by, successively, the UGC, the UFC and, after the Further and Higher Education Acts, 1992, the national funding councils. There was a naivety among its founders who were then surprised when it developed beyond a simple technicist exercise. The exercise was one manifestation of the 'value for money' agenda of the Thatcher governments and also reflected their mistrust of professionals and the autonomy they claimed on the basis of expertise. There was some justification for this: university academics were funded on an assumption that they did research as well as teaching, but the first two exercises showed that, for a considerable minority, there was no evident productivity. This marked the beginnings of the state as evaluative (Neave, 1998) for regulatory purposes (King, 2007): threshold compliance with a dual role expectation (research and teaching) seemed to be the aim. Little documentation was required and agreement from the universities was helped by a promise of increased funding for research.

Emphases changed with the coming of a unitary system in 1992 (polytechnics taking university titles) and a second phase of the exercise was initiated, moving from evaluative/productive to evaluative/qualitative, with increasing use as a policy instrument to promote institutional diversity. So, from baseline common compliance with a role specification, there was a move to research concentration as a strategy. The 1992 exercise involved all Higher Education (HE) institutions, giving ex-polytechnic and college staff their first access to systematic research funding. But submissions and funding allocation calculations were based round 'research active staff', not overall student numbers, where the less prestigious side of the binary line was clearly bigger (that may have influenced the shift in the equation). For the first time since the war some academics in the traditional universities – those not giving evidence of being research active – generated no funding. This led to an explosion in the quantity of published output, of productivity, but not necessarily to higher quality (Talib, 2000). Some outcomes were published as part works in successive issues of a journal, or even the same one, as people drip fed findings into the public domain. However, neither quality enhancement nor increase in outputs had been an objective – they were unexpected consequences within the initial naïve framework. Early evaluations (Williams, 1991; McNay, 1997) found agreement that research was better managed, but much less support for a claim that it was of better quality.

The new context set up a post-binary struggle. No extra funds were provided to take account of the much bigger exercise. That affected some units of assessment – Education, Business and Management, Art and Design – more than others. Some departments (previously unfunded) in the modern universities (ex-polytechnics) outperformed some in the traditional university sector. So, funds moved across the former binary line. In each succeeding exercise, possibly to counter that trend, and possibly as a result of 'network power' (Kahler, 2009) the threshold cut-off point for funding was raised. A top grade of 5* was added to facilitate discrimination and different funding levels among the very best. So, modern universities improved their submissions, but still gained little extra funding. One problem for those preparing submissions was that such decisions were not announced until after submissions had been made. The same was true of the ratio of quality grade allocated to the unit of funding awarded, which moved from a straight line graph to one weighted heavily towards the upper end, where traditional universities, with a much longer history of funding, were disproportionately represented. So, tactics for the game (Lucas, 2006) were devised in ignorance of the rules of funding, which increasingly favoured the elite.

That lack of clarity also applied, to some extent, even to the basic grading criteria. HE has tolerated ambiguity to create space for flexible interpretation of policy, but the context here was seen not as permissive but as punitive. This was particularly the view among staff in the newer entrants to the exercise who saw the ruling elite making changes to protect their own interests (Harley, 2002) and dominating membership of the panels that set the rules: some discipline areas where there were more students outside the traditional universities than inside had no representation on the related panel. Sharp and Coleman (2005) relate this to grades awarded, and, in my sub-panel experience, the influence of institutional status could affect decisions on submissions at the threshold between grades: one submission was below expectations but put above the line because of a long history and an assumption of underlying quality; one submitting for the first time was kept down because of the lack of such a record. One could argue for a reverse decision, where the newcomer is rewarded and encouraged for doing well despite lack of resource and the older department should have done better given its well-established base and previous funding.

There were also concerns about equity of treatment for some sub-disciplines. Harley (2002) records the preference for 'hard' economics/econometrics, and Marks (1995) shows the higher grades in psychology going to lab-based departments. The feedback from the 2001 panel in education urged more work on large scale, quantitative, long-term studies. This was outside the realms of realism for smaller emergent departments. Perhaps Veterinary Science took equity to an interesting length – for 2001, all six Units of Assessment (UoAs) were represented on the panel and all six were awarded Grade 5.

The quality grade was allocated on the basis of individual output, and of individual staff (as in, e.g. New Zealand) but was awarded to a 'unit of assessment'. One of the naïve assumptions in those early days appeared to be that teaching and research were conducted in the same organisational structures – discipline-based departments. The assessment of interdisciplinary work has been one abiding issue: many research teams crossed several disciplinary boundaries and drew on several departments. Staff and their outputs were, then, disaggregated into disciplines aligned to the panels, and assessed divorced from the context of the research – the project team. Since part of the assessment grade was context-related – assessing the quality of the research environment – this led to some creative accounting and in some cases exclusion of active researchers who were 'outliers' in the collective (Lucas, 2006) so as to present a misleading picture of coherence. That added to the basic problem of staff management faced by heads of department.

The grading criteria also encouraged exclusion. For a Grade 5*, there needed to be

> Quality that equates to attainable levels of international excellence in more than half of the research activity submitted and attainable levels of national excellence in the remainder.
>
> (RAE, 2001)

A Grade 5 required

> Quality that ***equates*** to attainable levels of international excellence in up to half of the research activity submitted and to attainable levels of national excellence in ***virtually*** all of the remainder.
>
> (RAE, 2001, my emphasis)

The two terms in bold lack precision, but it was the (implied) exactness (all of 'the remainder') of the 5* criteria that cost at least one unit a star when a very small number of items or staff included were deemed to fall below national excellence. That assumes that all four items for each individual were part of the grading, but the History panel decided to take account of only one, deemed the best, as an indication of the quality that could be attained, and with no penalty for including weaker work (McNay, 2003). There were similarly loose framings for other grades, so there was no consistency or equity within the 'rules' of the game. Staff managers inside institutions were then faced with making judgements on whom to submit: higher numbers to motivate staff by deeming them research active, or fewer numbers to include only those of higher quality and so make a higher rating more likely. The ignorance over the financial arithmetic, noted above, made this another element of the game played in the dark. I was twice involved in situations where the politics of personnel management may have over-ridden the politics both of image/reputation and of income management.

In one, a member of the directorate, before signing it off, added two people to the submission, when I had judged their output to be below national standard; in the second, soon after an internal merger, with attendant politics, there was a reluctance to be rigorous about inclusion/exclusion of people from the other partner. In both cases, a lower grade was achieved than might have been the case with different decisions. Had we known that a Grade 4 in 2001 would mean more than three times as much money per person as a 3a, rather than 1.5 times as in 1996, a different decision might have been taken and a more selective group of staff submitted. (Note: the ratio gradients were much flatter (fairer?) outside England.) The consequences were stark when funding was cut from 3a graded departments. So, our quality was maintained, but funding was cut – to zero. There was a certain bitterness, too, since internal decisions had been taken to top-slice funding from two schools that generated it from 1996 onwards, to fund development in others to reach a funded grade. None did: investment in weakness had not proven to be a sensible strategy, but since funding came to institutions and was not earmarked for the successful UoA, it allowed senior managers to use it for internally determined purposes – 'strategically'.

Such decisions also assume a common understanding of 'national' and 'international excellence', which there was not. As a sub-panel member in 2001, I sought a benchmark against familiar ratings – master's theses, for example – but got no clear guidance. In 2001, for History, national excellence included 'highly *competent* work within *existing* paradigms which does not necessarily alter interpretations' (HEFCE, 1999), whereas History of Art work of that grade was expected to make 'an intellectually substantial contribution to *new* knowledge and understanding and/or *original* thought' (HEFCE, 1999, my emphasis). So, which panel would any good manager submit to? For 2008, when I sought clarity from the HEFCE Director of Research on the meaning of 'internationally recognised', he could not help, and advised me to wait for the panel statements. They did not help either. Johnston (2008) is scathing about the variations in interpretation of 'world-leading', the top grade in 2008. Gradings were derived from judgements on originality, significance and rigour which were applied to all UoAs, but with different understandings, and with different weightings for output, context and indicators of esteem. He identifies three clusters – those based on degree of significance or impact; those which form a point of reference and those that shift paradigms. The three could be mapped on to a Venn diagram, but, Johnston asks, how many outputs in a five year period – from an individual or a unit – would you expect to shift paradigms in a discipline? Very few, he suggests; not the high percentage – 17 per cent – recorded in the 2008 results (HEFCE, 2008).

Those results gave more reason for friction among what Watson (2009) calls the HE 'gangs'. There had previously been a recommendation in a review of the exercise (Roberts, 2003) that the best researchers in lower graded units should be seconded to higher graded ones, probably never to return, like postgraduate students from developing countries sponsored to study in the USA. The 2008 results, on a profile basis, not a single grade average, showed that world-leading work – the new mantra – was widely distributed. Of 159 submitting institutions, 150 had at least one UoA with 5 per cent or more of its work at level 4. As Adams and Gurney (2010: 1) wryly note: 'it appears that the policy of selective funding, while leading to a fair [sic] degree of concentration of research funds, had not led to quite the concentration of research excellence that might have been expected'. That is hardly a resounding endorsement of twenty years of a policy in operation. The commitment of the funding council, HEFCE, to fund excellence wherever it was found resulted in a swing of funds away from the elite, redressing the trend of the previous decade. Pressure immediately came from the elitist/protectionist universities to require a minimum critical mass as a criterion of quality, so excluding from funding outstanding individuals or small departments, mainly in the modern universities (Corbyn, 2009), with 90 per cent of funding to go to about 25 institutions, mainly members of the Russell Group (the elite universities). In Wales, one institution – Cardiff – got over 60 per cent of funding in successive exercises. That was followed by pressure from the small but beautiful gang – the 1994 Group – to withdraw funding from PhD students where there were low numbers (Newman, 2010). The counter-pressure, from government representatives, and resisted by those elite groups, was to move 'impact' from meaning only influence within the academic community, with citation levels as an indicator, to affecting policies, practices, people's lives on a much wider canvas, and within a culture closer to the former polytechnics. In the end, the pendulum swung back, with an announcement in February 2010 that the funding gradient would be adjusted, again, to favour higher grades disproportionately.

There had been previous criticism, from quite powerful quarters (HoC, 2004; ESRC, 2004), of the failure to give enough esteem to work based on professional practice – what the Victorians called useful knowledge (*phrenesis*) or to apply findings to policy initiatives. Even when a major critique was produced relating to education among other professional domains (Furlong and Oancea, 2005), the panel refused to change its criteria. The HEFCE consultation then responded to this pressure by proposals to isolate impact, treating it as an endorsement to work deemed excellent under traditional criteria rather than as an essential criterion of excellence, and excluding representatives of research users from the main panels. For those who define their research agenda by reference to practice, and build in user involvement as part of initial project design, that was disappointing, but perhaps not unexpected. I have a vivid memory of a presentation by a director of research at a major pharmaceutical company who summed up the attitude of the academics to research user members as 'go and sit in the corner and we'll come back to you when we've made our decisions'. Lewis (2002) was scathing about the panel on social policy and social work, where the importance of research to better understand the professional context has recently been shown to be essential. The Academy of Management response to my survey for HEFCE urged a 'double discourse' with different dissemination for academics and professionals in the field (McNay, 1997). There is a widespread practice of planning and assessing research as a discrete activity, almost hermetically sealed, and with no relation to teaching or even enterprise and regional development (McNay, 2009), though some departments with high student numbers were closed as a result of the RAE grade and research capacity fell in some regions (Evidence Ltd, 2003). Not even the surplus from higher fees could save them.

We may now be entering a new phase in the role of the exercise, announced by Gordon Brown when he was Chancellor, pursued by Peter Mandelson within DBIS, the ministry responsible for universities, and then adopted by Vince Cable and David Willetts for the 2010 coalition government. Research is now a major element of competitive strategy in a global knowledge economy, so we have the evaluative/competitive state, where rankings in global league tables are important. Within national boundaries, this may again favour the modern universities, who, even before the impact debate, had been shown to have a better gearing ratio in generating supplementary research funding than the elite institutions with comfortable state funding (Adams, 2005). In the hard times to come, better added value of this kind may be a major plus factor in reputation with government funders.

The other battle over the next period will be about process and evidence, with two camps pitching their banners for continuing peer review by expert panels and others urging more use of quantitative measures, such as citation counts. This has generated a lot of heated debate, but the outcome is likely to be a blended/hybrid model (Michelson, 2006).

We have seen the struggle to introduce assessment, initially seen as reducing academic autonomy, though my work (McNay, 2007) suggests this is more about internal exercise of power and is limited in its effect: high graded researchers have enough capital to resist and those in low rated departments are given freedom to do almost anything . . . unpaid. There has been gang warfare as each of the mission groups exerts network power to influence and interpret policy to favour their agenda. Policy has changed as the place of research in the national agenda has changed, with university staff, who have long survived the vagaries of politics, seeking a favourable gloss on official documents, and trying to find a comfort zone of accommodation. Even within the academic discipline communities there has been a struggle for dominance in defining the boundaries and topography of a subject.

The discussion in this case study has raised questions about 'what is research for?' If quality is judged as 'fitness for purpose', any assessment exercise needs to be clear about the purpose of research. Meanwhile, in operational process terms, the struggle continues to get an exercise that satisfies more fully the criteria the RAE claims for itself (HEFCE, 1999):

- clarity of documentation
- consistency across academic areas
- continuity between exercises as far as possible
- credibility to those being assessed
- efficiency in the use of public funds
- neutrality over research approaches
- parity across different forms of output
- transparency.

This narrative suggests there is a way to go.

7

The elephant in the room: evaluating postgraduate education in South Africa

Christine Winberg

Introduction

The focus of this chapter is an evaluation of postgraduate education in South Africa that was commissioned by the South African Council on Higher Education and undertaken by the Centre for Research on Science and Technology at the University of Stellenbosch. The evaluation report is titled Postgraduate studies in South Africa: a statistical profile (South African Council on Higher Education (CHE), 2009a), and is a quantitative account of postgraduate education in South African Higher Education (HE) institutions.

There are 23 state-funded HEIs in South Africa (eleven 'traditional' universities, six 'comprehensive' universities, and six universities of technology). South African HE continues to be beleaguered by inequalities inherited from the apartheid past, when black South Africans were largely excluded from HE, particularly from research-based studies. Since the demise of apartheid, a cluster of policies and laws have been passed with the aim to normalise South African HE. These have included mergers (that to some extent do away with previously segregated institutions) and policies to promote the participation of black students in both undergraduate and postgraduate education.

The policies that promote postgraduate education place pressure on South African universities to become more internationally competitive, while at the same time requiring them to respond to local needs (Bunting, 2002). Policy directives to increase the amount of masters and doctoral graduates in the South African context are part of a specific 'high skills' development strategy supported by the South African government and its partners to 'overcome the historical imprint of a particular low skills regime' (South African Ministry of Education, 2001). HE institutions have, for the most part, been receptive to these policy directives, with each institution making efforts to increase masters and doctoral enrolments through a range of means such as fee waivers, offers of research fellowships and competitive scholarships (South African Council on Higher Education (CHE), 2009b).

The term 'high skills' was coined in the late 1980s in the United Kingdom by educational theorists who sought to explain the divergence and variability in the performance of the advanced economies. The key to this diversity, they argue, is the interrelationship of social, cultural and historical factors that underpin economic development; in addition, a combination of conditions is necessary if an economy is to achieve a 'high skill equilibrium' (Finegold and Soskice, 1988). Later theorists expanded on this work by developing what they call a 'political economy of skill formation' (Ashton and Green, 1996; Crouch et al., 1999; Brown, Green and Lauder, 2001). These writers argue that both skill formation and economic performance are socially constructed; they are experienced differently within social institutions such as universities or commercial enterprises and can be organised in divergent ways in different national contexts.

There has been renewed international interest in postgraduate education and its relationship to a high skills economy (European University Association, 2007). The importance afforded to postgraduate education in South Africa is informed by arguments around the development of a high skills economy, in particular the critical contribution of postgraduates to knowledge, innovation, national wealth and welfare (Kraak and Press, 2008). The policies driving HE in South Africa have in common a concern with postgraduate education, particularly doctoral education, as the basis for the production of high-level skills. Arguments that link postgraduate education with a high skills economy are reflected in the national funding framework for HE and in several of the new programmes launched by funding agencies and science councils (e.g., South African Department of Science and Technology, 2009; South African National Research Foundation, 2007). These documents make the assumption that there is a direct relationship between postgraduate education (particularly in the applied sciences, engineering and technology) and the development of a high skills economy.

Context: findings of the evaluation report

In this section, the findings of the evaluative report (CHE, 2009a) are summarised, using as sub-headings the main categories identified by the evaluation team.

Postgraduate enrolments

In the years immediately following the establishment of a democratic government in South Africa, the HE system experienced substantial growth as undergraduate enrolments almost doubled (from 385,700 in 1994 to 715,800 by 2005). First enrolments for masters degrees similarly grew after 1994, reaching a peak in 2003, and thereafter declining somewhat. Currently masters enrolments comprise 6% of total university enrolments, which is well below targets. In the case of doctoral enrolments, there was growth up to 2001 which thereafter levelled off. Doctoral enrolments currently make up only 1% of total university enrolments.

Graduation rates

Graduation rates for both masters and doctoral programmes remain small, with significant field differences. Overall, graduation has been highest for the social sciences (11.6%) and lowest in the applied sciences and engineering (6.2%).

'Pile-ups'

Many candidates remain enrolled for their degrees for longer than expected (or desirable), resulting in a 'pile-up' in the system. Nearly two out of five (37%) of all enrolled masters students, and three out of five (59%) of all enrolled doctoral students, are recurrent enrolments. The number of masters graduates as a proportion of total enrolments has remained the same (20%), but the situation for doctoral students has deteriorated from 14% in 2000 to 12% currently.

Completion rates: time to degree

Those masters students who do graduate (20% of masters candidates) take three years on average, and those doctoral candidates who graduate (12% of doctoral candidates) take approximately 4.5 years from enrolment to completion. These rates are comparable with those recorded in Europe, Australia and North America (UNESCO Institute for Statistics, 2008).

The burden of supervision

Due to increased enrolments and the 'pile up' effect, South African academics are increasingly burdened with an unrealistically high number of postgraduate students to supervise. The number of postgraduate students has doubled over the past 15 years, whilst the number of permanent academics has only increased by 40% over the same period. The average supervision load is seven masters postgraduate candidates. There are considerable disciplinary differences, with the burden of supervision in the social sciences estimated at nearly 12 students per supervisor. This is high by international standards (CHE, 2009b).

Participation rates

The participation rate refers to the number of masters and doctoral students (in first-enrolments and graduations) per 1,000 of the population of those aged between 25–34, and 35–44 years. Overall the rate of participation by masters students increased from 0.88 to 0.98 (per 1,000 of the age cohort 25–34) and for doctoral students from 0.12 to 0.15. South Africa has 0.05 doctoral degrees in science, engineering and technology (SET) fields per 1,000 of the 25–35 year old population. This compares unfavourably with developed nations.

Demographic shifts

There have been some increases in the number of black and female masters and doctoral enrolments and graduates, but the pile-up effect is more prevalent amongst female students and higher for black students at the masters level. No gender or race differences were found at the doctoral level. The number of white masters first-enrolments is substantially higher than that of any other race group in the 25–34 year age group, and this has continued to increase over time. Black first-enrolments have the lowest participation rate. The extent of the challenge is illustrated by the gap between white and black participation rates at the doctoral level (1.43 compared to 0.05). This means that whites in the age group 25–34 are 28 times more likely than their black counterparts to engage in and complete doctoral studies in South Africa.

Using the RUFDATA framework to analyse the postgraduate evaluation

In this section, the RUFDATA framework (see Chapter 1) is used as a tool to explore the nature of the evaluation practices in the report discussed above. I have changed the order of the categories, and have concentrated on the particular focus of the evaluation.

Agency

The evaluation was commissioned by the South African Council on Higher Education, a body formed to advise the ministerial Department of Higher Education and Training on a range of issues in HE. The evaluation was undertaken by the Centre for Research on Science and Technology which has considerable experience in conducting evaluations of HE policies, programmes and institutions. Commissioned by a statutory body of the Higher Education Ministry, the evaluation is strongly framed by the terms of the evaluation brief.

Reasons/purposes

A number of government programmes, support mechanisms, as well as locally and internationally funded capacity development initiatives have supported South African masters and doctoral graduates over the past fifteen years, and there was a need to evaluate the effectiveness of these policies and programmes. The evaluation was thus undertaken for reasons of accountability.

Timing

The evaluation was published in 2009, to coincide with the life-cycles of a cluster of policies and funding programmes that specifically promote post-graduate studies in the applied sciences, engineering and technology fields.

Uses

The evaluation was intended to provide the evidence to diagnose at least some aspects of the state of the production of postgraduates in the South African public HE system (CHE, 2009a). The report findings are thus intended for use by the ministerial department, HE managers, academic planners and others who would like to make the HE system more efficient.

Audience

The evaluation report was published in the Higher Education Monitor, an on-line publication of the Higher Education Ministry that produces several issues each year on the state of HE in South Africa; it is generally read by HE practitioners, funders, and government officials.

Data/evidence

The evaluation brief confined the researchers to a quantitative survey and statistical analysis of the postgraduate data captured by the Higher Education Management Information System. The statistical measurement of the amount and nature of postgraduate outputs enabled the evaluation team to assess the efficiency of the system, but did not allow for closer or more detailed analyses of postgraduate performance and practices.

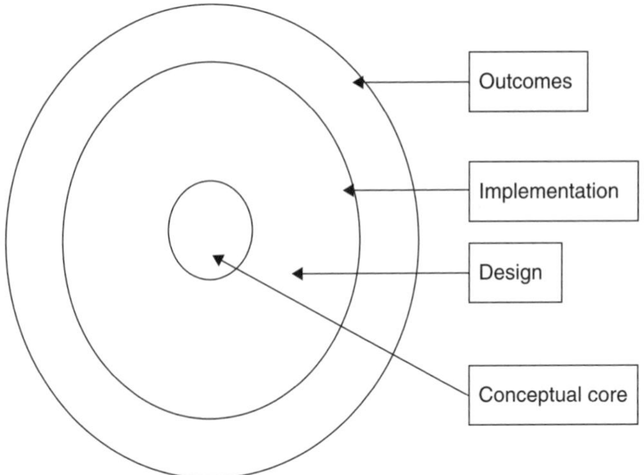

Figure 7.1 Levels of analysis in an evaluation

Focus

Evaluating programmes, policies and systems is a complex and multi-layered task. At least four levels of analysis can be distinguished in most evaluations: 1) an analysis of the conceptual core of the programme, 2) its design, 3) factors affecting its implementation, and 4) its outcomes (see Figure 7.1).

Because of the complexity of the objects of evaluation, a focus for the evaluation is needed. Evaluators might study a slice, through different components of the programme in order to understand the effect of conceptual clarity (or confusion) on design, how design issues affect implementation, and the cumulative effect of the inner layers on the programme's outcomes. In the postgraduate evaluation report discussed above, the evaluators were required to focus only on the outer layer, the outcomes, in this case, the number of postgraduates going into the system, getting stuck in the system, and emerging from the system. They were not required to address implementation issues, such as the selection of masters and doctoral candidates and their levels of preparation for postgraduate work (several studies (e.g., Manathunga, 2005) suggest that many PhD candidates are under-prepared for doctoral research); neither did the brief require the evaluators to consider the capacity of current academic staff to supervise masters or doctoral candidates: of the 41,383 academic staff employed in South African public HEIs in 2009, only 6,806 had doctoral degrees (16%) and 14,033 had masters degrees (34%) (CHE, 2009b). It should be pointed out that the distribution of highly qualified academics is uneven; the historically white traditional universities have considerably more staff with PhDs than comprehensive universities or universities of technology (CHE, 2009b).

In the preface to the report, the evaluators explain that the brief required a focus on the outcomes, and the evaluation was not intended to assess 'the effectiveness of any of [the] initiatives and policies', nor was it 'explicitly [required to] suggest the reasons for the success or failure of any policy' (CHE, 2009a). Yet the presence of assumptions about how postgraduate students are produced, and why South Africa might need them is, like an elephant in a room, difficult to ignore.

The elephant in the room

The high skills theorists argue that there are historically evolved relationships between educational systems, labour markets and the broader economy – and they place great emphasis on these interdependencies (Ashton and Green, 1996; Crouch et al., 1999; Brown, Green and Lauder, 2001). This is because the interactions between sectors are understood as constituting important social processes, and it is these interrelations that construct either a low skills or high skills equilibrium. Consequently, any attempt to change a low skills economy to a high skills one can only succeed if there is alignment across all social institutions. The introduction of a single reform (for example, the promotion of postgraduate education) without systemic changes in related socio-economic structures and processes is unlikely to affect the desired transition. The underpinning individualism and the implied power of individual agency in the South African policy documents avoid analysis of the cultural and social conditions of knowledge production and transfer.

The way forward

The challenges to developing the next generation of scientists and academics in South Africa cannot be addressed in the short term (Cloete and Galant, 2005). While policies and incentives have increased postgraduate enrolment, and have resulted in some progress towards gender and race parity, they have had practically no impact on the South African economy. Notwithstanding the importance of strengthening postgraduate studies in South African universities, just how valid are the policies and mechanisms that promote postgraduate education? In which ways can masters and doctoral graduates contribute to a high skills economy? And how useful is a high skills strategy in a developing country?

The quantitative data of the evaluation report provides a 'snapshot' of the general state of postgraduate education in South Africa; but the conceptual confusion in policies and programmes that link the creation of a high skill economy to the production of postgraduate outputs needs to be addressed. The critical voices that have been raised about the conceptual coherence of initiatives and policies intended to develop a high skills society in South Africa (Ashton, 2005; Kraak, 2004) are needed as a critical and constructive lens for analysing policies and practices – and locating these within a 'sociology and political economy of skills' (Ashton, 2005) that will enable researchers and planners to understand the trajectories of skills strategies over time as well as the importance of South Africa's history. These matters need to be understood before policy makers can begin to address the legacies of South Africa's past and plan constructively for its future.

8

Evaluative practices and outcomes: issues at the national level

Paul Trowler

> Evaluation findings can serve three primary purposes: rendering judgments, facilitating improvements, and/or generating knowledge . . . and some evaluations strive to incorporate all three. [B]ut in my experience one is likely to become the dominant motif and prevail as the primary purpose . . .
>
> (Patton, 1997: 65)

The case studies in this section have raised six interrelated issues for evaluation practices at the national level, each of which bears, directly or indirectly, upon the RUFDATA categorisation of approaching evaluation. These are:

Issues associated with the relationship between national evaluative practices and those on the ground: they revolve around RUFDATA's Audience for an evaluation and the Uses to which it is put. I want to raise issues about engagement with evaluation outcomes, about evaluation approaches in this regard and the motivations of those on the ground to engage. My comments here will address in particular the chapters by Prosser and Vaira.

Issues around interpretation of evaluative data: they address the D in RUFDATA, Data and evidence, but also refer back to my comments in Chapter 2 about the ideological underpinning of evaluative design and practices. While not explicitly addressed in the RUFDATA questions, this issue underpins them all. Mike Prosser's chapter is central in this discussion.

These first two issues are intimately connected and so below I will deal with them together.

Related to the first two is the issue of meanings generally, which in this area as anywhere else cannot be taken for granted. Discursive differences and the presence of different interpretive communities mean that what seems self-evident is not so for everyone, for example in what is being evaluated, or the nature of the thinking underpinning that object of evaluation. Thus, in their very different contexts, Winberg raises the question of the meaning of 'high skills' in postgraduate provision and McNay raises that of 'internationally recognized research' in the evaluation of research quality.

Indeed, underpinning that is the meaning, and purposes, of 'research' itself. The meaning and significance of concepts like these is negotiated and developed over time, and this has important repercussions for what is being evaluated.

Issues of power are highlighted in both McNay and Vaira's chapters; this is the question of Agency (the second A in RUFDATA). McNay shows how resources are mobilised within universities to make the research assessment process work to the benefit of some and the detriment of others, while Vaira's account highlights the relative lack of power of evaluative agencies to effect change. In both cases the operation of power was very evident, with significant effects on the outcomes of evaluative practices for other areas of practice. But in each case that 'power' was different in nature and very different in how it played out.

Important questions about the focus, and the choice of focus, of evaluative practices are raised in this section as elsewhere in the book, particularly in Winberg's chapter where issues about the level of analysis are raised. Here both the R and the F in the RUFDATA typology come into play, the Reasons and purposes and the Focus of evaluative practices.

Finally, there is an issue of particular significance at the national level: is there an HE system at all? If there is, then a single evaluative approach, at least in a defined area like learning and teaching or research, will make sense. But if there is not then the application of a single approach may have deleterious effects for some. In the absence of a single system then the most appropriate answers to each of the RUFDATA questions may be different in different places.

I will address each of these points in turn.

National evaluative practices and ground-level practices: the reception and implementation of evaluative outcomes

In both Mike Prosser's chapter and Max Vaira's we see issues about the relationship between the evaluative activity undertaken and the reception and implementation of its outcomes (or not) on the ground. Evaluators usually expect or hope that their work will be carefully analysed and taken into account by those who commissioned it and those whose work was being evaluated. This is often not the case, as Patton notes in a section he heads 'Reality Check: evaluations largely unused' (1997: 7). As Vaira's chapter shows, even for 'official' evaluations it is perfectly possible for the reports to sit on the shelf and have no effect and essentially no audience, especially where it is in no-one's interest on the ground to act upon findings, and where there are no carrots and no sticks.

Moreover, that problem is compounded by another; where evaluations are put to use they can in fact be misused. Their findings are misinterpreted, misunderstood, selectively applied, miscommunicated or simply reinterpreted into something more palatable or desirable.

One might imagine that in the case of national-level evaluations, often funded by or at least authorised by the state, such phenomena would not occur, and that evaluative exercises that involve much expense would themselves need to have demonstrable value by having real impact and bringing about enhanced practices on the ground.

Sadly this is not always so. The example of the Quality Assurance Agency's Subject Review process in England and Northern Ireland provides a rather sad illustration of my point. Here the teaching and learning provision in every department in universities was reviewed every 5 years by a team from the QAA. The system of review proved very expensive (at least £75,000 for each department) and involved huge amounts of work for departments. It did not result in useful findings and so did not help compare or judge the value of departments (most departments scored between 21 and 24 out of 24). It bureaucratised quality, tending to turn 'quality' into a score, and its evaluation a ritual to be followed (and one, interestingly that paid almost no attention to gathering direct data about practices in classrooms). In fact the exercise probably detracted from the real quality of provision because it directed effort away from learning and teaching. Eventually the reality of this became obvious, but only after a revolt by some universities and the resignation of the head of the QAA. In 2001 Subject Review came to an end, after 8 years of operation and nearly 3,000 reports (QAA, 2003). Even the QAA's own reflections on the extent to which Subject Review achieved its aims is cautious, particularly on what could be argued is the most significant aim: 'to provide a link between funding and the enhancement of quality'. Most academic observers argue that Subject Review provided a language which departments nationally could use to reflect on their own learning and teaching practices, but little more than that. That evaluative exercise proved to be at best ineffective in bringing about change.

Meanwhile selective exposure theory should alert us to the dangers of misunderstanding or misinterpreting the messages from evaluations. Klapper (1960) for example showed how we tend to be predisposed to selective exposure (paying attention to those messages we want to hear, avoiding those we don't), selective perception (perceiving messages in ways conditioned by pre-existing viewpoints) and selective retention (processes of remembering, and forgetting, similarly conditioned by pre-existing viewpoints). While Klapper was discussing mass media messages, the same theory could well be applied to evaluation messages.

More sinister, though, is deliberate selectivity for political purposes, either by those commissioning the report or during the process of subsequent publicity surrounding the evaluations. An example occurred with the so-called Three Wise Men report into the state of primary education in the UK in the early 1990s (Alexander et al., 1992). Despite being commissioned by the Department for Education and Science under a Conservative government, which selected three very much 'on-message' academics to conduct the review, much spin was applied to its conclusions by the Department and its head, Kenneth Clarke. This emphasised the parts of the report which were critical of progressivist teaching methods and claimed that the report stressed the urgent need for more traditional teaching methods in primary schools. This interpretation was further exaggerated by the reporting in the media, to the extent that one of the authors had to write a rebuttal of this depiction of the report (Alexander, 1992).

Another example occurred closer to home and more recently. Lancaster's Department of Educational Research conducted a commissioned evaluation of the Scottish Higher Education system's quality enhancement framework over a three year period, discussed by Lent and Machell in Chapter 13. The final report was picked up by the Times Higher Education Supplement and read through the lens of media news values. The headline ran *Scotland Slams QAA's Methods* (Tysome, 2007) and the story was one of dispute and conflict between Scottish and English approaches to quality assurance and enhancement. This was not of significance in the report, which, when comparisons were made, did not frame them in confrontational terms. Clearly such reporting had the potential to do considerable damage to reputations and relationships, though media sources seem unconcerned about this.

Of course, such events can be understood within the frame of social practice theory. Essentially the results of an evaluation are filtered by the symbolic structures, the orders of meaning, found in different social fields: the political sphere, editors and producers in the media and so on. Ozga (2005) talks about different *assumptive worlds*, the 'mix of perceptions and beliefs that constitute an understanding of the environment', which constitute an aspect of the social practices there. Evaluative practices in one way or another can involve the engagement of a number of fields: the funders; the evaluators; those on the ground; politicians; the public. At different points in the evaluative process each selects, interprets, filters and acts in ways conditioned by pre-existing social practices. This perspective implies a nuancing of Patton's three purposes of evaluation, quoted at the head of this chapter. There may be avowed evaluative purposes from one group involved, but these purposes may be subverted by others. Moreover, the stated purposes may be simply one dimension of what is going on. Evaluations may be put into place to, say, permit education 'consumers' to have more information on which to base choices, but beneath this rhetoric may be others. Purposes are unstable and sometimes rhetorical or deceptive in character. Moreover it is easy, as Prosser shows, to misinterpret the data from evaluative reports, even where there is no deliberate 'spin' being applied to them and even discounting the effects of previous standpoints that lead to selectivity in interpretation.

So how could the link between outcomes of evaluation and practices on the ground become more tightly coupled to bring about enhancement? As we saw in Chapter 2, Bleiklie (2002) points us to four broad policy instruments which might be applied, in different ways, to this end. But evaluative practices themselves have a role to play. One important issue is about practices of engagement with users. Evaluators may see their role as simply providing an end-of-study report, published for funders and perhaps more generally. But this is at one end of a continuum of possibilities which ranges from there through to, at the other end, on-going engagement and discussion with a variety of 'stakeholders' during the course of the evaluation and a range of engagement practices towards its end, and beyond it. These may take the form of workshops, presentations or other more hands-on activities where evaluators and others have the opportunity to grapple with findings and their implications for changing practices. Prosser provides an example of this end of the continuum in his account of how Flint and colleagues engaged with the Students Union in a series of events to investigate why students had responded as they had to a national evaluation, and only then taking institutional action (Flint et al., 2009).

We saw in Chapter 1 that social practices are not easily changed, and it would be rare indeed for a chunky report alone to bring about this challenging task. More fundamental though, is the very purpose and conception of evaluation; whether it is utilisation- (and user-) focused in the first place and whether the answers to the RUFDATA questions will lend it credibility among those who might be expected to change their practices. As Laughton (2003: 309) suggests in relation to Subject Review, discussed above:

> If academics are not convinced of, or do not actively support, the values and methodologies associated with teaching quality review, then there is little chance that these will either produce accurate or meaningful assessments of teaching quality, or act as a spur to the quality enhancement of this aspect of individual and institutional activity.

Discourse and meaning

The point made above about the multiple social fields involved in evaluative practices and their reception foregrounds questions of discourses and multiple meaning. To assume that there is intersubjectivity (shared meaning and understanding) between all parties involved in an evaluative process, or that meanings are stable for any length of time, would be an error. Social fields develop into interpretive communities where there is a degree of intersubjectivity, where a word or phrase has been collectively 'built' to mean the same thing to most participants. However, wherever multiple social fields are involved issues will almost inevitably arise (though not always be surfaced) around meaning.

Two examples arise in this section: Winberg's discussion of the significance of 'high skills', the evaluation of South Africa's postgraduate provision, and McNay's discussion of the meaning of 'internationally recognised' and 'research' in the evaluation of research quality in the UK. There is a Frascati definition of 'research', but that concerns purpose, not process (OECD, 2002). Purposes of research will differ dependent on context, so degrees of international recognition of the same output will vary in the way they are perceived: in some countries research is still an essential element of 'nation-building', and in some cases, for example Hong Kong, that is a criterion in evaluation. Where meaning shifts, or is contested in and between different social fields, the evaluative process is made more complex: precisely what is being evaluated in situations where there are contested concepts? As Winberg says in discussing the focus of her piece, 'the presence of assumptions about how postgraduate students are produced, and why South Africa might need them' is an elephant in the room: very obviously there, but deliberately not mentioned by the participants. To point out the elephant would be to expose the different assumptive worlds present. It would lead to fundamental questions about some very basic issues such as 'Is it really possible to achieve an homogenously "high skills" economy through this approach?' and 'Where are the contradictions between that goal and that of socio-economic transformation in post-apartheid South Africa?'. Keeping the concept of 'high skills' fuzzy (ignoring the elephant) helped avoid this, but did not permit the evaluation to get to the heart of the matter. In that case evaluative practices needed to uncover and analyse in a rigorous way the multiple meanings at play, and their effects. The evaluators should have vigorously pointed to the pachyderm.

Power issues

The exercise of power permeates social practice in daily life, and this is just as true of evaluative practices and processes as elsewhere. Power can be understood in relatively concrete ways: as using advantage to secure desired outcomes; as the ability to set the agenda and exclude issues from the agenda; as the manipulation of discourse to shape views of the world (Lukes, 2005, who talks about these as three dimensions of power). Alternatively it can be seen as the use of localised mechanisms, techniques and practices in the workplace, where it is shifting and fluid in character, not just lying in the hands of one person or group (Foucault, 1980; Ball, 1990). A de-faced theory of power goes further still. Here power is 'not . . . an instrument some agents use to influence the independent action of others, but rather . . . a network of boundaries that delimit for all the boundaries of what is socially possible' (Hayward, 2000: 3). Whichever understanding of power is deployed, the issue of Agency (the second A in RUFDATA) arises.

Each of these conceptualisations has purchase in HE, and we can locate their operation in the evaluation projects discussed here. McNay's chapter illustrates several of them very clearly. Power can be seen at play both in the RAE process itself and on the ground in an attempt to achieve the best outcome from that process. Different agendas were brought into play (for example the politics of personnel management) and position was used to secure desired outcomes (Lukes' first dimension of power). There was the perception that those in positions of power dominated the subject-specific assessment panels in order to protect their own interests by being able to set the agenda for decision-making (Lukes' second dimension of power). Assumptions about 'quality' based on discourses around universities and their histories influenced outcomes of the evaluation (Lukes' third dimension). Meanings of significant terms were unstable and contested, as noted above, and this left space for different and inequitable applications of them in different contexts in a fluid way (Foucault's 'network' view of power).

Meanwhile the limits of what is socially possible (the de-faced theory of power) works in ways which are harder to see, but are nonetheless significant. A good example comes not from these case studies but from the case of Subject Review, discussed above. There were 2,904 review reports published between 1993 and 2001, at a conservatively estimated cost of £218 million. In only 16 cases was it reported that the providers were not meeting their own aims and objectives (the test applied in Subject Review). In only one case did a re-review lead to a second non-approved judgement. There were no funding implications for either high scorers or those who failed; this would have been a step too far in England and Northern Ireland at that time, even though one of the stated aims of Subject Review was 'to provide a link between funding and the enhancement of quality' (QAA, 2003).

Vaira's chapter too illustrates the play of power, and in that case the absence of any ability among evaluative agencies to affect practices on the ground. In his narrative of the Italian case it is very clear where power lies, and in that case a fairly concrete view of the nature of power seems to fit the situation best. It is possible of course that the national systemic evaluation did produce knowledge about the system which was not there before, and allowed judgements to be made (two of Patton's three purposes for evaluation) but the primary avowed purpose of the evaluations, to improve practices, simply did not happen.

Both the macro- and the micro-mechanisms of power, these case studies tell us, will infuse both evaluative practices and practices on the ground in relation to the evaluative process and its outcomes. Evaluators need to be at least conscious of this, and its effects, even if they often cannot do much about it.

The focus of evaluative practices

Both here and in Chapter 10 the issue of the appropriate focus of evaluative practices arises: where the evaluative eye is most appropriately directed. This issue is taken up in Chapter 27, the concluding chapter. Both the R and the F of RUFDATA are mobilised in addressing this question: the Reasons and purposes behind an evaluation and its Focus. Winberg's chapter raises the question of the appropriate level of analysis of evaluation. Too low (as in the case study she discusses) and the significant locus of change is missed, too high and the effects of practices on the ground are ignored. In the case of the evaluation of postgraduate provision in South Africa, Winberg points out that without systemic changes in socio-economic structures and processes at the national level, the single reform being evaluated had almost no chance of being effective. Yet that systemic level was outside the remit of the evaluation. Moreover the coherence of the concepts underpinning that reform at the national level themselves needed to be evaluated. The brief for the evaluation set the level of analysis far too low and so the evaluation itself was (to take Winberg's argument further than she takes it) almost pointless.

Another example, taken from outside these pages, will illustrate the point. In the USA the Fund for the Improvement of Postsecondary Education (FIPSE) provides funding for projects seeking to enhance learning and teaching in American universities and colleges (http://www.fipse.aed.org/). It has done this since 1994 and no doubt has brought about significant changes over its period of operation. It requires careful evaluation of each project funded, the outcomes of which are available on the web. Yet no evaluation has been conducted of FIPSE itself, at the level above the individual projects. Such an evaluation could address the thinking underpinning its approach to change (project funding) and its effectiveness in terms of its goals compared, for example, to other comparable organisations elsewhere in the world which have adopted different strategies (for example the UK Subject Centres). Again, the object, the focus and the level of analysis of evaluation have been significant in what has been learned, and what questions have not even been asked.

Evaluation and 'systems' of Higher Education

Finally there is the related question of the extent to which HE in any national context is a 'system' at all. The word system signifies that there are a number of interacting, interrelated, or interdependent elements forming a complex whole. But in some contexts, and arguably more and more in the UK, the national HE scene really consists of several sub-systems. The division between the Russell Group of universities ('the 20 leading UK universities': http://www.russellgroup.ac.uk/), the 1994 group (promoting 'excellence in research and teaching': http://www.1994group.ac.uk/) and the University Alliance (with a 'balanced portfolio of research, teaching, enterprise and innovation': http://www.university-alliance.ac.uk/) arguably now comprise three different systems, or at least two. This may not be a 'bad' thing. The 1963 UK Robbins Report on HE addresses this point eloquently:

> Higher education has not been planned as a whole or developed within a framework consciously devised to promote harmonious evolution. What system there is has come about as the result of a series of particular initiatives, concerned with particular needs and particular situations . . . there is no way of dealing conveniently with all the problems common to higher education as a whole. . . . The absence of a plan for everything is not necessarily an indication of chaos. . . . [W]e are not demanding that all activities should be planned and controlled from the centre. We

> set great value upon the freedom of individuals and institutions in any academic system. . . . Our point is that the central decisions that have to be made should be coherent and take account of the interests of all sectors of higher education, and that decentralised initiative – and we hope there will always be much of this – should be inspired by common principles. . . . We ask indeed that there should be co-ordination, some principles of policy commonly accepted, some organisation providing for rational allocation of scarce resources. But we should hold it to be the very bankruptcy of constitutional invention if such conditions were thought to be incompatible with the scope for individual and institutional initiative that . . . [is] one of the main essentials of intellectual and spiritual health.
>
> (NCHE, 1963, paragraphs 18–39)

The question is: should the different subsystems of HE be evaluated in the same way, or does a single set of evaluative practices operate to favour some and disadvantage others. Does it serve to 'stifle individual and institutional initiative'? RUFDATA itself may be applied at the wrong level of analysis in some national environments.

Part Two

Programmatic evaluative practice

9

Programmatic evaluative practice in Higher Education: design diversity and degrees of programme alignment

Murray Saunders

> As evaluators, we undertake our studies with the intention of helping decision makers make wiser decisions. We provide evidence that shows the successes and shortcomings of programs. We identify some of the factors that are associated with better and worse outcomes. And, we often try to explain how the program works in practice and why it leads to the effects we observe. We expect that these data will feed into the decision making process and influence the actions that people take at the staff level, at management levels, or in the higher reaches of decision making.
>
> (Weiss, 2005: 286)

This section is concerned with the kinds of evaluative practice which have characterised the evaluation of specific interventions, initiatives or programmes into Higher Education (HE) institutions at sector-wide level. This type of evaluation has been termed programme evaluation. As Carol Weiss suggests in the opening quotation, such evaluations are closely aligned to the provision of resources to stakeholders, usually the commissioners of evaluation in the first instance, concerning the quality, value and worth of a planned, funded and designed intervention with a time limited life.

This type of evaluation, its theory and its practice have a relatively long history, beginning in the US. In the introduction to the *Handbook of Evaluation,* Mark et al. (2007: 7) identify the plethora of evaluation theories, approaches and models in the programme evaluation tradition. They quote the work of Shadish, Cook and Leviton (1991) who, in a comprehensive review of the work of seven programme evaluation theorists, offer a stage model which attempts to describe the development of major evaluation theories up to that point in time. This section cannot attempt such an overview. What it will do is provide some cases of contemporary practice in the evaluation of interventions into the HE sector. These evaluations have not always followed an explicit evaluation theory but may have been informed by social theory of a more general kind, to provide an explanatory frame with which to make sense of the evidence of a programme's effects.

As Mary Henkel has pointed out (Henkel, 1998: 291), evaluation is no stranger to HE. We could argue that HE practice is predicated on evaluations of the quality and worth of the knowledge produced by research within HE institutions. However, the evolution of the way in which 'programmes' have been evaluated in HE is less familiar, simply because programmes which have emanated from outside the institution, mainly from government sources, have only a recent history. This can be explained to some extent by the relatively separate positioning of HE with respect to the State. However, we find that that this relative autonomy has diminished as the connection between HE and the State has moved from a relatively 'loosely coupled' one to a much more tightly coupled relationship. The purpose of these kinds of interventions and their evaluation is the focus of this section.

There are still comparatively few instances of evaluations where the State has systematically intervened in the internal practices of institutions via specific programmes. In the European context we can see the way in which interventions and invitations to engage in 'funded project activity against set criteria' suggest that the conventional HE curriculum and teaching and learning practice, which these interventions address, is regarded as having become 'dysfunctional' in some way, or certainly in need of some improvement or enhancement from sources outside the institutions themselves.

We can argue that they never did function in quite the way the proponents of a tighter 'fit' between HE and either economic or social sectors suggest, or that the traditional connections have become out of sync. However, this perspective is dominant and embodied in the location of the State's management of HE in the UK in the Department for Business, Innovation and Skills with no mention of education or universities in the title. On commenting on the challenge to the UK from other countries, John Denham's speech in 2008 endorsed by the DBIS site, suggests:

> They will challenge us in every area – research; teaching; our links with business and employers; and our links between research, innovation and enterprise.
>
> (Denham, 2008)

Denham, the Secretary of State, suggested that, over the long term, a one percentage point increase in the size of a country's tertiary educated workforce increases GDP growth by around six percentage points. The closer a country is to 'the technological frontier' (as measured by patenting activity), the more dependent is its growth on a highly educated workforce. For these countries – and regions – innovation, so dependent on higher level skills, is particularly important to their economic progress (Denham, 2008).

However, although the functional connections in the 'technical' sense are where the emphasis lies and the State, at least in the UK and in the EU, premises its interventions and programmes in HE on the basis of that prescription, other processes, for example of cultural and social reproduction, form equally potent functions of HE. The work of Bourdieu and Passeron (used for example by Reay et al., 2005) in their overview of the way in which HE helps to reproduce difference, and the work of Brown and Scase (1994) suggests precisely the same perspective by emphasising the continued role of cultural capital and the stubbornly resilient tendency of HE to reproduce material advantage through cultural differentiation. Most state interventions, however, eschew such analyses and draw on a more optimistic stance in which they note that there has been a new 'crisis of confidence' in the capacity of HE to deliver a much more 'relevant' graduate in terms of their knowledge, skills, capacity and habitus. We have had, therefore, a succession of programmes and interventions in the UK that can be depicted in the following way.

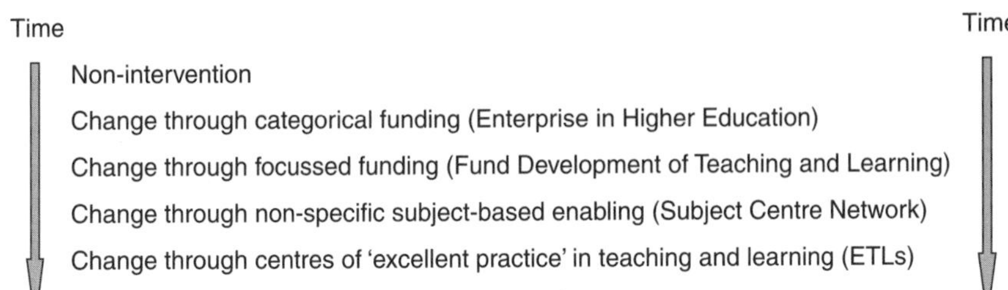

Time
Time
Non-intervention
Change through categorical funding (Enterprise in Higher Education)
Change through focussed funding (Fund Development of Teaching and Learning)
Change through non-specific subject-based enabling (Subject Centre Network)
Change through centres of 'excellent practice' in teaching and learning (ETLs)

Figure 9.1 Shifting programme mechanisms in the UK

Emanating from the EU, we have had a similar succession of 'calls' for research and development projects that further the Commission's aims to influence the 'coupling' of HE to the needs of the EU as a trading partnership. The mechanisms used involve funding driven activities through the development of 'demonstrator projects', learning approaches and curricular developments that embody what might be termed 'human capital' needs in the future. The EU's most recent advice for the procurement of funding, from its *Practical Guide to EU Funding Opportunities for Research and Innovation*, for example, opens its text with the following:

> The knowledge economy – with its emphasis on education, research, technological development, innovation and entrepreneurship – is at the heart of the renewed Partnership for Growth and Jobs, a programme to develop Europe's economy and guarantee quality of life for its population.
>
> (ftp://ftp.cordis.europa.eu/pub/fp7/docs/practical-guide-eufunding_en.pdf (accessed 20.8.10))

These interventions, encapsulated in the cases in this section, are 'categorically funded' in nature (funding which is time limited, against set criteria, based on invitations to submit proposals, closely monitored and evaluated) and have embedded within them a theory of how they might create or sponsor changes. Evaluations in this context will have practices that embody this imperative and are tasked with variously identifying the 'impacts', uses, worth and value of the funded project.

The uses to which the evaluations are put constitute a practice cluster. This category of consideration is best understood in terms of the kinds of recurrent behaviour associated with particular circumstances, at specific times and places. It can for example refer to strategic use of an evaluation output for change purposes within an institutional or national context (i.e. discussion by a key agency or committee leading to the cessation of funding or the rejection of a particular approach for wider use or its use as a professional development resource). The focus for these kinds of programmatic evaluations will vary of course, depending on the character of the intervention. What is of interest in our cases, however, is how the foci for the evaluation are reached, the practices associated with their identification and whether the cases refer to aspects of programme experience which are relevant to quite diverse stakeholders. It is also interesting to note the extent to which the foci are intended to provide so called formative resources to the programme or more concerned to provide estimations of programme effects or impact. The diagnostic power of the evaluation for programme participants will depend on the balance between these two dimensions.

Key also is the forms taken by the evidence or data deemed essential to address the dimensions or foci selected as core indicators of the extent to which or how a programme is working. Our cases demonstrate the range and diversity in what counts as 'legitimate' evidence. We have depictions, narratives and vignettes derived from interviews mainly and we also have evidence which is rendered numerically in some way. Part of the character of practices within this level of evaluation concerns the issue of timing and agency. In other words, who is doing the evaluation, where do the evaluation designs come from and what is the derivation of key indicators of 'effect'. Our cases construct the constellation of practices from four very different perspectives but all embody the core issues of programmatic evaluation as we have outlined them here.

The first contribution from Murray Saunders lies at the centre of what we have identified as programme evaluation practice in that it unequivocally references known evaluation approaches (utilisation focused and theory driven evaluation). The CETL (Centres for Excellence in Teaching and Learning) programme was a time limited central government (via the Higher Education Funding Council) investment which called for an external evaluation. The approach outlined in the Saunders' contribution was based on an examination of the central 'theory' to improve teaching and learning in HE, embedded in the CETL programme. It has a strong articulation of the idea of policy, policy instrumentation and the mechanisms that were developed at the level of individual CETLs. It also has a clear interrogatory framework (Innovation trajectories) by which the way the practices encouraged by CETLs evoked different responses from potential stakeholders. The evaluation approach adopted in this example enables a judgement to be made on the extent to which the theory embedded within the CETL programme worked as a change strategy.

John Owen's piece analyses the evaluation of a new pre-service program (ITEP) which was devised to overcome some perceived weaknesses in the traditional approaches to teacher preparation. It allowed for the influence of a mentor to act as a bridge between teacher-education institutions and supervisors, evidence-based knowledge to support the work of the mentor. A key aspect of ITEP was that the locus of action was more embedded in the day-to-day work of a school than was the case for conventional models of teacher preparation. It was expected that the more conceptual aspects of teacher education would inform what students encountered in the schools. This was in effect a 'theory informing practice' approach. The chapter emphasises the way in which an evaluation designed to create effects on practices, must itself, generate practices which enable or enhance the chances of its outputs being used for onward action. In some quarters this pre-occupation is associated with evaluation use or, put another way, engaging with the evaluation outputs. The chapter emphasises the importance of practices associated with negotiating the terms of reference for the ITEP evaluation with programme stakeholders in order to 'nest' potential use.

This negotiation is a first sign of evaluator-client interaction that should commence at the design phase, and manifest itself in the adoption of responsive dissemination techniques. These actions are consistent with practices of sustained interactivity which means more than providing a readable report. Audiences need information about the evaluation as well as what the evaluation has found. In the ITEP evaluation, meetings with the evaluation team were held regularly during the year to discuss how the programme was progressing, and towards the conclusion to discuss the final report. While experience has shown that we cannot always count on instrumental use of our findings, this chapter suggests ways of aiming for a high level of conceptual understanding among audiences.

Alan McCluskey offers a unique critique of the way in which evaluation was embedded in a European funded project. His chapter draws on a recent evaluation designed as part of a large international research programme entitled PALETTE. The idea behind the project was to trial a range of learning environments, broadly termed the 'participatory development of services and use-scenarios' in order to enable better non-formal learning processes. The key concept underscoring the project was the idea of a 'community of practice'. The communities participating in the project were drawn from HE, vocational training and industry. He identifies five interrelated aspects of the project for particular attention and looks at these from the perspective of evaluation as a deep learning activity.

Evaluation in this context was embedded within the project and was considered first and foremost as 'formative'. Within this complex environment, three aspects of the evaluation experience emerged successively during the trajectory of the PALETTE programme and it is these he problematises. They are claims concerning the participatory nature of the evaluation, the evolution of the evaluation into an expert based process and evaluation as an informal and more formal practice. The remaining two aspects in this chapter address the impact of the wider context on the work of evaluation and the role of evaluation in handling complexity.

The perspective or lens through which this dynamic is analysed highlights the 'connective tissue' and contradictory assumptions that characterise a complex project with ambiguous aims and diverse expectations. Of particular interest is the focus on the way in which informal, embedded and tacit forms of evaluation are being undertaken by project participants but these practices are not identified as evaluative as such. The argument is that to tap into this rich vein of practice and build upon it would be an effective strategy in such complex evaluative environments. However, he demonstrates how the 'project' environment characteristic of EU funded activity, inhibits this approach and militates against its legitimacy.

Lent and Machell provide an analysis of the way in which a policy of 'enhancement,' operating sector wide in Scotland, contains several mechanisms to improve the quality of teaching and learning. They highlight, in particular the evaluation of 'Enhancement Themes' (for example 'employability') which bring together a focus, a range of resources and events that are intended to foreground a specific area of development. This dimension of the policy works in a similar way to a programme intervention in that it has a timeline, specific resources associated with it and it has an embedded theory of the way in which change might be brought about. They identify the alignment between the thrust of the enhancement policy on the one hand and the design integrity of the evaluation on the other.

They argue in their chapter that in the light of the shift away from an audit-based approach to review and evaluation implied by the introduction of the Quality Enhancement Framework in Scotland, it would be inappropriate for the design of the evaluation to adopt standard audit type evaluation methods based on attribution. They argue for evaluative alignment for two reasons. First on the basis that summative evaluations are unlikely to engender the degree of openness or sense of ownership among institutions and practitioner necessary for the QEF to be successful. Secondly, the degree to which ownership of the framework needs to permeate through the Scottish HE sector means that the 'system' being evaluated can usefully be viewed as a number of different systems (including the QEF, sector-wide agencies, HEIs and disciplinary-based groups) interacting through a variety of networks that make reductive attribution impossible.

These contributions demonstrate the diversity of practice in the evaluation of programmes within the HE sector. The insights they offer will be considered in the commentary at the end of this section.

10

The national programme of Centres for Excellence in Teaching and Learning (CETLs) in England and Northern Ireland: a theory driven evaluation of change

Murray Saunders

The CETL programme

'Centres of excellence' were first announced in the 2003 Government white paper, *The Future of Higher Education*. Following a consultation and a two-stage bidding process in 2003–4, the Higher Education Funding Council (HEFCE) initially announced funding for 74 Centres for Excellence in Teaching and Learning (CETLs) in January 2005 (the change in the preposition from 'of' to 'for' was significant). This approach to the improvement of teaching and learning in Higher Education has an embedded theory of change i.e. it constitutes a strategy with the intention of bringing about improvements in teaching and learning by establishing centres of excellence in teaching and learning. This embedded theory focuses on the following propositions:

- reward and recognition,
- excellent teaching produces excellent learning,
- recognising individual and institutional excellence in teaching and learning promotes excellence across the sector.

The CETL programme evolved into an investment of some £350 million pounds by the HEFCE in England, HEFCW in Wales and the Department for Employment and Learning in Northern Ireland. After the initial announcement (see above) it finally established 81 Centres in England, Wales and Northern Ireland to reward and recognise excellent teaching in a variety of disciplines and cross disciplinary practices. In England this investment is an intensification of the work undertaken under the teaching quality enhancement fund.

However, the programme was not overly prescriptive, thus encouraging a diverse range of expressions across most HE disciplines. The CETL programme can be described as an example of 'categorical funding' that is a resource-driven mechanism to produce change against specific criteria, over a time limited period, usually with an evaluative component. It is the latest in a line of approaches to interventions or change strategies in teaching and learning in HE that have all been characterised by degrees of openness appropriate to the culture of relative autonomy in the UK system.

CETLs were a novel strategy, complementing work already achieved through the device of other learning and teaching strategies and through central initiatives such as the Subject Centre Network and then the HE Academy.[1] They give credit to a commitment to teaching enhancement at a time when the research assessment exercise might distract attention from teaching.

Interestingly, the CETLs do not constitute a managed programme. This can be illustrated by comparison with the Subject Centre Network, which was also evaluated by the same team (Saunders et al., 2002). The CETLs are supported by the Higher Education Academy and HEFCE provides some support as well but the strong sense is that these are like independent countries located on the same continent – they certainly do not constitute a 'United States of CETLs' let alone an empire. A CETL might be discipline based or have a more cross-curricular brief but its raison d'être is to act as a 'beacon' of innovative practice that might be replicated elsewhere.

The theory of change embedded in the CETL programme

Importantly, the CETLs were launched with an explicit 'change theory' associated with the idea of excellence, or more precisely, 'beacons' of excellent practice and the way its reward and further resourcing might act to encourage further innovative practice across the sector. From an evaluative perspective, the programme had a clearly stated policy objective (to improve teaching and learning in HE) derived from the seminal Dearing Report on Higher Education in the UK (Dearing, 1997), through a particular instrument (Centres for Excellence), using a variety of mechanisms (at the level of individual CETLs these included for example buildings, research, curricular development, staff fellowships) to create desired effects (better teaching and

[1] The HE Academy provides support to the HE sector by working with individual academics. The network of discipline-based subject centres provides a range of services to subject departments. Its website states that it works with UK universities and colleges, providing national leadership in developing and disseminating evidence-informed practice about enhancing the student learning experience. http://www.heacademy.ac.uk/

more effective learning). This way of analysing policy builds on the work of both Vedung (1998) and Pawson and Tilley (1997) and is captured in Figure 10.1 in which the elements construct a conceptual hierarchy. The dimensions of the policy, its instruments and mechanisms are outlined.

It is clear that the CETL programme did have a theory of change embedded in its stated purpose and acted as a policy instrument. To be explicit, the existence of a Centre for Excellence was intended to have wider effects on the sector as a whole. According to HEFCE, 'the purpose of CETLs is to reward excellent teaching practice and to invest in that practice further in order to increase and **deepen its impact across a wider teaching and learning community**' [my emphasis] (HEFCE, 2004).

The key phrase in this extract is emboldened to emphasise that the CETL programme was designed as a strategy to maximise the impact of excellent practice across the whole sector. The key metaphoric phrase 'deepen its impact'

Policies (e.g. widening participation, massification, closer HE employment connections, improved teaching and learning): ***(the logic of policy intention)***

Instruments (e.g. resource allocations to universities for widening participation, ring fenced funds for targeted developments, Subject Centre Networks, creating Centres for Excellence for Teaching and Learning: ***(the theory in action of funded and targeted development)***

Mechanisms (in the case of CETLs, specific strategies used by CETLs to 'enact' programmes) e.g.

- Providing opportunities for visiting practitioners or fellows working with teachers and students.
- Awarding bursaries and grants for staff and students to undertake pedagogic research.
- Offering bursaries and grants for staff and students to experiment with new learning opportunities and curricula.
- Organising and supporting events (workshops, seminars, PD activity) undertaken to disseminate innovation.
- Developing digital and web-based events, affordances and other resources.
- Establishing partnership arrangements designed to widen opportunities and promote creative teaching and learning practice.
- Making creative and efficient use of buildings, plant and equipment.

(theories of change embedded in specific strategies)

Effects (positive changes in practices (economic, social, educational, health) brought about by the aggregated determination of mechanisms, instruments and policies)

Figure 10.1 HE 'Programme and policy enactment': environment and evaluation focus

signals this intention clearly. There are other ways of accomplishing these effects, so we can suggest that this particular intervention (the use of Centres for Excellence) had within it the embedded assumption, or theory, that creating and reinforcing existing good practice through CETLs would deepen impact.

Importantly, in the case of the CETL strategy, we can depict it as an example of a 'complex policy instrument', with an explicit theory of change that has particular implications for evaluation design. These instruments are designed to improve teaching and learning quality in HE but do not have detailed specifications. Key ideas that are loosely assembled to constitute an underlying theory-in-use are:

- HE is semi-autonomous, has complex cultures and affiliations and is used to generating its own momentum
- a relatively light touch is most likely to yield positive improvements through these instruments
- change tends not to be linear and happens unevenly, with some areas surging ahead while others take some time to shift or remain resistant to change
- change is brought about by complex causal mechanisms (carrots, sticks, sermons and partnerships) but also by the convergence of many long-term and short-term factors (opportunity, funding, policy change, new appointments
- change increasingly relies on many enabling features sometimes called affordances being put in place.

Implications for evaluation

There was however, a sense in which the CETLs were working at a level which was greater than the sum of their parts (mechanisms). By this we refer to the way in which the programme might reposition teaching and learning (T and L) practices at institutional and sector levels in ways that were difficult to determine precisely or predict. It was possible, for example, for CETLs to create 'ripple' effects through recognition that they were creating a shift in the way T and L practitioners are rewarded and resources and attention might be flowing toward T and L. We offered the framework (Figure 10.2) for understanding the way in which reward and recognition through CETL mechanisms might create 'deeper' effects across institutions and the sector. This model builds on the work of Hall and Loucks (1978) and suggests that at the outset of the CETL programme, excellent practice was essentially taking place in pockets within institutions and it is these pockets of practice that have been rewarded. We used the metaphor of an 'enclave' to depict these pockets of excellent practice. The categories in Figure 10.2 are used herein to denote how the CETL 'connects' to the wider organisational context or the sector as a whole. In many ways what matters is the way innovatory practice within a CETL might impact on the sector as a whole or across an institution. The theory of change used by the CETL programme is at

7. ***Refocusing:*** new practice clusters emerge marked by common contexts for action and new practices
6. ***Collaboration:*** bridgeheads spreading: becoming systemic, moving from enclaves to wider influence, working with others
5. ***Consequence:*** evaluation of bridgeheads with attention on impact on students, staff, departments and whole institution of new practices and processes, relevance, evaluation and implied changes
4. ***Management:*** attention on difficulties in the processes and tasks involved in developing new practices, processes and systems
3. ***Institutional/personal:*** bridgeheads beginning to form, begin to analyse effects and impacts on existing systems and practice
2. ***Informational:*** interest growing in new practices
1. ***Awareness:*** Initial awareness of innovative practice embodied in CETL enclaves

Figure 10.2 Innovation trajectories as a framework for evaluation

once its strength but also its weakness in that it is uncertain how these 'enclaves' of practice can exert influence outside their immediate environs.

An enclave is a set of practices that exists in a larger organisational setting but which has characteristics that are distinctive. Individuals within it subscribe self consciously to a different culture (or way of doing things) to the organisational norm and there are clear organisational, temporal and sometimes spatial differences that distinguish it from its organisational setting. The key evaluation question was 'To what extent and under what conditions does an enclave have an impact on the wider organisation?' We believe that the enclave begins to challenge wider practices in the organisation and so transforms itself from an enclave to a 'bridgehead' or platform for wider developments (Saunders, Bonamy and Charlier, 2005).

Related concepts which help to explain the relationship between an enclave and the wider context are the ideas of 'emergent' culture within a 'dominant' culture in an organisation (see Williams, 1980). It might be said that as long as the new culture remains in an enclave then there is not necessarily any change at the wider organisational level. However, once an enclave begins to develop as a bridgehead, then it can emerge as an 'oppositional' culture to the dominant culture and challenge its dominant position in the organisation providing the resources for a 'paradigm shift in practices'. We were interested to note the way in which and under what circumstances enclaves had evolved over time. Thus, practices were observed that remained in enclaves of innovation, mainly because they had no theory or strategy for change in the wider context. CETL practices were also observed that were making a limited impact in the wider context i.e. moving from enclave to bridgehead because CETL staff were adopting strategies for engagement which were influencing wider practice.

We were able to identify changes that moved through the enclave stage to developing 'bridge-heading' strategies and on to create changes in embedded or routine practice. What were the practice clusters associated with evaluation within this change environment, characterised by a clearly stated 'theory' associated with the intervention? We might look at the logic implicit in policy instruments. This evaluation worked with project or programme designers to foreground the logic of their change strategies, asking, in essence, on what basis did they think the existence of a CETL would lead to positive effects beyond itself. In other words, what was their theory-in-use? (Hughs and Traynor, 2000). In doing this, the evaluation team asked representatives from HEFCE to explain their assumptions about the ways in which their theories-in-use were expected to lead to the desired effects.

These discussions were at the level of policy instruments i.e. on what basis did key informants from Government, HEFCE and the sector as a whole think that CETLs would or would not achieve the objectives of teaching enhancement it was set. This level of inquiry formed a strategic assessment of the approach as a national strategy. It is interesting to note that the same broad focus also applied to the visits to the CETLs themselves. In this case, discussions moved towards a consideration of the way in which the mechanisms selected by the individual CETLs to act as change 'vehicles' were creating desired effects.

In order to adopt a social practice approach, the design of the evaluation was relatively open, focused on evolution i.e. on the ways in which CETLs had evolved over time. It was flexible enough to accommodate unanticipated events and effects. Rather than benchmarks or baselines, we might talk of the formative evaluation in terms of subtle 'situational analyses' that provide starting points for the journey through which change processes take us.

The process of deepening, we argued, involved the principles, ways, means and approaches that constitute excellent practice moving out from these pockets or enclaves of practice and influencing the wider case as 'bridgeheads'. To have deeper effects therefore, would involve the programme as a whole shaping practices at the consequential (5), collaborative (6) and refocusing (7) levels in Figure 10.2. Evaluatively, the emergence of recurrent practices that embody the ideas and activities promoted by the CETLs formed the principal focus for the later stages of the evaluation. In this way, the innovation trajectory model enabled the evaluation design to have at its heart an interrogatory tool which could depict the range of CETL 'effects' in terms of influencing improvements in practice.

The task of the evaluation was to render the interim effects of the CETL programme as a whole. The innovation trajectories framework for evaluation (Figure 10.2) was used to profile the programme as a whole. In terms of this model, we found the dominant mode was within stages 1–3. These stages involved wider emerging institutional awareness and interest in knowing more, thinking of implications for the institution or for other networks (such as subject or regional ones) and initial awareness of innovative practice embodied in the CETL. More importantly, it also initiated engagement strategies that began to establish new bridgeheads. However, some CETLs were beginning to move toward stages 4–5 involving more attention on the impact on students, staff, departments and whole institution of new practices and processes, relevance, evaluation and implied changes. At this stage, attention was on difficulties in the processes and tasks involved in developing new practices, processes and systems. We expected, toward the final period of funding, that CETLs would begin to experience activity at what we understand as stages 6–7 where attention was now on adaptation, major changes, alternatives to original ideas and creativity. This opened up the possibility of increased coordinating and cooperating with other stakeholders in using new practices, systems and processes (see Saunders et al., 2008).

Overview

The principal metaphors this evaluation used were narratives or stories concerning participants' experiences. The way networks operate and interconnect and activities in parts of the system work together, provide new types of focus for evaluation. These approaches are valuable because they are able to create broad evidence bases to represent participants' experiences. Evaluations that have important aspects designed by the change participants themselves are particularly potent. High-validity evaluations of complex change involve collaborations between many stakeholders to identify key questions. This was also a feature of the evaluation through networking fora that brought the CETLs together for exchanges of experience.

On the basis of this approach, we were able to say at a formative moment in the development of the CETLs that the various dimensions of this evaluation revealed an overall positive narrative for the development of the CETLs as 'nodes' of teaching and learning focused activities. Notwithstanding the tendency for newly formed entities like CETLs to have a strong sense of emerging identity, internal culture and excitement, the data pointed to a range of positive effects the existence of the CETL programme has enabled. These effects tended to be circulating around the direct beneficiaries of CETL resources (i.e. in enclaves) but there is growing evidence that effects are beginning to move out from the enclaves of practice within CETLs and, in some cases, are being used to strategic effect within institutions (see Saunders et al., 2008). The effectiveness of the strategy overall will stand or fall on the extent to which the CETLs established sustainable changes in recurrent practices beyond the direct beneficiaries.

I argue that formative evaluation has a particular role in complex change. It can help us, as learners and teachers in HE, to find short-term, provisional, creative solutions to the problems produced by change. They can help us to think more clearly about complex problems and themselves act as a 'bridging tool' to enable planning and decisions for future action. This means that survey, interview, visual evidence, discussion, narratives, vignettes and case reports can together provide enough knowledge for onward planning. And, to repeat the point, this knowledge is provisional, while also being secure enough to support deliberation, at many levels, about ways of continuing to make the best of the change process.

11

Foregrounding social interaction in programme evaluation: an evaluation of an innovative pre-service teacher education initiative in Australia

John M. Owen

Introduction

This chapter is designed to contribute to debate about effective program evaluation practice in the area of Higher Education (HE). The chapter is based on a recent commissioned study and report provided to a client of the evaluator (Owen, 2009). We provide a deconstruction of the evaluation process, based on a well-used framework developed by the author (Owen, 2009). Such a frame, which is super-ordinate to the plethora of models found in the evaluation literature, emphasises the importance of social interaction in the conduct of contemporary evaluation practice.

As the introduction to the programmatic section of the book suggests, we think of evaluation as the production of knowledge based on systematic enquiry to assist decision-making about a program. This definition expands (but does not replace) the view of evaluation as the determination of program merit or worth, to acknowledge that decision-makers may need timely information about a program that is in the design or developmental stages. During this period, assessing merit or worth based on determining impact is premature. The use of evaluative information to make decisions about a program as it is being delivered has changed the ball game for evaluators. Practices associated with responding to the needs of program managers and providers requires evaluators to be more responsive to clients, more pragmatic in choices about data sources, and more able to communicate effectively than is the case for traditional approaches to evaluation. The framework used here provides a structure to discuss these issues and analyses a set of interactive practices designed to foreground use and engagement.

Context: nature of pre-service teacher education in Australia

In discussing a given evaluation it is usually necessary to describe the evaluand or program in context. In this case the context is the supply of adequately trained teacher educators for Australian schools. That there has been considerable disquiet about this provision is evident by recent coverage in the broadsheet press (see for example Milburn, 2010). While academics have been sending messages about the need to reform pre-service teacher education, there have been few attempts to try new approaches to pre-service teacher education in Australia. There are several reasons for this, among which has been a marked reduction in Government funding for HE over the past decade. This has affected the potential of educational faculties in universities to resource innovations relating to the professional preparation of teachers.

Despite funding issues, conventional pre-service teacher education in Australia has managed to maintain partnerships between teacher education faculties and schools. The partnership assumes that professional preparation involves a linked combination of practical and theoretical inputs about teaching, schooling and education, and that the partners will act to produce synergistic outcomes for participants.

A simple cause and effect portrayal of conventional 'beginning teacher preparation' is summarised in Figure 11.1. This implies that school supervision is a major influence in teacher preparation, and that academics from university education faculties provide both direct and indirect influences on the development of beginning teachers.

A particularly important element of competency is the need to master basic pedagogical skills. Pedagogy can be thought of as the interaction between curriculum and teaching, or the juxtaposition of content knowledge and learning theories to provide rich experiences for students in classrooms and other environments. It is this area of pedagogical knowledge and

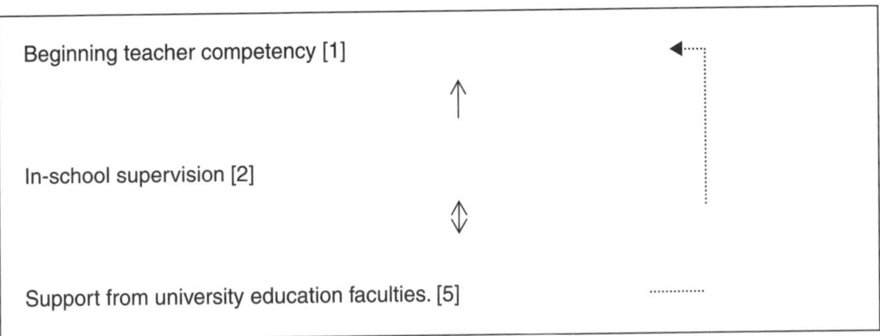

Figure 11.1 Conventional beginning teacher preparation

skills about teaching and learning, where in-school supervision is of fundamental importance.

Recent research on trainee teacher experiences indicates that the model has deficiencies in practice (Ure, 2009). There have been concerns that education academics are out of touch with the realities of schools, and so their contributions to training are irrelevant and out of date. At the same time, teachers involved in supervision have had little training to undertake their roles as supervisors. There has been a notable lack of innovative interventions involving co-operative links between education faculties and schools in Australia. All told, pre-service training gained a reputation for being stuck in a groove, and non-responsive to challenges that teachers will face early in the twenty-first century.

The ITEP Program: an innovative program of pre-service teacher education

During 2007 a new pre-service program was devised to overcome some of these concerns. For simplicity we will call it the Innovative Teacher Education Program (ITEP). The causal diagram to describe what ITEP hoped to achieve is depicted in Figure 11.2. This approach differs from that in Figure 11.1 in that it allows for: the influence of a mentor to act as a bridge between teacher-education institutions and supervisors [3], and evidence-based knowledge to support the work of the mentor [4]. This version of the model was developed by the auspices of the program, the Association of Independent Schools of Victoria (AISV) who also acted as a coordinating body with involved universities [5].

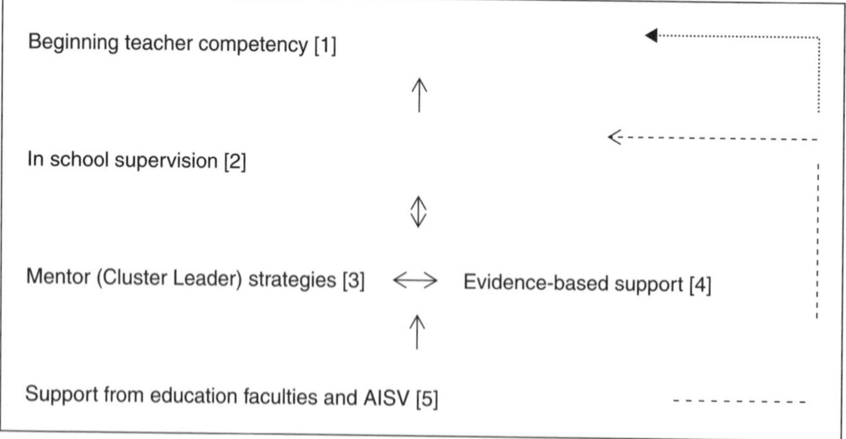

Figure 11.2 The ITEP approach to beginning teacher preparation

A key aspect of ITEP was that the locus of action was more embedded in the day-to-day work of a school than was the case for conventional models of teacher preparation. It was expected that the more conceptual aspects of teacher education would inform what students encountered in the schools. This was in effect a 'theory informing practice' approach.

During 2008, the ITEP model was trialled in three locations across the State of Victoria. Each location consisted of four or five schools working as a cluster to provide a base for approximately 25 pre-service students, so that students could meet together on a regular basis (usually in one of the schools in the cluster). Operation of the model involved: (a) appointment of a mentor who was subsequently defined as a cluster leader, (b) support for these leaders during the year from the AISV through a series of meetings and administrative backup from key AISV staff, and (c) the appointment of a consultant who provided evidence-based support for the cluster leaders on a need-to-know basis. Cluster leaders were experienced teachers who had personal and professional attributes that made them acceptable to other parties in the program. Of particular importance was that they be accepted by supervising teachers due to their recent school experiences.

Purpose and key questions for the evaluation

Fundamental to good evaluation practice is to negotiate the terms of reference with clients, among other things to identify the audiences for the study. It became clear that the AISV saw themselves as both client and primary audience (a secondary audience was the Commonwealth Department of Education, Employment and Training, (DEEWR), that oversees tertiary level education in Australia). As part of an evaluation we like to push audiences about the potential use of findings. In this case AISV policy makers wished to know how key parties involved in the delivery of ITEP 'made sense' of the initiative, with a view to informing further adoption of this model in the future. This was in recognition of the prototypic nature of the first implementation of ITEP. Our experience is that in social and educational contexts, in Australia, new programs are often prototypic (a term adopted by Lee Cronbach), that is, launched without a full specification of how a program will deliver outcomes. Lack of specification can occur at all levels of social provision. As this is being written there is considerable publicity about a national policy designed to make Australian homes more energy efficient. A key program designed to achieve this objective, the insertion of ceiling insulation, has failed due to the proliferation of untrained installers, with consequences, such as deaths among workers and fires in homes. The Commonwealth Minister in Australia is under pressure to justify the design of the intervention and his position.

AISV also were required to provide indications to the DEEWR about the potential worth of the model. A key question for DEEWR was whether the model added value to the conventional model, and to what extent. This was essentially a question about the enhancement of existing practice through the adoption of the new practices embodied in the ITEP approach.

The following policy related issues were negotiated with AISV:

- What is the nature of an effective mentor supported practicum?
- To what extent did the ITEP practicum model make an impact on pre-service teachers? Is it superior to the existing conventional model?
- What advice can be provided about the future implementation of the model if it is shown to add value to conventional approaches?

Establishing key questions is fundamental because this provides focus for the evaluation design, decisions about data collection and analysis. The evaluation questions led to the following decisions about the evaluation design and the management of the evaluation more generally.

- Question 1 was a descriptive/interpretive enquiry about delivery. This required comprehensive collection of evidence about implementation over the life of the program (12 months).
- Question 2 was an enquiry about outcomes. It was necessary to get some indications of implementation effects on participants. This is consistent with a process-outcome approach to determining program effects. Key audiences were warned that this was a prototype version of ITEP and effects on participants might be small.
- Question 3 was an enquiry about the future of ITEP. The evaluation design made allowances for the collection of information that could elicit advice about the future design of ITEP. This included 'what if' based enquiries to those with direct experience of prototype delivery.

Findings

For a chapter of this size and orientation, it is not possible to outline details about the conduct of the evaluation design over the year of the program. In summary, a key feature of the evaluation design was to undertake a systematic comparison of the three site deliveries of ITEP using a range of complementary methods, e.g. interviews with cluster leaders, observation of cluster meetings involving leaders and students (Question 1).

In addition interviews with key observers, such as school Principals hosting ITEP students reinforced the finding that students in ITEP were better prepared than students who had undertaken the practicum in their schools in previous years. Interviews with providers, including the three cluster leaders, using 'what if' questions, provided a basis for establishing an 'ideal model' for ITEP. These findings were presented as a logic model for ITEP designed to guide future delivery of the program.

We found that the ability of the cluster leader to coordinate the work of schools and the university staff varied markedly. The most effective cluster leader provided a strong bridging facility across the entities and materially added to the satisfaction of pre-service teachers involved. Furthermore, teachers and principals in schools valued the role of the cluster leader and saw the ITEP model as a considerable improvement over conventional teacher education courses.

Effective cluster leaders played an important brokering role, working with other key parties involved in the practicum. That cluster leaders could convey student concerns back to supervisors in a diplomatic way ensured that supervisors had additional understanding of how students were handling their classroom performance. That cluster leaders have the potential to inform university staff of similar concerns about factors such as the relevance and extent of formal assignment work added further potential to their brokering role.

The ITEP model also had the capacity to allow student discussions that allowed relevant theory to be linked to the practices they had undertaken in classrooms. We saw these sessions as highly desirable as they offered an opportunity to link students' practice with theory. The model also included a contribution from evidence-based practice as a way of informing cluster leaders about research on teacher education. Cluster leaders were supported through discussions of relevant research on matters such as effective supervision. These aspects highlight the contribution that timely injections of relevant research can make to the pre-service education if there is adequate planning and resources.

We used a set of teaching standards set by the Victoria Institute of Teaching, to construct and validate an instrument designed to allow pre-service teachers to comment on their readiness to teach as a frame. We also took an opportunity to collect the same data from a cohort of students not in the program as a comparison group (Question 2). These data were collected at the end of the academic year as students were completing the program.

We recommended that a fully specified ITEP would have the cluster leader at the core of the model, with direct influence on students in their day-to-day work in schools, and an indirect influence on schools on one hand, and on involved university based staff on the other. Moreover, while the direct influence was well established in good clusters in 2008, indirect influences, especially with university staff would need more attention from AISV policy makers for the program to achieve full potential.

Dissemination and engagement practice

A key difference between evaluation and most social research is the attention given to dissemination of information to audiences. In some quarters this pre-occupation is associated with evaluation use or, put another way, engaging with the evaluation outputs. Simply put, there is little point in undertaking evaluation work unless there are strategies designed to engage those audiences. Earlier in this chapter, we emphasised the importance of practices associated with negotiating the terms of reference for the ITEP evaluation with program stakeholders. This negotiation is a first sign of evaluator-client interaction that should commence at the design phase, and manifest itself in the adoption of responsive dissemination techniques.

These actions are consistent with practices of sustained interactivity, a commitment to ongoing linkages between evaluator and client, which build on what is known about the utilization of social research (see for example, Huberman, 1994). This means more than providing a readable report. Audiences need information about the evaluation as well as what the evaluation has found. In the ITEP evaluation, meetings with AISV were held regularly during the year to discuss how the program was progressing, and towards the conclusion to discuss the final report. Oral presentations encourage audiences to 'make meaning' of the findings and allow evaluators to provide information that they may not have included in written form, consistent with the adage that 'we know more than we can say'. While experience has shown that we cannot always count on instrumental use of our findings, we should always aim for a high level of conceptual understanding among our audiences.

Reflections on the evaluation process

An issue for this book is the degree to which this evaluation of a HE program differs from one focussed on a program at other levels of education, or in other areas of social provision. In another place, we have suggested that effective evaluation practice consists of three interlinked phases

- negotiation of an evaluation plan
- development of an evaluation design, and
- dissemination strategies.

It can be seen that evaluation practice based on this framework involves two phases involving social interaction and one phase involving technical social research skills.

We contend that these three phases provide a common cluster of practices for all evaluation studies that are responsive to the knowledge needs of identified audiences. An evaluator might then call on an existing model as the basis of the evaluation design phase of the evaluation study, but even in this research oriented phase, we find that evaluation work usually relies on the adoption of what some have labelled 'pragmatic principles' of action to get the job done within time and budget constraints. (See Datta, 1997)

We see no reason to depart from this generic framework in tackling evaluation work in HE. What might be necessary in this sector, however, is an increase in commitment to evaluative practice in general and that which is interactive in particular. While there has been long-standing evaluative activity in primary and secondary education sectors in Australia, there is considerably less evaluative action at the HE level. For example, it is rare for conferences of the Australian Evaluation Society to include presentations of evaluations of university teaching programs. It is possible to assert that curriculum and teaching in HE are under investigated in this country. As many evaluations are directed to assess new practices the comparative inactivity of evaluators at the tertiary level may signify the lack of innovatory teaching and learning approaches in universities.

12

Evaluation as deep learning: a holistic perspective on evaluation in the PALETTE project

Alan McCluskey

Introduction

This chapter draws on recent research in the context of a large international research programme in Higher Education (HE), vocational training and industry entitled PALETTE dealing with the participatory development of services and use-scenarios for learning in communities of practice. This chapter singles out five interrelated aspects of the project for particular attention and looks at these from the perspective of evaluation as a ***deep learning activity***. Evaluation in this context was embedded within the project and was intended first and foremost as 'formative', that is to say, as a major learning practice involving all actors in the ongoing process of understanding and steering project processes at all levels. Within this complex environment, three aspects concerning different approaches to evaluation emerged successively along the trajectory of the PALETTE programme: participatory, expert-based and evaluation as a practice. The remaining two aspects address the impact of the wider context on the work of evaluation and the role of evaluation in handling complexity.

The programme context

The aim of PALETTE, a three-year integrated R and D project funded by the EU IST programme,[1] was to 'facilitate and augment individual and organisational learning in Communities of Practice (CoPs)'. To achieve that overarching aim, 'an interoperable and extensible set of innovative services

[1] Sixth Framework Programme, Technology Enhanced Learning (IST-2004-2.4.10) EU R and D Fund

as well as a set of specific scenarios of use will be designed, implemented and validated in CoPs of diverse contexts.' Many of those contexts involved HE, both through the partners taking part and the fields worked on. The R&D process in PALETTE took place within the framework of a participatory design methodology (PDM), which was set up to establish 'a good balance between technological and pedagogical experts.' (PALETTE, 2006: 4)

A participatory logic

The initial PALETTE description of work explained that evaluation was to be integrated into the project process '*to provide direct, frequent and detailed feedback*.' The evaluation had three specific aims: assessing the methodological approach adopted in the project; providing ongoing formative evaluation; and establishing how a community of practice could be supported more effectively by a participative approach to developing tools and services and drawing up descriptions of practices. The form that evaluation took evolved over the three-year trajectory of the project. Initially, echoing the participatory logic that was central to PALETTE (the participatory design methodology), chosen actors from all the work packages were actively involved in project-wide evaluative activities. This approach was based partly on RUFDATA (Saunders, 2000), which was conceived, amongst other things, as an instrument to extend awareness and capacities of those that were required to carry out evaluation but who were not necessarily recognised evaluators, with the intention of inducting them into a community of practice of evaluators. As Saunders puts it: RUFDATA was '*a "tool" for those in the process of induction*.' The intention was that the actors thus 'inducted' into the community of evaluators were to act as relays and advocates of evaluation in their own areas of activity. Reflecting ideas emanating from writings about communities of practice, such actors were to straddle the boundary (Wenger, 1998) between their own professional community and that of evaluators, and in so doing were to stimulate potential change and innovation in ways of working.

To get a better idea of the notion of 'participatory', let's begin by what might be called an inclusive participatory approach to evaluation, by way of comparison with empowerment evaluation, considered to be one of the strongest 'expressions' of the idea of participatory. Such evaluation could be understood as strengthening community commitment, resources and skills by enabling all participants to plan and carry out their own evaluative activities. One way of doing so involves minimising the distance between the expert evaluator and the programme participant in what Meyer calls 'co-discovery' (Meyer, 1996: 75). To achieve its aim, such evaluation must involve a majority of participants and be seen by them as an integral and meaningful part of their everyday activities in what is called elsewhere a 'deep learning' process (see Entwistle, 1988).

The situation in PALETTE was somewhat different. Firstly it involved participation by delegation, that's to say where one person takes the place of a large number of others and acts as their voice and agent. This approach, which is familiar from many democratic systems, seeks to make the most of the advantages of participation while minimising the cost of wide-scale involvement, especially in contexts where available time and means are limited. Secondly, given the intent of RUFDATA to induce these 'delegates' into the larger community of recognised evaluation experts, they are distinguished from their colleagues by their status as those who 'discover' (and learn) in lieu of others. They are then confronted with the dilemma of communicating their own 'deep' learning to others in circumstances in which they are only able to call on 'surface' learning i.e. by reports and syntheses. Thirdly, the meta-level preoccupations of those piloting the evaluation, centred on such issues as overarching project processes and perceptions of formative evaluation, were diversely perceived by those involved in the everyday working of the project; their appreciation of it ranging from pertinent to irrelevant.

An expert-driven approach

Despite the use of delegation in evaluation at the beginning of PALETTE, the workload was still seen as too high given the pressure to fulfil other project objectives as dictated by contracts and descriptions of work. As a result, the participatory approach to evaluation through delegation was dropped after the first year in favour of an expert-driven approach in which a separate, much smaller group of experts carried out the evaluation. Many project actors perceived this shift as resulting in a distancing of evaluation from the project that was experienced as either essential or unfortunate, depending on the people questioned (McCluskey et al., 2008). This added 'distance' or possible 'marginalisation' brought into sharper focus the challenge of communicating evaluation outcomes to project partners and the management in particular and raised the question of evaluation design in relation to the communication and the uptake of results.

If evaluation is perceived from the perspective of learning, in the sense that it develops essential knowledge for both individual and team functioning, then an expert-based approach has certain limitations. The knowledge developed by experts in evaluation seen as a learning process needs to be 'communicated' to those who most need that knowledge and who must 'translate' it into operational terms. The word 'communicate' used in conjunction with the notion of the spread and uptake of knowledge evokes a mechanistic perspective on learning in which it suffices to pass on what is to be learnt for appropriate learning to take place. The degree of learning (if one could imagine a scale ranging from surface to deep learning rather than considering them as mutually exclusive) could never attain the same depth as that of the original learning of the 'experts' in situ. This raises the further question as to whether the economies achieved by assigning an expert to learn for others are not counterbalanced by the cost of then trying to bring others to 'learn' or at least to 'make sense of' what has been learnt by experts.

The presence of multiple perspectives on project reality amongst participants in this trans-disciplinary project further complicated the 'communication' of learning, in the case of PALETTE, particularly between those responsible for project management and those carrying out evaluation. This learning process could be facilitated by the design of the evaluation. For example, the use of depth interviews with key players contributed both to increased individual and collective awareness but also to the development (in some cases) of a more reflexive practice. The possibility of modelling the design of evaluation to favour deeper learning depends largely on the perceived role of evaluation both by evaluators and by those mandating the evaluation. If evaluators see evaluation in terms of providing knowledge rather than stimulating learning then there is no incentive to design evaluation that is conducive to deeper learning. In the same way, if decision-makers, such as project managers, see evaluation as the production of material to facilitate or justify their decision-making, then the investment in evaluation as learning may be seen as pointless.

Evaluation as a practice

The third and final change in the integration of evaluation in the project came with the emergence of the notion of moments of evaluation. The phrase was coined to cover a set of widely found practices that retained some of the characteristics of evaluative practices as recognised by experts in evaluation without necessarily being seen as evaluation by those carrying them out (or by those people who were professional evaluators). Evaluative moments generally entailed a number of related phases that might include the negotiation of work to be done with actors concerned, the process design and the creation of tools, the collection or generation of data, the analysis and/or reorganisation of that data and the integration of this (new) knowledge in a process. The exploration of evaluative moments in PALETTE made it apparent that many of the people conducting those moments neither saw themselves as evaluators nor work of this reflexive type as evaluation. This contrasted with the expectations of the RUFDATA approach aimed at induction and suggested an alternative way of looking at evaluation as a subset of those practices that characterised a wider set of professional communities.

This shift in perception from evaluation as uniquely the activity of a community of practice (CoP) of evaluators to evaluative practices as belonging to a wider set of practices embedded in the different professional communities taking part in PALETTE had a potentially emancipatory impact on the notion of evaluation (McCluskey et al., 2008). Such a perspective (of multiple communities, each with its own practice of evaluation) might also provide a more satisfactory framework for understanding the 'community' of evaluators within which many differing, if not diverging, practices cohabit.

It casts a new light on the division between so-called lay and expert evaluators. Evaluation carried out as a subset of activities in a given community of practice by actors of that community proved to be just as professional and possibly more appropriate in the given context than those carried out by experts of evaluation. At the same time, in examining such evaluative practices, it became clear that they were not always well designed, especially those that were tacit and informal, indicating that attention needed to be paid to the design and implementation of such activities by way of increased awareness of their nature without necessarily over formalising them.

Finally a word of caution is necessary about the distinction between evaluation carried out as an integral part of the activities of a community of practice not given over entirely to evaluation and evaluation carried out by specialists of evaluation. The research carried out in PALETTE indicates that moments of evaluation are invariably an integral part of a project process that couldn't work without them. In comparison, the evaluation carried out by specialists of evaluation often plays a more tangential role, in which the use and impact of its work depends on an additional will on the part of participants to integrate it into their work. This is particularly the case when evaluation addresses meta-level considerations and process innovations. Seen from this perspective, it raises the question of the contribution of evaluation design in engaging participants in addressing meta-level and process-based issues and the possible impact of such an engagement in founding change and innovation on deeper learning.

The dilemma of the wider context

No scene setting of the PALETTE project would be complete without a mention of the wider context, in particular the so-called Lisbon strategy of the European Commission to favour a social model which protects the environment and improves the quality of life (see the EU 2010 strategy) thanks to economic growth aided, amongst other things, by the development of ICTs and their uses. In the field of learning and innovation, that strategy is based on the underlying conviction that knowledge development should be accelerated and consequently improved by the reification of knowledge, shifting knowledge from tacit to more formal so as to enable ever increased knowledge exchange. Strategies employed to do so include peer exchange, peer learning, communities of practice and the identification and exchange of best practices. The PALETTE project is an integral part of this movement, centring its contribution on finding effective ways to promote and extend the reification and exchange of knowledge with the aid of ICTs within communities of practice.

Given the central nature of these assumptions and beliefs both to the project and to the European programmes that finance it, there is no legitimate or 'safe' way to question them within the project. Seen in this light, the scope of evaluation is always bounded by the limited context in which it takes place. Although factors beyond that boundary may have a decisive impact on the project and its success, in our current paradigm that handles complexity and the related interconnectedness of the whole by fragmentation; those factors cannot be addressed or questioned from within. Maybe the assumption that well-being can be improved by the wide-scale acceleration of learning is misguided, but this question cannot be raised within a project working towards that aim, even if evidence should appear in the evaluation of the project that points in that direction because project participants are not contractually, or morally, or paradigmatically allowed to call into question such a 'fundamental' issue.

As part of the wider context, the administrative structure that framed such R and D projects had other implications that were both important for the project and, in particular, its evaluation but which were beyond the accepted scope of evaluation within the project. European funding was granted on the basis of a project description that lay down detailed objectives and listed deliverables before the outset of the project, despite the fact that the area of research was one of the fastest changing (see McCluskey et al., 2008). The project was granted funding because it was judged to be appropriate to the needs and thinking of the Commission at that time. Although mechanisms were in place to permit periodic modification of the project trajectory should it prove necessary, the 'description of work' represented a contractual obligation leaving little place for unintended or unexpected outcomes or developments including those in the wider context.

Compliance with contractual obligations was the subject of regular reviews by the EU Commission, which, although supposedly formative in nature, were tied to a decision about granting the next stage of funding. Understandably, preparing for and responding to the considerable demands of the annual external review process run by the Commission was uppermost in priorities of participants as the continuation of project funding depended on it. As an evaluative exercise, it consumed a considerable part of the overall time project partners were prepared and able to grant to evaluation. Internal formative evaluation was not of such a high priority. As anecdotal evidence of priorities, two monthly steering committee meetings were entirely given over to preparing the annual review whereas the discussion of evaluation outcomes was generally placed at the end of the lengthy meeting agendas. When asked, individual participants' visions of formative evaluation diverged, ranging in general from an activity that marginally influenced individual perception to one that formed the shared understanding (see McCluskey et al., 2008).

The role of evaluation in handling complexity

The inherent complexity of PALETTE went beyond that of the difficult dialogue between actors from technology and pedagogy that lay at the heart of the participatory design methodology employed in PALETTE. As a transdisciplinary project, it brought together not only experts in educational technology and in pedagogy but also animators of CoPs in learning contexts, especially in HE, alongside experts in evaluation and in project administration. As a trans-European project, it also brought together participants from differing national cultures and languages. In this context, one of the challenges of the evaluation was to enable actors to make sense of the complexity. To do so, rather than trying to reduce complexity by searching for common solutions or systematised approaches, with the aim of creating a stable framework that tries to harness change, preference was given to an evaluation framework that helped participants within a developmental process to create situated provisional stabilities (see Saunders et al., 2006). Provisional stabilities assist decision-making processes and serve to combat entropy by enabling the emergence of a simpler order from complexity, albeit temporarily. Complexity as a paradigm, although very much in vogue in certain circles, is not nearly as widely used or deeply seated as those metaphors rooted in mechanics, telecommunications or cybernetics. For an evaluative approach based on the paradigm of complexity to be effective, the fact that approaches via other paradigms might be inadequate needs to be granted some credibility both by management and by individual participants. It also requires that time and effort be invested in understanding the multiple perspectives at play in the project as part of a deeper learning in creating provisional stabilities that enable us to handle complexity, contributing both to the success of the project and the development of each participant. The pressure to deliver which typically characterises this sort of research project, the related tendency to handle complexity by fragmentation and the associated type of funding based on deliverables will militate against spending time on activities that are consequently seen as accessory or pointless unless there is a strong, project-wide commitment to such an approach.

13

A social practice approach to the evaluation of enhancement strategies in the Quality Enhancement Framework for Scottish universities

Neil Lent and Joan Machell

Introduction and background

The Scottish Funding Council's (SFC) Quality Enhancement Framework for Scottish Higher Education (SFC, 2006) is a sector-wide policy that is intended to bring about systemic changes in the Scottish HE sector by focussing on the enhancement of teaching and learning experiences of undergraduates in Scottish Higher Education Institutions (HEIs). The QEF is a policy consisting of five elements. Each of these elements may be understood as programmes through which the policy framework is enacted. CSET (Centre for the Study of Education and Training) at Lancaster University has been commissioned by the SFC to evaluate the framework. The five elements that make up the QEF are:

- Subject reviews undertaken by Scottish HEIs
- Enhancement-Led Institutional Reviews (ELIR) undertaken by external reviewers
- Improved public information tailored to the needs of various stakeholders such as employers and students
- A greater voice for students in institutional review procedures
- A national programme of Enhancement Themes, aimed at encouraging academic and support staff and students to share current good practice and collectively generate ideas and models for innovation in learning and teaching.

The CSET evaluation is mainly focussed on the whole framework rather than considering each element separately. Nevertheless we are expected to draw some evaluative conclusions in relation to these separate elements. The evaluative approach we take is informed by social practice theories such as

Bourdieu and Wacquant (1992), Wenger (1998) and Engestrom (1999) where we focus on practices developed in specific contexts and how they relate to the values espoused in the QEF.

It is important to note the emphasis given to 'enhancement' in the framework. It has been argued that thinking about quality in terms of maintaining standards is becoming less relevant and needs to be replaced by a more developmental approach to quality (Gordon and Owen, 2008). This change is reflected in what can be seen as a rebalancing in Scottish Higher Education's (HE) own evaluative practices where there is a shift in emphasis from quality assurance based on audit, compliance and 'concrete data' to an emphasis on ownership, partnership, openness and development of improved practices among HE professionals. To a large degree, 'ownership' of the QEF and its processes now lies within the Scottish HE sector itself. This can be seen as a necessary condition for the shift towards enhancement. As assurance is associated with inspection, policing and summative judgments linked to the provision of resources, such regimes tend not to encourage openness because revealing shortcomings can lead to sanctions. Conversely, an enhancement approach emphasises the need to identify issues in need of further development. Openness and honesty are, therefore, essential elements for any enhancement-based policy. The quality assurance regimes pervasive in UK HE have been described as 'Coercive accountability' associated with an audit culture (Shore and Wright, 2004). The required change in practice in the Scottish sector requires a change in the prevailing quality culture that will allow new enhancement practices to be developed.

This broad approach marks a shift from practices associated with external inspection as part of previous audit-based review systems to practices where the sector is now expected to take a much greater ownership of quality systems and activity. This means that instead of developing a range of 'impression management' practices in which the imperative is to show themselves in the best possible light to an external auditor, institutions are now asked to be confident enough to identify those areas of their operations that can be improved and to be prepared to discuss how such areas can be enhanced. This shift has important implications for what might be termed 'systemic trust' in which the institutions need to feel confident such openness will not be abused in some way or that invidious comparisons might be made be made between 'open institutions' and those who have been more strategic.

Quality assurance inspection practices tend to be relatively bureaucratic with an emphasis on data gathering and verification. This includes making sure that the correct policies and procedures exist in written form (reified systems) without necessarily taking account of the practices on the ground. The focus on changing cultures and practices emphasised in the QEF and its attention on the experience of students within the sector suggests another shift. 'Enhancement' in this context is not about getting paperwork in order and making sure the 'right' statistics and 'impression' is made for inspectors. Instead, it is about taking account of practices taking place throughout whole institutions, including what happens in classrooms in terms of day-to-day teaching and learning practices. This spreads ownership of the framework, and responsibility for quality, across whole institutions.

The framework can be seen as existing within a complex network of diverse stakeholders that include sector-wide agencies such as the Scottish Funding Council and the Quality Assurance Agency Scotland, UK-wide agencies such as the Higher Education Academy (HEA) and also individual HE institutions. The network becomes more complex as each of these individual entities can also be seen as a network. For example, a university can quite easily be viewed as a network made up of various different groups from senior management, academics in various different disciplines, various forms of manager and administrator, through to the students that attend the institution. This view can be seen as an extension of Becher and Trowler's (2001) analysis of the diverse nature of academic communities within institutions in that we include non-academic stakeholders. The complex networked nature of the Scottish HE sector together with the culture shift implied by the emphasis of the framework on enhancement means that there are important implications for the evaluation of the QEF with which the authors of this chapter are involved. Given the shift away from an audit-based approach to review and evaluation implied by the introduction of the QEF, it would be inappropriate for the CSET evaluation team to adopt standard audit type evaluation methods based on attribution through cause and effect relationships. Considering the ubiquity of audit culture (Power, 1997), methods based on measurement and 'benchmarking' could adversely affect the success of the QEF in addition to providing information that is of no use in gauging a change in culture.

An evaluative approach

Our own practices need to be aligned with the shift for two reasons:

- Summative evaluations are unlikely to engender the degree of openness or sense of ownership among institutions and practitioners necessary for the QEF to be successful.
- The degree to which ownership of the framework needs to permeate through the Scottish HE sector means that the 'system' being evaluated can usefully be viewed as a number of different systems (including the QEF, sector-wide agencies, HEIs and disciplinary-based groups) interacting through a variety of networks that make accurate attributional judgements impossible.

In this chapter, we use the example of our evaluation of the Enhancement Themes to illustrate how our evaluation practices have responded to the challenges of programmatic evaluation. The work in the sector on the Themes serves to illustrate the complex networked nature of the sector. Work on the themes is led by the Quality Assurance Agency Scotland but involves direct formal inputs from academic institutions, disciplines, the Higher Education Academy and NUS Scotland. As such this case study functions as an illustration of our wider evaluation approach and practices in relation to the whole of the QEF.

According to the Enhancement Themes website (QAA, 2008), the 'Scottish higher education Enhancement Themes aim to enhance the student learning experience through identifying specific areas for development'. Also, 'Enhancement Themes encourage academic and support staff, and students collectively to share current good practice and to generate ideas and models for innovation in learning and teaching.'

The currently active themes are:

- Graduates for the twenty-first century: integrating the enhancement themes
- Quality cultures and systems and structures for enhancement

Past themes have included:

- Research-teaching linkages
- The first year
- Integrative assessment
- Flexible delivery
- Employability
- Responding to student needs
- Assessment

We should also state that while evaluating the themes (and the QEF more widely) we consider ourselves to be actors within the networks in which we are interacting. We do not see ourselves as impartial observers collecting objective data but as participants in a process of co-construction with other participants in the network. In essence we see ourselves as visiting participants with some role in shaping the object of our evaluation. This is a very important element in shaping our own practices. The notion of co-construction was important in our practices from the design stage onwards. As such RUFDATA can be used to illustrate the design concerns for the evaluation and our responses to these.

As a component of the QEF, the Enhancement Themes are intended to enhance the student learning experience in Scottish HE by identifying specific areas for development and encouraging academic and support staff and students to share current good practice and collectively generate ideas and models for innovation in learning and teaching. In other words: to provide nodes of concentration where practitioners and HEIs can develop their practices in relation to issues within the sector that have been identified as important areas where practices can be enhanced. We are looking for examples of a shift in culture taking place and whether the changes in culture are *consistent with the values associated with enhancement.* This is an important point: rather than basing our evaluation practices on a simplistic notion of attribution, we use an 'inferential' approach where evidence of embodied practice is sought. Our approach, therefore, puts a premium on what is happening, rather than the lost cause of cast iron attribution.

The Themes are broadly intended to lead to enhanced practices that will improve the experience of Scottish HE students. The uses to which our evaluation will be put are to gain understanding of how Themes are used in the Scottish HE sector and to optimise their use by stakeholders in ways that are aligned with the cultural values associated with the QEF. It is assumed that practices will develop within the various contexts to be found within the sector relating to different institutions, different disciplines, varying student needs, management cultures etc. The findings of the evaluation can be used to understand the role of values and practices that are aligned with the values of enhancement in developing a culture of enhancement. These need to be sufficiently flexible to allow for the likely diversity to be found in the Scottish HE sector. It is useful to be mindful of Saunders' assertion in Chapter 1 that 'A framework should provide a generic context for action in which some recognisable shaping characteristics are evident but within the shape a wide range of actions is possible.' As evaluators we need to recognise that 'enhancement' can take different forms in different places. For the Themes, this may mean that some Themes may be more relevant than others for different institutions or disciplines or that they need to be dealt with in different ways. We can therefore expect that different stakeholders in the Scottish HE sector may well use the findings of the evaluation in different ways that relate to their own specific contexts.

Foci: Within the overall Quality Enhancement Framework the enhancement themes have their own focus in terms of dealing with the development of new practices in a practitioner-led way that are intended to have a positive impact on student experience. Bearing this in mind, the focus of this part of the evaluation is on the practices of stakeholders in relation to the Themes and their judgements on how useful these are. We are also interested in the relationship between the Themes and other elements of the QEF. To an extent we will be evaluating the evaluations of stakeholders working with enhancement themes.

Data and evidence: The emphasis on culture shift and the complexity of the Scottish HE sector means that a quantitative approach that seeks to establish direct cause and effects between the Themes and changes in institutional values and practices is, as we have said, unlikely to yield useful results in evaluation terms. As evaluators we were concerned to build up a 'theory' of enhancement and culture shift through on-going dialogue with the evaluation commissioners and with other stakeholders. This involves building up an holistic view of the sort of cultural values that might be associated with enhancement. This is fairly generic and not prescriptive in that it should provide a generic context for action in which some recognisable shaping characteristics are evident as mentioned above. Therefore our evaluation practices must be able to take account of the likelihood that a wide variety of practices may well emerge in different areas of the Scottish HE sector that may look very different but are all aligned with the shaping characteristics of the framework. We approach the evaluation using largely qualitative means such as case studies, focus groups and group or individual interviews. For example, we conduct loosely structured interviews with stakeholders. We recognise their own expertise and make it clear that participants are free to dictate the topics discussed. In many respects our 'interviews' might be more usefully thought of as 'conversations'. Likewise many of our focus groups tend to take on a flow led by participants, often with very little active contribution from the evaluators.

Through these activities we are trying to build up a picture of how people at various levels of the Scottish HE sector view quality enhancement. We do this largely through enquiring about respondents' own practices, how they claim these are shaped (in both positive and negative ways) by their interactions with institutional, disciplinary and other relevant cultures, values and practices. Our evaluative judgments are shaped by the extent to which the cultures, values and practices articulated by our respondents are in alignment with the cultures, values and practices we have associated with enhancement cultures. We accept this may take a different 'form' in different parts of the sector. The degree of ownership offered also suggests that we should be looking at practitioners' own evaluative practices (perhaps better labelled 'reflective' practices) as a marker of success for the Themes and the Framework as a whole. We also need to be reflexive about our own evaluation practices. This includes resisting any urges to apply summative 'hard data' driven judgements and also to recognise our own status as actors within the sector.

Audience: Bearing in might we are looking at a complex networked sector it can be argued that the evaluation has multiple audiences. The 'bottom line' audience is the body that has commissioned the evaluation (The Scottish Funding Council). Other audiences include sector-wide bodies such as QAA Scotland, NUS and the HEIs themselves as well as other 'stakeholders' with a remit for, or professional interest in, quality in HE – including, most importantly – students and HE practitioners. For the Themes in particular there is an emphasis on practitioners, HEIs and academic disciplines bearing in mind the emphases within the Themes on developing practices. We need to be aware that the evaluation and its findings should be accessible to these groups.

Timing: We submit regular written and verbal reports to a time-scale agreed with the evaluation commissioners. There are also channels of communications being established with various groups within the sector. In relation to the Enhancement Themes, we have regular contact with QAA Scotland and with the Scottish Higher Education Enhancement Committee (SHEEC)[1] and also more informal communication with practitioners

---

[1] The Enhancement Themes are planned and directed by the sector through the Scottish Higher Education Enhancement Committee (SHEEC). SHEEC members are drawn from the sector and have institutional responsibility for teaching and learning.

through conference attendance and institutional visits. It is important that our evaluation findings are communicated in a timely fashion so stakeholders can utilise the information while it is still relevant.

Agency: The evaluation is carried out by external evaluators (CSET) although the form of our activities is negotiated with the commissioners and evidence is co-constructed with stakeholders to a degree. Again the point made above about our own reflexivity is important, we are also actors within the system and our evaluation activity of itself will have an effect. Although retaining the necessary lack of bias of external evaluators, we are not, in any sense, 'distant' observers.

Evaluation as 'practice'

To summarise, we have constructed a vision of the intentions of the QEF commissioners and a wide range of stakeholders and have built a 'theory' of evaluation based around alignment of values and practices taking place with those that might be associated with an enhancement culture. This theory recognises the diverse nature of the Scottish HE sector and therefore the diverse nature of potential enhancement. This means our practices need to be interpretive: we need to understand what practitioners are doing, how this relates to their particular circumstances and how (within context) this can be viewed as enhancement (or not).

Obviously we are not applying a pre-agreed set of measures to themes in an attempt to quantify how effective they are. Our approach is based around discussions with practitioners in the HE institutions and with practitioners who are able to have a wider sector-level appreciation of the enhancement themes. We attempt to gain an understanding of how the Enhancement Themes (and the other elements of the QEF) relate to problem areas identified by practitioners and the practices they develop to surmount these. In terms of usefulness for practitioners, we look for how the various Themes might enable practitioners to understand an issue and also the extent to which Themes are drawn upon as resources in dealing with specific issues. Although we use a number of different techniques, the fine details of our practices are built up through our own on-going involvement in the system(s) we are evaluating.

Although we are not from the Scottish HE sector, our status as 'fellow academics' allows us to be seen as non-threatening peers who have a basic understanding of, and sympathy for, the work of academics rather than as consultants set on applying the latest externally derived management models to HE. Through this we try to build up mutual trust and understanding with practitioners in the sector so that we can be confident that participants in our evaluation are being open with us. Part of this is being clear with those we involve in our evaluation that our work is intended to help them in what they do, not to provide another layer of bureaucracy to be dealt with before they can get on with their 'real' jobs. In essence our practices are intended to be flexible enough to cope with the variety thrown up within complex systems and aligned with the cultures and values of those systems. The flip side to this is that, no matter how we present ourselves, we are acting on behalf of the funding council and are expected to make evaluative judgments. This can understandably lead to the take up of a defensive stance among the stakeholders we interact with (especially where they are particularly used to dealing with audit-style approaches to quality in the past). One important part of our evaluative practice is to make very clear that the judgements we have been commissioned to make are in relation to the framework and the whole Scottish HE sector, not individual, institutions, departments or people. The people we interact with as we undertake the evaluation are sources of data not the objects of our evaluative gaze.

14

Insights into programmatic evaluative practice in HE: a commentary

Murray Saunders

Introduction

As we note in the introduction to this section, the case studies are drawn from the experience of programmatic evaluative practice from four different contexts, two from the UK nations, one from Australia and one from Europe. Two cases refer to programmes designed to improve teaching and learning in Higher Education (HE), one case on the preparation of teachers and a fourth on the way in which evaluation is embedded within an EU funded project.

One way in which these cases can illuminate evaluative practice is by using the following categories for comparative purposes.

Purposes and 'visions' for evaluation

We can see in these examples the way in which evaluations are justified and their focus emerges or even evolves rather than presents as a high fidelity design. We might call this practice as 'visioning'. By this we mean the behaviours associated with defining and articulating what the evaluation should be about.

While the evaluators were interested in a modified form of theory of change, in the case of the CETL evaluation, and this was drawn from the experience of previous evaluations, there was some resistance on the part of the commissioners to the idea of 'testing' a 'theory of change' in a full sense. The commissioners were clear that there were two purposes for the CETLs: they were to reward excellent teaching practice and to invest in that practice further in order to increase and deepen its impact across a wider teaching and learning community. This clear representation suggested a steer for the evaluation and to provide its principal purpose. Its vision was to examine the 'fidelity' of the strategy i.e. the extent to which it was able to achieve the effects its proponents desired. At the same time it attempted to provide formative feedback to the commissioners in order to strengthen and improve the programme.

It characterised the 'problem' as how the 'change environment' might be evaluated. A place it started was to look for the logic implicit in policy instruments. The starting point for an evaluation could be working with project or programme designers through the logic of their change strategies, asking, for example, on what basis they think activity X will lead to effect Y – in other words, what is their theory-in-use of themselves as change agencies?

In doing this, they might ask informants to explain their assumptions about the ways in which their theories-in-use are expected to lead to the desired effects. We might characterise this stance as a propositional vision, in which the evaluation asks 'Did this way of attempting to bring about positive changes work, i.e. bring about positive changes?'. Of interest in this case, was the search for the conditions under which 'bringing about changes' were likely to occur over a sustainable period.

In contrast, the vision of the evaluation role within the PALETTE project was quite different. Here we have an evaluation work package within a large European project in which the vision of the evaluation was contested, opaque and multi-layered. All projects of this kind are required to have an evaluation but its nature is unspecified by the funders. The positioning of the evaluation in relation to other work packages is similarly unspecified but the expectation and requirement is that the project design will have a full and coherent account of the evaluative dimension. The evaluation of the project then takes place at two levels. On the one hand is the embedded evaluation (to which McCluskey's chapter refers) which has the brief of both the provision of formative feedback as well as a knowledge based one in which it was required to assess the efficacy of the design methodology (participatory) within the project. To this extent, it was an evaluation vision for both knowledge and for development. At another level an expert panel is appointed by the EU project manager which undertakes periodic reviews of the overall project, including its evaluative dimension, and makes a final judgement of its acceptability. McCluskey demonstrates the way in which this process skewed the internal evaluations by pre-occupying participants disproportionally with these regulatory mechanisms rather than with the evaluative processes for 'learning' which formed the substantial dimension of the internal evaluation design of the project.

This process, along with modification of a participatory internal evaluation approach, to one which was essentially external to participants (although part of the project) and at the same time 'expert,' had two effects. First it reduced the potential of the 'learning' dimension of the project evaluations and secondly, it foregrounded and emphasised the 'evaluative moments' within the participants' practices which were often tacit and unacknowledged. We could call this a learning vision in which the evaluation both tacitly and explicitly provided learning resources for participants but which was susceptible to subversion and a reduction in effectiveness for both regulatory and pragmatic reasons. In this case, visioning, like most European projects, did not exist as a clear initial starting point but 'evolved' over the lifetime of the project.

In John Owen's case of the evaluation of the ITEP programme, we can discern the evaluation having an efficacy vision. This was a vision in which the evaluation was designed to answer questions associated with modelling and improving future practices on the basis of a new way of doing things, in this case the added value of having embedded mentoring support within a school. The evaluation was able to suggest conditions under which the new practices implied in ITEP might be best supported. This is clearly a form of policy learning but one in which the 'object' of learning was highly proscribed and contained within a tight design for delivery.

In the case of the evaluation of the enhancement themes within the QEF in Scotland, reported by Lent and Machell, we have a different kind of visioning practice which combined an acknowledgement of a espoused value set associated with 'collegiality', sector ownership and enhancement and alignment. While the commissioning of the evaluation was undertaken in a conventional way, there were strong expectations on the part of the commissioning agency that the evaluation's style, tone, justification and focus was aligned to the espoused values. In other words, the evaluation was not being 'done' to the HEI but was designed to establish the existence, or not, of sets of practices associated with the messages in the themes. It was described as an investigation into the existence of a 'culture shift' through the examination of narratives of stakeholders focusing on the 'experience' of the enhancement themes. 'Visioning' in this case consisted of aligning the evaluation practices with those associated with the object of the evaluation. In this sense, the Scottish case, is an example of an evaluation associated with a cultural change vision.

It contrasts with the PALETTE project in that the expectations and practices associated with the use of 'learning outputs' or artefacts by the 'client' or commissioners were clearly articulated and embedded. In this case, visioning was undertaken in collaboration with this stakeholder. In the case of PALETTE, the visioning took place at the level of project design by a group of participants who were completely disassociated from other groups of participants in other work packages. In the context of no guidance from funders, visioning in PALETTE was adaptive, evolving and remained opaque for many participants.

While there may be other visions and visioning practices in programmatic evaluations, these cases illustrate some interestingly contrasting approaches to the question of 'purpose' or 'vision' in evaluations within HE, as illustrated in Table 14.1.

Key actor interactions and 'legitimate practice' in the evaluation process

The examples of programmatic evaluation demonstrate the diversity of interactions between the stakeholders within evaluative practice. This can be a

Table 14.1 Visionary practices in programmatic evaluation

Type	*Practice*
Propositional	Testing of a theory of change involving discerning and identifying the intended effects from an intervention design. This vision is derived mainly from texts based on programme design at the point of evaluation design. This vision is similar to the use of a logic model.
Learning	Embedding an evaluation within programme or project practice to enhance or encourage learning either about project process or about project 'objects' (participatory design). This vision is derived iteratively during the project lifetime by continual adjustments and renegotiations.
Efficacy	Establishing 'what is working' in terms of specific piloting of strategy, method or professional practice before wider implementation. The vision is derived through close discussions with commissioners and estimations of the future use of evaluation outputs.
Culture change	Designing an evaluation which is aligned to the espoused tone, ethos and style of the object of study (QEF) and derived from previous experience in the sector and a theoretical estimation of the way culture change might be assessed.

subtle process whereby the evaluation is given authority by key stakeholders in the process; these stakeholders however, may have differently situated interests which will assert influence on the way they perceive both those providing data and evidence and those who are undertaking the evaluation. It is entirely possible that there may be contradictions in the way in which legitimacy is attached to the evaluation by different stakeholders.

In the Scottish and Australian examples, the values and 'tone' provided by the commissioners and partners became critical in the legitimacy of the evaluation. There was continuity and convergence in the levels of legitimacy between the 'sector site' of the evaluation or the professional constituency (the HE system as a whole in the case of Scotland and the Teacher Trainer sector in the case of Australia) and the commissioners. In each case, convergent legitimacy enabled the evaluators to undertake their work with high levels of cooperation from those asked to provide data and evidence, there were ready channels through which to maximise the use of the evaluation outputs and the suggestions or implications of the evaluation were given weight and authority.

To some extent this characterisation depends on the way in which the evaluation was billed, essentially, as a way of improving the processes and practices associated with a programme of intervention which had already been given, itself, legitimacy by those who were 'policy recipients'. The evaluation therefore, was not seen as a way of policing or inspecting 'fidelity' between the expectations of policy promulgators and the way in which policy enactors had interpreted and developed new practices in its name. It was much more associated with improvement and development.

However, in the QEF evaluation outlined by Lent and Machell, we have a context which has its ambiguity. On the one hand is an approach which was broadly 'owned' by the HE sector in that enhancement themes were seen as a mechanism designed to help and support developments in teaching and learning. On the other hand, the 'mechanism' itself was open to some critique i.e. it attracted the 'usual suspects', neglected the hard to reach and skipped too quickly from one theme to another. So, while the overall instrument might win legitimacy, specific mechanisms might be more problematic.

This finer grained analysis of practice in the evaluation of programmes might also yield other tensions in an otherwise convergent model. In the Scottish case, there is an unclear positioning of the focus and direction of 'culture change' within the vision of the policy which impacts upon the relationships between the actors. Who might be leading it, from whence do the ideas come and who are the sponsors? If any of these questions can be answered that it was by a source from outside the universities themselves, then evaluating the change also changes the dynamic for the evaluation weakening the idea of policy ownership.

Legitimacy in the way we have outlined it is part of the story. In both cases, however, we have other forces at play in this convergent model. They both have a track record of 'negotiated development' and what John Owen calls sustained interactivity which has created early warnings concerning expectations, uses and ways of practising that have helped to create a consensual approach.

However, when we look at the relationships analysed in the other two cases, we have a different picture. The relationships between the stakeholders in the chapter by McCluskey and by Saunders suggest a more fractured or at least complex dynamic. In the case of the CETLs in which a lightly managed intervention created relatively high levels of individual CETL autonomy, a strong local sense of identity and a 'local' evaluative culture, there was a danger that the evaluation of the whole programme, at this interim moment, might have low legitimacy with the individual CETLs. In the event, the relationship between the evaluators and the CETLs was legitimised by having a clear justification for the evaluation which focused on testing the efficacy of the policy instrument (spending money on CETLs) at the national level rather than attributing worth, externally valorised, on the work of individual CETLs.

The relationship between the commissioners and the evaluators in this instance was supported by Owen's sustained interaction which began with the agreement that the evaluation should be about exploring the theory-in-action associated with centres for excellence (reward and beacons) that they could act as a mechanism for enhancement across the whole sector not just those in receipt of time limited resources.

The relationships between actors in the PALETTE project on the other hand evolved through practice during the lifetime of the project and were often tacit and inexplicit. Previous experience and expectations about the nature and role of evaluation led to some diverse and contradictory expectations about the relationships between actors as far as the evaluation was concerned. These divergences were strongly related to the focus of the next section below on the 'object' of the evaluation. What an evaluation should be evaluating is an important determinant of divergence. McCluskey shows that PALETTE actors had very different views on what the evaluation should be doing which ranged from policing, validating, providing management information, undertaking primary testing of solutions and finally, examining the efficacy of some core operating principles. At the same time, the projects 'real' evaluation was being undertaken externally by EU appointed reviewers through the imposed periodic review sessions at key moments of the project life cycle.

Through intense negotiation and the development of social networks, the relationships between actors in the orbit of the evaluation became more effective. As the various views of the evaluation, in practice, became redundant or not born out in practice, actors began to give some legitimacy to the 'conduit' role evaluation might play, even though it resulted in only partial fulfilment of expectations. McCluskey shows how the position of formal evaluation remained uncertain throughout the lifetime of the project when faced with the core paradox associated with formative evaluation within a contractual environment which allowed unintended outcomes or unexpected developments little scope. His chapter shows how the compliance framework of European projects of this type was the single most important influence on all relationships between actors in PALETTE, including evaluation.

We can see that these contributions provide illumination of the way that actor interactions around programmatic evaluation are shaped by interlinking factors which provide greater and lesser degrees of legitimacy to evaluative practice. Interestingly, the degree of 'externality' on the one hand or 'ownership' of the evaluation on the other, may not be a key factor in determining legitimacy. Clarity of purpose and sustained interaction emerge as core dimensions of legitimacy. While projects and programmes in receipt of resources from a funding body may not 'enjoy' an evaluation, it might be considered appropriately justified on the basis of testing a theory of change, providing resources for improvement or identifying examples of interesting or innovative practice.

What is the 'object' of an evaluation?

In Chapter 27, we review the use of this term to denote the evaluation focus. Here within the context of programmatic evaluation, we can see some interesting nuances in the way the object-as-focus is expressed. The chapters by Saunders, Lent and Machell, and Owen all take the policy of improvement as a 'given' and do not challenge the basic assumptions behind attempts to improve teaching and learning.

When the object of the evaluation is the policy instruments (e.g. resource allocations to universities for widening participation, ring fenced funds for targeted developments, subject centre networks, creating Centres for Excellence in Teaching and Learning), the focus of the evaluation might be the theory in action of those instruments. In the Saunders chapter, it was the idea of the Centre for Excellence as a way of improving practice across the sector which formed the object of the evaluation. The chapter by McCluskey explicitly critiques the policy instrument and points out the way in which it was excluded from the object of the evaluation.

When the object of the evaluation is at the level of a mechanism (in the case of CETLs, specific strategies used by CETLs to 'enact' programmes), the object would be the theories of change embedded in specific strategies, for example how a small scale research grant worked.

When it is an 'effect', the object refers to positive changes in practices (economic, social, educational, health) brought about by the aggregated determination of mechanisms, instruments and policies. Programmatic evaluations rarely have the opportunity to continue long enough to have as their object, the longer term effects of the programme. This problem has given rise to the increased interest in the meta review or synthesis as an attempt to capture the aggregate or longer term effects of a series of programmes or interventions. This said, the Lent chapter outlines an approach to evaluation objects which aspired to charting the way 'practices' had shifted to absorb some of the thematic messages.

As well as understanding the evaluation object as a progressively focused continuum (as above) between policy and effects it can also be understood as a logical series of evaluation objects which flow from an initial experience of awareness through a learning process which includes the 'reconstruction' of learning in new practices.

Object 1: Quality of the experience of the intervention

This incorporates consideration of how the intervention is experienced by the target group 'at the time', essentially this level of evaluation object is concerned with the tone, pitch, quality of resources, space, timing and relevance of the engagement activity or adoption of a programme. In many cases this diagnostic tool is used as a quality check, customer service tool or 'happy sheet'. It is important as a diagnostic tool for the quality of the delivery of an engagement strategy or estimations of awareness. This object was present in the chapter presented by McCluskey in which the way PDM was experienced became the evaluation object. However, and this was the main thrust of the chapter on PALETTE, the object of the evaluation was contested. The variations gave rise to questions about the relevance of the evaluation for different stakeholders. A further insight offered by the PALETTE example is how the object of evaluation can be embedded into on-going developmental practice and not 'discerned' by those engaged in it as a discrete practice. McCluskey's 'evaluative moments' alerts us to this process.

Object 2: Quality of the situated learning outcomes

If the engagement had specific learning or knowledge based outcomes in mind on the part of the target group, this object is concerned with measuring what these may be in learning environments; these might be specific skills or new knowledge acquisition. These outcomes are important. Because, while not corresponding to new behaviour or practice on the part of the target group, they might be considered a necessary condition for changes in practice.

Object 3: Quality of transfer or reconstructed learning in new practices (effects)

This is probably the 'gold standard' in terms of evaluation object as effect and is a direct reference to the extent to which strategies have produced more routine, longer term changes in the attitudes, capacities, confidence and identities in the target group. This level of consideration can be addressed by quantative indicators with relatively little diagnostic potential (inclusion rates associated with the target group, stay on or drop-out rates, types of courses etc.) but might also include indications of experience involving more narrative inquiry techniques.

Object 4: Quality of institutional or sector effects

This object shifts the focus from the experience of individuals or small populations to the extent to which strategies are promoting 'new ways' of doing things at the institutional level in terms of new systems, routine systemic practices and assumptions which are framed by the widening participation agenda). As an evaluation object, other key stakeholders (undergraduate and postgraduate officers, teaching and learning committees, teams engaged in learner support practices, teachers engaged in routine teaching and learning practices) will form the source of evaluative evidence.

Object 5: Impact on macro or long term strategic objectives

It may be interesting to work with individual evaluations at institutional level (concentrating on levels 3 and 4) to develop a meta perspective on how the policy is achieving positive effects overall. There may also be a case for commissioning an independent evaluation with level 3 and 4 concerns that provided a meta evaluation of trend through the sector. We return to a consideration of effects in Chapter 27.

In McCluskey's case, the use of semi-structured interviews was shaped, in part at least, by the nature of the evaluation object, that of participants' tacit or unacknowledged knowledge of how the PALETTE project process was being experienced. In this case, another way of putting it is to discuss the way the 'focus' for an evaluation is presented, identified and exemplified. This might mean, as well, what is not identified. As we note above, the primary 'policy logics' that might give rise to a particular programme (as its instrument) are not normally accepted as a legitimate evaluation object by commissioners. In other words, it raises issues about how we decide about what counts as an evaluative object within programmatic evaluations within HE. Invariably, they tend to be associated with mechanisms, 'what works' type preoccupations and a range of second order issues which do not challenge basic policy assumptions. This is entirely predictable given the desire of commissioners either to use evaluation to problem solve operational issues or to legitimate existing decisions at policy level.

In summary, we can say that the object of evaluation has profound implications for method of inquiry as well as evaluation approach. It raises issues that centre on the capacity we have to attribute value for example, that involve clarity on establishing the effects of an intervention or programme. For many commissioners, the most desirable yet illusive evaluation object is the existence or not of an unequivocal causal link between what is happening and the stimulus for change provided by the programme or the intervention.

Variations in evaluation use

To some extent this is a 'Cinderella' area of consideration. While it seems axiomatic that evaluations should be used, a planned and rehearsed approach to the way this may happen is rarely undertaken. Of course we have the seminal contribution to this debate offered by successive editions of 'utilization focused evaluation' by M. Q. Patton (1997) in which he asserts that the potential for use is largely determined a long time before 'a study is completed', he argues that 'utilization-focused evaluation emphasises that what happens from the very beginning of a study will determine its eventual impact long before a final report is produced' (Patton, 1997: 20).

For Patton, an evaluation which is focused on use, 'concerns how real people in the real world apply evaluation findings and experience the evaluation process . . . it is about intended use by intended users' (Patton, 1997: 20). He acknowledges that in an evaluative environment there are likely to be an array of evaluation users as well as uses, but he argues for a particular emphasis on primary intended users and their commitment to specific concrete uses. Further he argues for the highly situated nature of these kinds of decisions, which, broadly is the stance taken in this book.

What are the situated practices associated with the cases we have included that illuminate issues associated with use?

While commissioners and users of an evaluation are not synonymous, they can be collapsed for the purposes of this commentary. It is self evident that once an evaluation enters the public domain, if it does, then anybody can be a potential user of the evaluation if they have access to it. This is one of evaluation's great potentialities and suggests the urgency of establishing the levels of public access to evaluations very early on.

Building on earlier work, the thrust of earlier points implies both process use (see Patton, 1998) and access to the products of an evaluation by a wide range of stakeholders is an aspiration. When we view the process use available in our cases we can see that it refers to the unintended effects of carrying out an evaluation, i.e. the effects associated with the practices of asking questions, focusing on specific dimensions of a programme experience, organising visits etc. In this way, the act of carrying out an evaluation can:

- foreground new or unacknowledged issues,
- draw attention to 'hot spots' or problem areas during the course of questioning and informal feedback,
- force attention on difficult implementation areas or contested experience,
- provide a 'voice' for the powerless, disaffected or the 'unheard',
- draw attention to time-lines and act as an implementation tool,
- make participants think about 'audience' and 'users',
- police aspects of programme implementation.

A general rule should be that if the evaluation is in the realm of public policy, promulgated by public policy-makers, then the evaluation findings should find their way into the public domain. There has long been a debate within evaluation circles about the relationship between an evaluation product (report, analysis, synthesis, etc.) and the way an evaluation might be used. Should an evaluation contain recommendations for example? The position that evaluations should not make recommendations in the strictest sense of the word is persuasive. How can evaluators be in a position to do this? What they can do is engage in a 'conversation' that might outline options according to different stakeholders' experiences, or against stated objectives where we might be able to infer likely gaps, etc. We can also engage with decision makers as participants in the decision-making process as evidence is discussed and implications for policy-making are reviewed. None of these things are the same as offering recommendations. This essentially is the position taken up by McCluskey in his case. It is based on the failure of the evaluation to be used effectively by most of the stakeholders within the project.

It is also possible to check on the way evaluation evidence is used and presented, to offer a critique when it is distorted or used selectively, and to point out the effects certain programme directions might have on what the evaluator knows about a stakeholding group. The role of the evaluation is to provide resources on which these decisions might be made but not to make the decisions themselves or to imply a 'latent' decision. This is not just a hair splitting exercise. Evaluations are constantly put under pressure by commissioners and designers of programmes to make recommendations. Sometimes this pressure is designed as a way to avoid any negative political fallout arising from evaluation implications and displace responsibility on to the evaluator.

More often than not it is simply a matter of not making clear at the outset, what the limits and possibilities of an evaluation might be. To some extent in the case of the CETL evaluation, evaluators did come under pressure to present a positive overview in the knowledge that the programme legitimacy was contested.

The process of establishing the voice of the user at the outset of the evaluation and building into the design a real 'rehearsal' of the way in which an evaluation might be used, seems to be both neglected and important. Not to do so all too often results in missed opportunities for any use at all with evaluation reports languishing on dusty shelves overlooking meetings where decisions are being made. Imagine a real situation in which evaluators and users are sitting around a table and discussing what is going to happen to an evaluation report on an organisational change process. This means identifying a list of specific practices. When we look at the cases outlined in this section we see the range of practices from tabling the report at a meeting, to assessing its implication, to exhibiting empathy with the stakeholding groups (we return to these issues in Chapter 27).

The evaluator can help this process by presenting the evaluation report in such a way that the logic of the findings makes it clear what the decision-making options might be. A simplistic example to demonstrate this point might be the analysis of positive effects of a programme on the one hand and the cost on the other. Both these elements of the depiction should be faithfully recorded for the users in order for them to make a decision on what the balance should be. This is a useful act and the voice or needs of the users are present but it does not trespass into the realm of recommendation. The cases describing the CETLs and the ITEP programmes demonstrate this type of use.

Using evaluations involve politics. While evaluators should not say what decisions might be made, they should be realistic and sympathetic to the world in which decisions are made. Users of evaluations have these considerations as central. Unpalatable findings might require presentation in a particular way, at a particular strategic moment to a particularly strategic audience in the first instance. Evaluators should be sympathetic to these realities and have little power to insist.

In presenting the voice of the commissioner, I have dwelt on the planning and design stages and the final stages of reporting an evaluation. But, an obvious part of the obligation of an evaluation is to meet the expectations of users that the findings are strong enough to bear the weight of important decisions. In other words the depictions offered by an evaluation are valid and reliable. In my view, normal social science standards pertain here. The way we collect evidence should be subject to those rules and conventions. This does not imply any social science paradigm, merely that the work complies with whatever standards are required for a given approach. What is important is that the claims that can be made on the basis of different approaches must be part of early conversations with users.

There is an emergent culture in the 'developed' world that holds that the public seems reluctant to allow expert groups (teachers, health workers, judiciary, etc.) to police themselves. The assumption used to be that their internalised professional values acted as a discipline on their practice and ensured the highest standards (in theory at least) and that their pronouncements could be trusted. This aspect of the social contract has broken down. It seems that governments, some would say the public at large; no longer trust these groups to discipline themselves. What has replaced it is a proliferation of evaluative mechanisms that are designed to control the quality and standards we used to allow the practitioners themselves to assure. In this sense, evaluation is in danger of becoming a universal policeman. This increases the burden on evaluators to take seriously their role in developing honourable practice. More optimistically, with this proliferation, we can see possibilities in the use of evaluation as part of social capital building. It has a role in the civic voice as it acts to bring states and organisations to account for the way they undertake their work and spend our money on our behalf. This goes some way in counterbalancing the policing role.

In summary, there are some further distinctions we might make which help this discussion. They centre on the difference between use on the one hand and usability on the other. These categories refer to the interaction between the organisational environment into which an evaluation output might be intervening and the design of the evaluation output itself. Both these features interact to determine the extent to which an evaluation output or an evaluation process can create effects. We return to a full discussion of these issues in Chapter 27.

These cases have helped to redefine some of the preoccupations of programmatic evaluative practice. It has demonstrated the richness of approach and the way in which the attribution of worth and value are nested in an array of practices which are highly situated and context determined. While this is true, we have attempted to show that there are some common generic concerns which the categories of consideration have highlighted and which will be picked up in our final chapter.

Part Three

Institutional evaluative practice

15

Institutional evaluative practice: quality, enhancement and regulation

Veronica Bamber

Introduction

This section of the book focuses on how institutions decide on the quality and merit of their internal practices, and how groups of stakeholders (teachers, researchers, students, external collaborators) decide on the value of what is done. As previous chapters have established, evaluation is strongly connected with the contexts and policies which constrain or enable it (Jacobs, 2000; Perrin, 2002), and institutional evaluation can't be divorced from the wider HE environment, such as the need to present positive public data in a competitive market, and the need to match internal evaluation to external evaluative practices.

Quality practice as evaluative practice

The purpose of evaluation in institutions is usually to improve quality (Potocki-Malicet et al., 1999), and the trajectory of evaluative practice in universities parallels the rise and fall of quality cultures. Figure 15.1 summarises this trajectory over three key periods (Pre-1990s, the 1990s and the mid to late 2000s) and in three sections: the Quality Environment, the Tenor of Evaluative Practices in that environment, with Examples of these Evaluative Practices.

What Figure 15.1 shows is that evaluation became a serious, more formalised business in UK institutions following the rise of the quality culture and managerialism in the early 1990s (Ball, 1998), since quality in research and teaching could only be assessed if data and evidence were available. The flow away from discipline-based peer review and towards centrally-coordinated systems for evaluation meant that administrators at the centre of institutions presided over the move from academic decision-making to administrative data collection and decision-making, with a consequent redistribution of power (Kogan, 2002). This era was also characterised by the colonisation of

	Pre-1990s	*1990s*	*mid to late 2000s*
Quality Environment	Self-regulation. No top-down, external accountability imperatives (but government latterly rattling sabres about linking funding and teaching quality)	Quality Culture in full flow: top-down institutional and subject-level audit of increasingly mass education HE, led by Funding Councils. Power moving from academic departments to central administration of universities. Sectoral mutiny in mid 1990s with creation of QAA in 1997, and the start of quality audit 'lite'	Funding Councils steer from a distance. Increasing emphasis on (overseen) self-evaluation by institutions
Tenor of Evaluative Practices	Informal, implicit, intuitive evaluative practices, and discipline-based peer review. Assumption of shared values. Older universities trusted to manage own quality	External, subject level review: external (peer) reviewers interrogate assessment performance, observe classes and make quality judgements; benchmarking across sector to share good practice	Enhancement rather than (solely) assessment and assurance of quality; institutional drive towards own management information; emphasis on alignment of university systems (eg HR) with institutional objectives
Examples of Evaluative Practices	Ad hoc, self-driven informal feedback in pre-1992 institutions, along with peer-review of examining; post-1992 sector already subject to HMI[1] and CNAA[2] inspections	Practices to match external review and institutional quality cultures: module feedback questionnaires, interrogatory monitoring and review procedures, led by administrators in central university services	National Student Survey; listening to 'the student voice'; QAA review aiming for greater reflection and collegiality

Figure 15.1 A brief chronology of evaluative practices, within the frame of UK Quality Assurance

Note:
1 HMI: Her Majesty's Inspectorate
2 CNAA: Council for National Academic Awards

educational policy by economic imperatives (Ball, 1998), and decreasing links between educational practices and evaluative ones. Following institutional protests in the 1990s against what was seen to be quality agencies 'getting too big for their boots', the curve turned again and the 2000s brought what Henkel (1998: 285) called a shift from a positivist to a hermeneutic paradigm. In the late 1990s, the government sanctioned a move from external departmental/subject audit to institutional review as the basis for its QA regime (Filippakou and Tapper, 2008), with greater emphasis on critical self-reflection (Filippakou and Tapper, 2008). This is especially visible in the Scottish sector, where Enhancement-Led Institutional Review means that institutions examine and monitor their own quality processes, and the Quality Assurance Agency carries out quinquennial reviews to check the findings. As mentioned in a previous chapter, the jury is still out on the extent to which enhancement-led review is fundamentally different from previous incarnations of quality assessment, but what is clear is that institutional self-evaluation is central to current evaluative practices. It is also clear that although certain values (such as respect for institutional diversity) are commonly held, context does matter, and the more context-specific an evaluation, the more likely it is to be effective (Henkel, 1998).

Having briefly traced the evolving cultural and political environment for institutional evaluative practices, these practices can now be framed conceptually, to provide us with a tool for analysing particular examples.

In Figure 15.2 we have depicted the way the intersections between content and processes associated with external imperatives, and internal responses to evaluation, unfold. We apply the term 'Discretion Framework' to a model which refers to the relative control an institution may have on the way it undertakes its internal evaluative practice. The nexus operates around

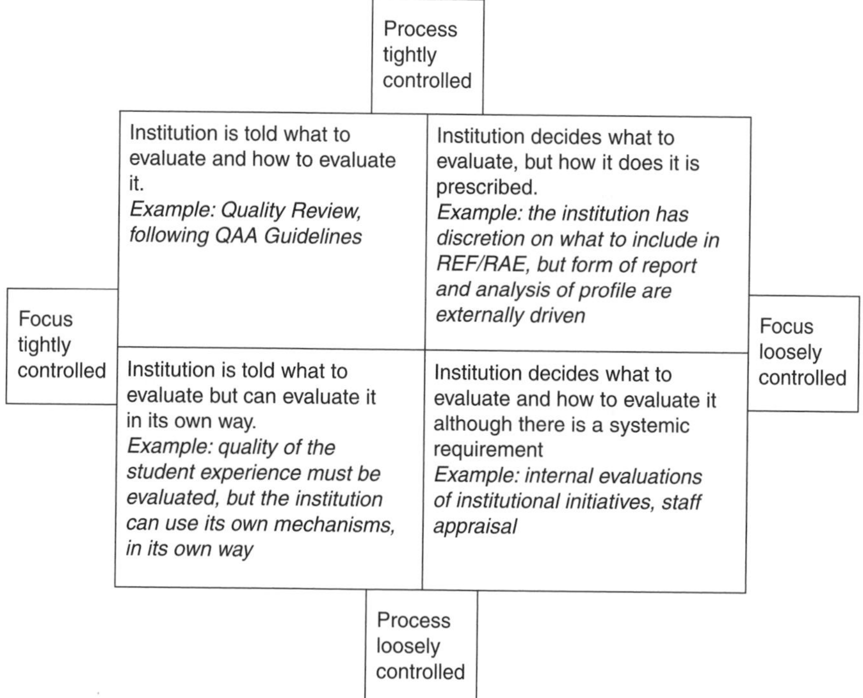

Figure 15.2 Discretion Framework for evaluative practices in institutions

control over what is evaluated (the focus of evaluation) and how evaluation takes place (institutional processes and practices). Thus the matrix demonstrates the level of discretion which an institution has in deciding how or what to evaluate in particular aspects of its activity. The Discretion Framework matrix helps us by giving us a language to describe what goes on in evaluative practices, and might help us decide what is appropriate in different contexts. This matrix may operate differently at various levels in the same institution. For example, in a particular institution there may be loose control of both process and focus, but a particular subject group or department may have its own evaluative practices, which are much more tightly controlled. If we imagine diagonal lines pulling from the top left hand corner down to the bottom right hand corner, or vice versa, then we can visualise the pull between different political and cultural tensions : is evaluation being driven by top-down, central forces (such as increasingly powerful and specialised central administrative functions), or is it rooted in bottom-up initiatives, such as reflexive institutional questioning?

As institutional evaluation has grown, so has the deep tension between Henkel's (1998) positivist and hermeneutic paradigms – the need for pseudo-scientific 'data' versus competing claims of subjective interpretation. In reality, of course, both sides of the divide are joined in a continuum, although this has not always been clear in the political and epistemological conflict between proving worth and interrogating it. At the macro policy level, there has been recognition over time of the need to give institutions more say in how they assess and enhance their own practices – perhaps within the social practices of the institution; the UK Cooke Report (2003: 51) acknowledged that 'quality enhancement should be owned by the institutions, with the agencies providing support through focusing upon activities which are best done collectively for the sector'. Tavenas (2003: 50–51), from the European perspective, indicated that universities should have prime responsibility for their own evaluation, and that these evaluations should be cognisant of local circumstances. Filippakou and Tapper (2008) confirm that institutions are, indeed, responsible for their own quality standards, and that institutional review aims to ensure that they have procedures in place to achieve and maintain them.

Nonetheless, tensions continue, and the pull between the quadrants in the Discretion Framework in Figure 15.2 depict some of these tensions. The Framework serves to highlight conflicts of direction, but can also illustrate some of the types of evaluative practice which you are likely to be familiar with if you work in a university. At the macro level, institutions are evaluated in order to meet government quality assessment agendas, and to demonstrate value for money in what can look like an 'economic-rationalist interpretation of quality' (Prosser and Barrie, 2003). As mentioned in previous chapters, the Funding Councils in the UK employ the Quality Assurance Agency to carry out institutional evaluations, assessing institutions against their own aims and objectives. This type of evaluation could be placed in the top left hand quadrant of the Institutional Discretion Framework, since universities have little control of how they are evaluated and what is evaluated. Evaluative practices in externally-driven institutional review are tightly controlled in both process and focus.

Institutions' own quality reviews are derived from the quality reviews carried out by external agencies, and could be located further into the bottom left hand quadrant of the Discretion Framework; these evaluations are tightly controlled in focus, but not in process; in other words, universities are obliged to demonstrate the value of what they do in key areas, but have some discretion in how they do it. For instance, they have to demonstrate 'student engagement' in quality processes, but they will have different ways of ensuring that engagement, and of evaluating it. Nonetheless, in spite of the greater levels of internal discretion, the close relationship between institutional review and external review will continue to produce close parallels between evaluative practices in the two arenas – what Hannan and Silver (2000: 139) refer to as 'systemic by-products' of quality review.

One of the difficulties in institutional review is the requirement for universities to reflect (usually in a self-assessment document) on their own performance. This usually takes the form of a written description of the academic context, curriculum, learning and teaching, support, etc., accompanied by an analysis of how well each aspect of provision is operating. Much is at stake, and the natural tension between self-protection and honest reflexivity is a high wire act which institutions have become increasingly adept at walking. Although some 'green shoots' of reflexivity have been able to emerge in the move towards enhancement-led review, the reality of walking that tightrope means that true reflexivity is unlikely to happen in large, public evaluations. More amenable to reflexivity is localised, bottom-up evaluative practice, led by those whose interests are at stake. Where 'truth' and 'data' are recognised as complex, contextual and often contradictory, more learning is likely to happen. The challenge for evaluators is not only to design appropriate methods for evaluation, but also to accommodate the realities and practices of academic life.

Related to institutional review is departmental or subject review, as the evaluation process drills down through the levels of the institution. One aspect of this is the course validation and review process, in which peers within the university support a central quality unit in assessing the quality of specific courses. In theory, this activity might again fit into the bottom left hand quadrant of the Discretion Framework, since the evaluation of courses is loosely controlled in process, but tightly controlled in focus: the university must evaluate the student experience and the appropriateness of the curriculum, but can decide for itself how best to do this. However, in reality, institutions have again adopted the 'systemic by-products' (Hannan and Silver, 2000: 139) of external review, down-scaling some of the global evaluative practices at the local level. Levels of discretion in this type of evaluation are perhaps only cosmetic.

In the chapters which follow, case contributors from England, Australia, Germany and Switzerland take us through their experiences of institutional evaluative practices. Having had institutional management experience over the period when university league tables came into being, Rob Cuthbert addresses the question in Chapter 16 of how senior managers can meet their accountability commitments, but not be drawn down the tunnel of league table myopia. He advocates fresh thinking about managing, to find social practices which embody the values needed to transcend managerialist pressures. In Chapter 17, Kerri-Lee Krause describes how a combination of imperatives at Griffith University led the institution to review its approach to evaluating the student experience; in this case, data sets and league table-type data are a key part of their holistic approach to evaluation.

Uwe Schmidt and Christoph Rosenbusch, in Chapter 18, discuss the links at their institution – Johannes Gutenberg-University in Mainz – between quality assurance and evaluation. The quality unit's strategy is deliberately research-related, and straddles the fields of quality and organisational development. Bernadette Charlier's Chapter 19 also focuses on organisational development, discussing the development of evaluative practices in a Swiss university, and the evaluations which underpin a parallel staff development programme. It argues that there is a risk of staff development evaluative practices being in tension with institution evaluative practices, and considers how to improve alignment between the two.

What all of these writers have in common is a desire to make the most of evaluation, and to ensure that it is seen as an intrinsic aspect of institutional development and change, rather than an isolated activity. This means that they link evaluative practices with the social practices of their university context, as the following chapters show.

16

Failing the challenge of institutional evaluation: how and why managerialism flourishes

Rob Cuthbert

Governments spending billions and individuals spending thousands of pounds on Higher Education (HE) rightly expect accountability for how the money is used. But pressure for accountability has accelerated the spread of managerialism, jeopardising rather than improving quality and posing dilemmas for managers trying to reconcile internal and external pressures. In the managerialist dialectic, unthinking resistance meets unthinking control, an unwinnable battle between the stereotypes of 'academic populism' and 'new managerialism' (Watson, 2009: 77). Managers and staff could respond more effectively to the challenge of evaluation by thinking differently about managing, to find social practices embodying the values needed to transcend managerialist pressures. In this chapter I use the case of league tables and draw on theory and practice (including my own experience as Pro and Deputy Vice-Chancellor in a large 'mid-table' university) to sketch an alternative approach.

Managerialism is a set of constituted and constitutive social practices involving actors inside and outside the institution, especially senior managers. It is associated with new public management, emphasising specification of outputs and targets, performance measurement as a means to its management, and business-inspired practices such as contracts for service, increased competition between HE providers, and a quasi-market framing students as customers (Dill, 1998). Such practices risk creating a managerialist ideology purporting to elevate managers above the managed, misrepresenting management as something more than a necessary means to making HE work properly (Cuthbert, 2007). Management can thus come to alienate the managed rather than be their natural support.

Resistance to managerialism rarely goes beyond simple opposition. El Khawas (1998: 319) argues: 'Resistance to a government policy is usually informal rather than formal, but it nevertheless has a systematic, not individual or idiosyncratic character.' Many HE staff resist league table evaluations which they believe present a reductionist, inaccurate view of HE (Eccles, 2002). This presents an institutional challenge faced by senior managers and their advisers in planning and institutional research offices, who occupy crucial positions on the 'implementation staircase' (Trowler, 1998: 55). Managerialism is a consequence of failure to interpret external demands for accountability in ways which make them constructively meaningful for internal staff and student audiences. But there is scope to develop alternative narratives for institutional evaluation, which satisfy external pressures for simple measurement and internal pressures for appreciation of operational complexity.

As the opening chapter of this book suggests, evaluation is a 'social practice bounded by the purpose, intention or function of attributing value or worth to individual, group, institutional or sectoral activity' (Chapter 1). Constructing and using league tables are evaluative practices. Reid's (2009) study of quality assurance in Australian HE showed how social practice can be shaped by discursive practice, itself derived from texts issued by a central agency which thereby became a central authority 'disciplining' universities to follow a particular approach. But in this process of establishing a discourse there is scope for senior managers to reconstruct policy in the way that Trowler (1998: 114) describes as the most creative option for academics responding to change. I will use RUFDATA concepts to develop the argument, suggesting interpretations and practices which might transcend rather than merely resist managerialism.

The use and construction of what have been termed 'league tables' involves public attempts to rank universities or parts of universities according to their performance on various dimensions. These tightly controlled evaluative practices (Chapter 13) apparently allow little institutional discretion: 'Institutions do not feel they have sufficient influence on the compilers and the methodologies used in the rankings' (Locke et al., 2008: 14). The best-known league tables are perhaps *The Times Good University Guide (UK)*, the *US News and World Report Rankings (US)*, and the global *Times Higher Education* and *Shanghai Jiao Tong Rankings*. The Funding Council's league table based on the National Student Survey is also very influential in the UK. League table proliferation has prompted rankings of rankings, notably by Yorke (1997) and Dill and Soo (2005).

League tables 'are being used for a broader range of purposes than originally intended' (Locke et al., 2008: 15) but the reasons and purposes can perhaps be reduced to two. For the media, they generate sales and readership; for institutions, governments, staff, students and potential students they offer a simple overall assessment, a proxy for reputation (Tapper and Filippakou, 2009) and a guide for policy and individual choices. Locke et al. (2008) showed how institutions deliberately use league tables 'as a short cut to reputation' (Tapper and Filippakou, 2009: 36). League table evaluations first command attention: 'The Board has set an institutional key performance indicator of improving the position in the league tables', then shape other practices: 'The aim of improving league table position . . . is encouraging moves to stronger central and corporate management for some functions' (Tapper and Filippakou, 2009: 38). As Reid's (2009) analysis suggests, the league table 'text' can lead to a dominant discourse within the institution which shapes managerial and other social practices. Managers may be in denial: 'although a whole list of key performance indicators have been devised that are aligned with performance-related rankings, there is reluctance to accept the description "league table-driven"' (Tapper and Filippakou, 2009: 36). Staff, who like managers are usually critically aware of methodological flaws (Mroz, 2009), are nevertheless subject to league-table-conscious supervision. If they cannot reconcile discrepancies between their own and the league table judgements: 'morale drops, and sometimes they blame senior management, other departments or those responsible for the data returns' (Locke et al., 2008: 39–40).

Problems arise from the variety of audiences and the corresponding variety of uses for league table evaluations. Politicians, journalists and potential students are glad to find an apparently simple and comprehensible guide for their own purposes, making league table evaluation extremely important for institutions and their reputations. 'Evaluation, however, takes on different meanings at an institution and system level' (Minelli et al., 2008: 170) – within institutions for improving practice, at system level for quality assurance, for disciplining the recalcitrant, and so on. Responding to external pressure can lead to internal uses in target-setting which overvalue or are perceived as overvaluing the league table. The agency producing such evaluations is usually a newspaper. Managers usually regard league tables, externally produced using official statistics, as beyond their individual influence, and aim simply to use rankings selectively for public relations.

A league-table-dominated managerial(ist) discourse alienates staff because it jars with their own experience, judgements, and values. Locke et al. (2008: 61) say: 'there is an onus on policy makers and HE institutions to promote greater public understanding of league tables and alternative sources of information about HE institutions.' But managers might make more difference if, instead of internalising league table measurements, they developed alternative approaches to evaluation which were a better fit with institutional mission and academic values. Such alternatives would improve morale and pride in the institution – effective weapons against inaccurate external evaluations. Managers have a choice: to accept and thereby to amplify league table evaluations, or to try to educate students, staff and lay governors about the work of the institution by developing a different discourse, using explicitly different terms, and ensuring alternatives are used internally.

This is familiar territory. 'Internalist evaluation is at the heart of HE. It is an essential component in the advancement of scientific knowledge . . . but also in the determination of academic reputation and rewards' (Henkel, 1998: 291). Systematic resistance to league table narratives should to a greater extent be reinforced through collaboration with other institutions, for example by building on benchmarking 'clubs'. It calls for different support from institutional research and planning officers, who in a managerialist regime focus on analysing league table positions rather than developing and supporting systematic alternatives.

Such an approach might also involve changing the foci of evaluation. Sponsler's (2009) US analysis called for policymakers to refocus rewards on institutions that promote equity, but this was simply a request for others to change. League tables encourage a focus on institutional reputation by reducing many complex activities to a single number or ranking. But reputation is the accretion of many achievements over time, and it can be rebuilt through alternative stories about successes in research, teaching and public service. The marketing offices to tell those stories already exist, and recognise the need for a strong institutional narrative or 'brand', to compete with the story told by a league table which places the university, 82nd, say, in a field of 150. But unless the brand narrative fits staff perceptions it too may become an alienating symbol of managerialism.

Reputation, which might once have been left to evolve, must now be managed: so must data and evidence. 'Data collection and verification is felt to be improving all the time and this is seen as the major consequence of the league tables' (Locke et al., 2008: 41). Mismanaging data can damage reputations: London Metropolitan University's long-running dispute with HEFCE over student enrolment data came to a head in 2009, doing major financial and reputational harm to the university (Newman, 2009). The university had been one of the few to opt out of appearing in most national league tables, by refusing to release data for their preparation. Vanishing from league tables has public relations risks, but there may in some cases be a dividend in protecting managerial and staff morale and reducing unproductive data management.

One major objection to league tables is that they 'count what is measured' rather than 'measuring what counts' (Locke et al., 2008). The goals of HE may be richly described (Robbins, 1963; Dearing, 1997) but they defy precise formulation and reduction to a single measure. The challenge to managers is to reconcile that inevitable truth with the equally inevitable wish of external audiences to find simple metrics for their narrow purposes. The managerialist turn has meant proliferation of measurement, target-setting, key performance indicators and other monitoring and regulatory devices which sit uneasily with the more qualitative commitment of many staff, motivated by higher ideals than ticking boxes in the corporate strategy. There is scope for using qualitative evidence – case studies, human stories, prizes, awards – to rebalance the league table story. And the cause is not hopeless: journalism thrives on human interest, and prefers stories to statistics.

Institutional evaluation is an instrument of political will for change (Henkel, 1998). Institutions cannot ignore and must therefore confront the challenge posed by new forms of evaluation, going beyond critique to develop alternatives to league tables. To reconcile internal and external demands, institutional evaluation must take forms acceptable to and usable by external audiences, but which also reflect academics' views of 'embedded issues of values and of the purposes of social inquiry' (Henkel, 1998: 286). The challenge is to find a synthesis which goes beyond Watson's caricatures of academic populism and new managerialism. Academic populism is unconstructive resistance; managerialism is undue domination of the practical 'wisdom' that in fact puts excessive reliance on an analytic-rational paradigm of management unsuited to much performance management in HE (Cuthbert, 2007). Both are inadequate responses to the legitimate challenge of institutional evaluation for accountability.

In responding to evaluations managers make choices often represented in either-or terms: summative or formative; improvement or justification; quality assurance or quality enhancement; playing the Government game or promoting educational values. But this reduces resistance to mere opposition, and we need to do more than change evaluation methods. Co-opting peer review, for example, does not necessarily imply greater legitimacy (Henkel, 1998), as successive Research Assessment Exercises (RAEs) have shown. The challenge is to transcend this 'dialectical managerialism' by seeking synthesis.

This means bringing different values and theories into the process of 'disciplining' institutions to conform to a model of global business organisation (Reid, 2009). In (social) practice this is unlikely to mean a few big decisions, or rewriting a corporate strategy. It is more likely to involve frequent reaffirmation of core educational/academic values in small ways, in particular reaffirmation by senior staff for middle managers, who might otherwise assume, perhaps wrongly, that managerialist thinking is expected. For example, my institution once ranked very low in a national league table for the proportion of first class degrees awarded. There was a danger that managers would press for more first class awards in a way that staff might have found anti-academic. A public announcement deprecating such moves would have been ineffective: 'they have to say that, but they don't mean it'. But if we were being unduly harsh we were disadvantaging high-achieving students, so as Deputy Vice-Chancellor I invited discussion by our Learning and Teaching Committee. They commissioned qualitative research which showed the low proportion of firsts was not, as many had supposed, due to the rigidity of the assessment framework, nor could higher proportions of firsts in some areas be attributed to the nature of the disciplines. Rather, our assessment culture and practices made it impossible in many areas for students to achieve much more than 70 on a scale supposedly stretching to 100. Publishing this research internally led to reflective self-appraisal by many staff and assessment boards, a spread of good practices such as differentiating between levels of first class achievement – and a small increase in the proportion of firsts, two or three years later. We had found a way to respond to a league table evaluation which stayed true to educational values and commanded academic support.

Without such responses, league tables will threaten institutional diversity. Dill and Soo (2005) argue that global league tables are converging on a common definition of academic quality, and Enders (2009) points to the danger of 'organisational isomorphism' as institutions indulge in a 'costly academic reputation race' and league tables become key influences in constructing the HE field by defining what matters most for globally leading universities. But collaborative work to develop alternatives is emerging, notably in the European Union-funded project by the CHERPA network. Such work, at international and national level, is urgently needed to counteract league table reductionism.

University senior managers may need to change how they think about managing, so they can respond better to staff expectations, student demand, financial restriction, public and journalistic scrutiny, government requirements, and more. These pressures point in different directions and demand creative management thinking as well as good judgement. Managers shape institutional narratives to make external ambiguity manageable for governors, staff and students. If they over-use rationalistic analysis, targets and key performance indicators as 'weapons' to respond to the 'attacks' they face, they may reinforce the very problem which causes the pressure – the inappropriately managerialist framing of evaluation questions. Mechanistic responses which do not sufficiently acknowledge academic and educational values reproduce external managerialist practices within the institution.

As tuition fees increase and public spending decreases HE faces major new challenges of accountability. HE's stakeholders have varying levels of understanding of, and varying interests in, the business of HE. There is a lack of trust between the parties involved, many institutions are financially at risk, and managers in these circumstances will struggle to assert and sustain alternative ways of thinking. The irony is that if they cannot, the excellence which league tables purport to promote will be denied. To make things better we must rise to the challenge of institutional evaluation and transcend dialectical managerialism.

17

Whole-of-university strategies for evaluating the student experience

Kerri-Lee Krause

Introduction

Evaluating the quality of the undergraduate student experience is now integral to institutional quality assurance and enhancement activities in universities. This case study reports on a range of strategies adopted at Griffith University, Australia to evaluate and enhance the quality of the student experience. It includes discussion of ways in which we are reconceptualising the evaluation practice to enhance student and staff engagement in the process, along with lessons learned and ongoing enhancement strategies.

National context

The quality assurance agenda in Australian Higher Education (HE) has increased substantially in scope and intensity over the past decade. Significant HE reforms are taking place at the national level, with quality and standards the cornerstones of the government agenda. The Australian Universities Quality Agency is to be replaced by the Tertiary Education Quality and Standards Agency with a mandate to accredit providers and carry out quality audits across the tertiary education sector. Complementary to these developments is the replacement of the national Learning and Teaching Performance Fund with a new quality assurance framework designed to improve institutional performance in relation to widening participation indicators and the quality of learning and teaching.

For the last five years the federal government has allocated a portion of the Learning and Teaching Performance Fund to universities on the basis of performance against a set of key performance indicators. These have included institutional scores on the Course Experience Questionnaire (CEQ) which is distributed to all graduates of Australian universities. Invariably the results of institutional performance on the CEQ each year lead to league tables and cross-sectoral comparisons. The results are also published in the Australian Good Universities Guide to Education, Training and Career Pathways (Hobsons, 2009) which includes the results of a range of institutional rankings, including indicators such as the CEQ student satisfaction and graduate employment ratings.

Similar to other HE systems in the western world, the focus on measuring and demonstrating quality in Australian universities has been accompanied by significant growth in the international student market, intense competition among universities, and a rise in the marketisation of the sector. These represent some of the main drivers behind institutional interest in evaluating and monitoring the undergraduate student experience. From a pragmatic perspective, funds and reputations are at stake; from a social justice standpoint, universities have a responsibility to ensure that they provide students from all backgrounds and abilities with the best possible educational experiences and outcomes. This combination of imperatives has led Griffith University to review its approach to evaluating the student experience, as outlined in the case study to follow. The university's strategies for monitoring the quality of the student experience are outlined first, followed by consideration of some of the challenges and opportunities afforded by a strategic decision to reconceptualise our evaluation approach through a whole-of-institution strategy.

Institutional approaches to evaluating the student experience

Institutional context

Griffith University is a metropolitan institution with more than 36,000 students across five campuses in Brisbane, Australia. The student population is diverse with approximately one in seven students designated in the low socioeconomic equity group, and around one in five international students. With such a diverse range of students across so many campuses, assuring and enhancing the quality of the student experience is a high priority for the university.

Four dimensions of the reconceptualisation process

The process of rethinking evaluation of the student experience at Griffith has included three critical dimensions of activity. First, the university needed to acknowledge explicitly that enhancing the quality of the student experience is a value held in high esteem across the institution, both by senior management as well as at the local department level. Articulating a value is not enough to bring about institutional change, however. The value needs to be borne out in the policies and practices of the institution. To this end, new roles were introduced and funded, each with a cluster of proposed new practices which embodied the changes. These included the First Year Advisor role, an academic position located in each department and designed to provide academic and pastoral care support for first year students in transition. The Dean (Student Outcomes) role was also introduced to support the collection, analysis and strategic dissemination of student experience data across the institution. Academic staff professional development programs and central support services and resources, such as support for blended learning, have also been progressively realigned to operationalise this value at the local level.

A second, and related, element underpinning the reconceptualisation of student experience evaluation at Griffith was the introduction of new accountabilities for learning, teaching and the student experience at the local level (i.e., faculty and department levels). Each academic department is responsible for its performance against key performance indicators such as student feedback on the quality of their experience in units of study and their degree program as a whole. While the many limitations of student evaluations of teaching and course experiences are acknowledged (Blackmore, 2009), the use of these evaluative data has provided an important focal point for a whole-of-institution emphasis on a shared set of indicators. Institutional funding attached to local achievement of targets provides an added incentive. Importantly, one of the indicators is overall student satisfaction as measured by the nationally regulated Course Experience Questionnaire. This mirrors one of the national indicators in the former Learning and Teaching Performance Fund.

The alignment of institutional and national indicators has been an important step for galvanising action in a tiered approach to rewarding activities that enhance the quality of the student experience and overall satisfaction. The promotion guidelines for academic staff have also been revised to include reference to the value attached to academic staff use of student evaluations to inform their teaching and curriculum design activities. It should be emphasised that student evaluations of teaching and their broader experience are but one aspect of the evaluation process. Feedback from peers, external moderation processes and self-review are some of the other strategies that are encouraged as part of a holistic approach to evaluation. For the purposes of this short case study, however, the focus is necessarily on the student experience dimension of the evaluation process.

A third dimension of this institutional approach to reviewing our evaluative processes is student engagement with the survey and feedback process. A common criticism of survey experiences from students is that they see no point in filling out surveys as they never hear about what happens to their responses once submitted. New practices associated with closing the feedback loop with students is an important step in improving student survey response rates and student engagement with the enhancement of their own experiences and those of peers at university. At Griffith, we have introduced a mandatory section in the unit (subject) outline distributed to students each semester, outlining the unit leader's response to student feedback from the previous semester. In some cases, improvements may have been made, in others it may be appropriate to explain why a particular strategy or text has been adopted as part of painting the bigger picture context for students. Another 'closing the loop' strategy includes providing brief summary reports for students on achievements and developments that have resulted from their responses to institution-wide student surveys. This strategy may be enacted through student newsletters or social networking sites, for example. Other strategies include posters, bookmarks and the like to alert students to ways in which their feedback has been addressed. These strategies mirror good practices shared by colleagues in other universities and are not unique to Griffith. Nevertheless, they illustrate the importance of a coordinated effort to engage students in the process of providing instructive feedback on a shared learning experience.

Finally, underpinning all of these activities is the fourth element involved in reconceptualising our evaluative practices: assurance of the data quality and robustness underpinning decision-making and actions to enhance the student experience. Like most universities, Griffith had large amounts of data, but these were not always deployed in the most strategic ways to enhance practice. Integral to this strategy was the importance of improving the rigour and timeliness of the data collection, analysis and dissemination processes. This included strategies such as: strategic sampling and analysis of data; easily accessible and targeted reporting of data for particular audiences and needs; and a range of efforts to improve student response rates. These processes are ongoing and essential to building confidence in the data as an instructive starting point for guiding curriculum design, resource allocation and other decision-making activities.

These four elements are works in progress. They are mutually supportive, complex, recursive processes that are best understood from a systems perspective on organisational learning and cultural change (Krause, forthcoming; Senge, 1990, 1999). Local ownership of the value of evaluating the student experience has been an important step along the way to engaging staff. The added dimensions of accountability and reward mechanisms are another important part of the picture. Student engagement in the process of providing informed feedback goes hand in hand with staff engagement, while the availability of reliable, valid, just-in time data is essential.

Challenges and opportunities

Reconceptualising our evaluative practices in relation to the student experience as a whole-of-institution priority has thrown up several challenges, along with opportunities for achieving strategic change and enhancement of the student experience. Three challenges, and associated opportunities, are explored by way of summarising a few important lessons learned.

Bridging the gap between policy and practice

Managing sustainable institution-level change requires us to address the challenge of making connections between high level policy imperatives and local level strategic implementation. In the case of student evaluation data, the national policy context is such that institutional student satisfaction and outcome data are gathered and published nationally. This has flow-on effects for university policy which in turn affects local level data collection and strategic priorities. The challenge lies in translating national policy imperatives into strategies that are meaningfully and feasibly adapted for local settings and needs. Building bridges between the national policy context, institutional strategic plans and local actions in classrooms, online and on campuses is fundamental to successful re-visioning of our use of student experience data to drive institutional improvement.

The 'think global, act local' mantra has come to mind on many occasions during this process of bridge-building. Addressing this challenge remains a work in progress. Morley (2001: 6) refers to the dangers of 'reductive and over simplistic' performance indicators that potentially alienate staff and reinforce boundaries between senior management and the rest of the university. Overcoming these challenges represents an important opportunity to facilitate regular, two-way dialogue and problem-solving between senior university leaders and staff – both professional and academic. Whole-of-university engagement is key to overcoming some of these challenges, as outlined below.

Whole-of-university engagement

Engaging the whole university in the process of reconceptualising the student experience and evaluation of it continues to be a high priority and a challenge. It includes consulting with Heads of School, Deans of Learning and Teaching, Program Leaders and others with responsibility for shaping the student experience, to determine their student data needs. It involves reviewing university-, faculty- and department-level strategic plans to ensure alignment of priorities and resources with the goal of enhancing the student experience. The engagement process also includes ensuring that the university's central and support services, such as facilities management, IT support, student services, and academic staff professional development are included in this holistic perspective on quality enhancement of the student experience. The whole-of-university approach has afforded opportunities to span traditional boundaries between academic and professional staff domains, as well as across campus and discipline boundaries. Importantly, student engagement with the process of providing feedback in various forms is a high priority also. One way of achieving this engagement is through a range of closing the loop strategies.

Closing the feedback loop for students and staff

It has been important to engage students with the process of providing their perspectives on the university experience through such avenues as surveys, focus groups, online polling and social networking sites. It is critical that this process represent a dialogue rather than a one-way flow of information from student to institution. It has been equally important to engage staff in this process using such strategies as ensuring that they are provided with timely data in accessible formats. This means providing reports to staff on a 'just-in-time' basis so that they can use the information to feed into course review and improvement processes, or department-based student orientation activities to support transition, for example.

A fundamental principle of student evaluation is to distinguish between 'reacting' and 'responding'. Reactive responses to student feedback tend to be rushed and impulsive, with a tendency towards 'quick fix' actions that may not be in the best interests of the students or the staff. Responding, on the other hand, connotes a more considered response, taking into account a range of contextual factors. The process of closing the feedback loop has provided a valuable opportunity for discussion about how to achieve a balance between these two approaches in addressing student feedback. In some cases, a quick 'reaction' is a viable and responsible one if a problem is easily addressed. On the whole, though, regular and timely responses to student feedback are the preferred option in order to keep students informed and to build their confidence in the feedback process. The process of reviewing and re-conceiving of the role and place of student data has offered important and ongoing opportunities to discuss these issues.

Concluding remarks

The case study outlined here is a work in progress, as stated earlier. It represents several challenges shared by other large organisations who are attempting to achieve cultural change and enhancement of the student experience by engaging all members of the university community in new practices. These challenges, however, provide valuable opportunities to forge connections between people and structural elements of a large organisation in order to improve the quality of the student experience while at the same time engaging staff. The use of robust evaluative data and the strongly reinforced value of enhancing the experiences and outcomes of all our students represent two key catalysts for effecting this significant change process.

18

Emphasizing the social dimension of scientific organizations: institutional evaluation at Mainz University

Uwe Schmidt and Christoph Rosenbusch

Introduction

As is the case in many other countries, the governance of Higher Education (HE) in Germany has changed significantly over the last few decades. This chapter will focus on the evolution and function of evaluative practices within Mainz University, with a particular focus on the tensions that are embedded in developmental and regulatory processes of evaluation as they are experienced by key institutional stakeholders.

Today, regulation of the HE sector places an explicit emphasis on autonomy and accountability at the institutional as well as at the establishment level and stresses the enhancement of competitive structures. Higher Education Institutions (HEIs) are increasingly seen as organizational or strategic actors (Krücken and Meier, 2006; Whitley, 2008) that actively seek to realize their strategic potential by analyzing and improving their structures and services. In this context, quite different forms of and approaches to evaluation of HE organizational structures and outcomes have come into being. The general function of these evaluation procedures can be described as the systematic collection and analysis of information, aimed at rendering possible 'substantiable' and plausible evaluative judgments.

A common classification differentiates evaluation procedures by their function or purpose (Chelimsky, 1997; Kromrey, 2003). While virtually all evaluation procedures fulfil the function of knowledge-gathering and or legitimation to some extent, there is a quite sharp divide between evaluations mainly aimed at controlling the success of programs or organizations and evaluations that are committed to the 'developmental paradigm'. This developmental paradigm can be characterized by the conscious effort to 'provide evaluative help to strengthen institutions' (Chelimsky, 1997: 100). As institutional evaluations – in contrast for example to program evaluations – mainly deal with ongoing social structures they usually bear the potential to initiate or at least facilitate organizational development as part of their interest. This is a potential that, as will be shown, requires especial mindfulness with regard to the social dimension of organizations.

Institutional evaluations in the HE sector focus on organizations or their sub-units that are characterized by a certain scale and complexity. In the German HE sector these evaluations have a comparatively short tradition. A starting point of sorts may be found in the context of German reunification. In the early 1990s the HEIs of the former German Democratic Republic (East Germany) had to be evaluated with respect to their scientific capacity and potential. Many of these evaluations led to significant reductions of budgets or the closing down of scientific facilities. This close conjunction of institutional evaluations and far-reaching political decision-making certainly cast a cloud over the acceptance of institutional evaluations in German HEIs. Nevertheless, since the mid-1990s, especially triggered by experience gained in the Netherlands, a combination of internal and external evaluation gained ground in the German HE sector. These evaluations were primarily organized by evaluation agencies such as the Association of North German Universities (Verbund Norddeutscher Universitäten) or the Central Agency for Evaluation (Zentrale Evaluationsagentur, ZEvA). Only a very limited number of universities developed their own system of evaluation and quality assurance (Bornmann et al., 2006; Schmidt, 2009). One of these universities is Johannes Gutenberg-University (JGU) in Mainz,[1] where dealing with measures and procedures of quality assurance already has a comparatively long tradition.

Needless to say, the way institutional evaluations are conducted depends to some extent on the characteristics of the organization being evaluated, i.e. there is a high degree of 'situatedness' in the expression of institutional evaluative practices. Similarly, it is certainly true that different evaluating institutions have developed their own approach towards institutional evaluation. This approach structures conception and proceedings alike. That said, the conception and conduct of the institutional evaluations carried out at JGU are closely related to the institutional character and history of quality assurance and development at JGU and the quality model that guides the work of its quality unit.

The institutional history of quality assurance and development at JGU began with the foundation of the 'project for the enhancement of studies and teaching' in 1992. Throughout the years this project carried out and/or evaluated more than 200 projects to promote studying and teaching.

[1] Johannes Gutenberg-University is one of the largest universities in Germany, organized in 11 departments (Fachbereiche). At Mainz there are three departments of natural sciences and four departments of humanities and social sciences as well as departments of theology, medicine, economics and law and a department for music and fine arts. The huge variety of subjects, is, compared with other German Universities, a quite specific characteristic of JGU.

In 1999 the project was transformed into an interdisciplinary scientific institution, the Centre for Quality Assurance and Development (ZQ). Its core responsibilities were defined by the senate of JGU and primarily lay in the fields of evaluation and the promotion of young academics. In the first years of ZQ's operation, institutional evaluation took centre stage. Following the well established method of internal and external evaluation (peer review process) with subsequent setting of development goals, the 'Mainz Model of Evaluation' features some specific characteristics.

First and probably most important of all, teaching and research are evaluated simultaneously. This practice differs significantly from the procedures applied in many other universities and evaluation agencies, where evaluations focus only on one of these two closely-related aspects at the same time. In our opinion this differentiation between evaluation of teaching and research does not measure up to the needs and complexity of organizational development in HEIs.

Furthermore, ZQ's institutional evaluations are based on a quality model that distinguishes between four different quality dimensions. The concept of Donabedian (1980) who differentiated three quality dimensions (structures, processes and results) is supplemented by a fourth dimension focusing on long-term goals of the social system in question. The inspiration for this widening of perspective stems from the system-theoretical theory of Parsons (Parsons, 1971; Parsons and Platt, 1973). Via the integration of a goal dimension, the four quality dimensions are substantially compatible with Parson's four functions of (social) systems (see Schmidt, 2007, 2008). Furthermore, the goal dimension reflects the experience that issues of goal-setting often do not receive a sufficient amount of attention in evaluation procedures.

Another specific characteristic of ZQ is its continuous efforts to integrate different quantitative and qualitative methods of analysis. In the actual procedure of institutional evaluation the main methods of data gathering are cumulative interviews with groups of students and staff members as well as interviews with professors. Concerning the scientific units of JGU, the resulting insights can be complemented by further data gained in different evaluation procedures, such as alumni surveys. Another interesting detail in this context is that in contrast to the usual internal and external evaluation of scientific institutions, the departments at JGU only provide a descriptive report while the analysis of strengths and weaknesses is provided by the staff members of ZQ. This proceeding reflects the experience that analyses offered by the scientific institutions themselves tend to play down weaknesses while strengths are overemphasized. At the same time, it should be noted that the evaluating institution needs a certain reputation and credibility if their analysis is to fall onto attentive ears in the scientific institutions.

Finally the 'Mainz Model' stipulates a distinctive role for ZQ within the process of evaluation. The work of ZQ is not restricted to the organization of evaluations in HEIs; ZQ acts more as a mediator between the departments and the executive board of the university; a position which is institutionally backed by its character as an independent scientific institution. Against this backdrop, ZQ's evaluations go further than measuring and evaluating in the above mentioned sense of providing a reliable knowledge-base for evaluative judgments. ZQ consciously engages in the field of quality and organizational development and thus slips into a position where it evaluates and gives advice at the same time. This position is not easy to maintain and is prone to conflict. At the same time, it is the strong belief of ZQ members and leadership that a mere concentration on evaluating in the sense of data gathering regularly leads to shortcomings with regard to the instructive potential of evaluations i.e. the purpose of evaluations under the development paradigm described above.

Over the last few years nearly all scientific units at JGU were evaluated. Furthermore all new study programs were accredited by an external agency or by ZQ in the context of 'system accreditation' (see Fähndrich and Grendel, 2007; Grendel and Rosenbusch, 2010). 'System accreditation' is a new way for German universities to conduct the mandatory accreditation of all their study programs. A correspondent pilot project at Johannes Gutenberg-University Mainz (JGU) plays an important role in paving the way for this alternative to the prevailing program accreditation. For more detailed information see Fähndrich and Grendel (2007) or Grendel and Rosenbusch (2010).

The following short sample of typical problems is not only based on the evaluations conducted at JGU but also includes lessons learned from evaluations conducted by ZQ in other universities in South Western Germany (Universities in South Western Germany form the 'Hochschulevaluierungsverbund Südwest', meaning that they co-operate closely in the field of quality assurance and development. JGU, that is to say ZQ, houses the liaison office for this consortium).

First of all, our experience has been that the majority of weaknesses found in institutional evaluations of scientific institutions are a result of typical processes of change in organizations in general and in science organizations in particular. Science continually branches into new sub-disciplines and there are regular shifts in the leading topics of disciplines. For example biology underwent dramatic changes during the last decades; several new research areas like genetics, microbiology or neurobiology prospered while at the same time some traditional areas of interest significantly lost relevance. Such developments require restructuring on the part of academic institutions and readjustments of the curricula. If evaluation aims at contributing to quality and organizational development it has to support these constant processes of change.

A second major topic often brought to light in institutional evaluations of scientific departments is that the coordination of curricula among faculty is often insufficiently institutionalized. Many institutes and study programs lack adequate coordination with regard to teaching content. This holds especially true for courses and study programs offered by different scientific disciplines and institutes, like for example 'Chemistry for physicians', or sociology or psychology courses in teacher training. Superficially this is only a problem of teaching organization but it is in fact a quite complex problem of communication and co-operation. These kinds of problems are significantly gaining relevance in the course of the ongoing Bologna reform as new bachelor and masters programs extend increasingly over traditional borders of scientific disciplines and institutes.

Furthermore, we often observe that there are no shared standards of performance for course achievement. Certificates or diplomas in the same subject are easier or harder to get, depending on the individual teacher. Similar to the above mentioned example, this shortcoming is less a problem of formal definition of respective standards but rather a question of continuous communication, negotiation and mutual adjustment.

These few examples may demonstrate why institutional evaluations should not be regarded predominantly as controlling instruments but rather as a starting point for the initiation or at least facilitation of organizational development. Most of the above-mentioned typical problems and challenges in scientific institutions are rooted in the social cohesion and communication in the respective organizations. From our point of view, the creation of solutions for these problems requires a certain amount of consultancy, based on knowledge in the field of organizational development as well as on practical experiences gained in other scientific units. From this point of view we decidedly take issue with an overly technocratic approach towards evaluation.

The main problem we see in an approach to institutional evaluation as a starting point for organizational development is the clash between being an evaluator and being a consultant, i.e. a clash of practice traditions. This double role needs to be balanced continuously and requires a high amount of knowledge and accountability on the part of the evaluators. At the same time, this dilemma is perhaps inevitable if institutional evaluation practice is aimed at initializing and facilitating the kind of 'institution-led change' (Clark, 2005) in scientific institutions that is becoming more and more crucial. This is particularly true in the light of the current shifts of HE governance mentioned in the beginning of this article. However, our experience quite clearly indicates that organizational learning and development is always only partially and temporarily realized. From time to time, organizations require external impetus to regain momentum.

19

Tensions between professional and organizational development: towards meaningful evaluative practices for all

Bernadette Charlier

Introduction

This chapter focuses on the development of evaluative practices in one Swiss university, and the evaluations which underpin a parallel staff development program. It argues that the risk is that staff development evaluative practices may be disconnected or in tension with the ones developed by the institution. How and in which conditions are these professional evaluative practices relevant to organizational development? In this chapter, after a clarification of the concepts of professional development and organizational development, this question is addressed. In doing so, some issues and challenges are raised that need to be dealt with in order to foster dialogue between the actors involved, and to contribute to building meaningful – and related – evaluative practices for all.

Like almost all universities in Switzerland, the University of Fribourg has experienced loosely controlled evaluative practices during the last 10 years which leave the institution more free to decide how to evaluate and what to evaluate. First, before 2000, the university decided to evaluate teaching quality through course questionnaires addressed to the students, and to identify and offer coaching to teachers for whom quality was less than average (loosely controlled content). In 2004, with the first audit organized by the Centre of Accreditation and Quality Assurance of the Swiss Universities (OAQ), the university designed a quality framework and procedures at different levels: teaching, administration, personal development etc. The university was told what to evaluate but could decide how to do it (tightly controlled in focus). In both cases, quality enhancement was owned by the institution. More recently, these institutional evaluative practices have evolved but remain the ownership of the institution.

During the same period, the Fribourg teachers' professional development system (Did@cTIC) was built and regulated through a series of needs analyses carried out in 2002, 2005 and the last one in 2008. These needs analyses guided the choice of training activities organized separately for teaching assistants and for professors. All the activities are guided by the following main principles:

- Related to practices and projects (personal projects, communities of practice, classroom observation)
- Flexible (4 programs: introduction, certificate, diploma, 'à la carte' modules)
- Open to: experts, and opened to other programs
- Bilingual
- Enhanced through the use of ICT (Information and Computer Technology).

All these activities are designed to support the professional development of each participant. Following the Staff and Educational Development Association framework (SEDA, no date), each participant defines his/her own specific objectives or training activities according to his/her own learning and professional project. The program is supported by a virtual learning environment in which information, communication and collaboration functions are available. Face to face training days are organized with experts as well as communities of practices in which each participant has the opportunity to describe, analyze, evaluate and enhance his or her own teaching practices. As part of all this, evaluative practices are undertaken by all the participants as well as by the Did@cTIC team responsible for the design, implementation and regulation of the program.

Professional development, professional learning and changing practices

According to Day (1999: 4) teachers' professional development includes:

> All natural learning experiences and those conscious planned activities which are intended to be of direct or indirect benefit to the individual, group or school and which contribute through these, to the quality of education in the classroom (. . . .) It is the process by which, alone and with others, teachers review, renew and extend their commitment as change agents.

In this definition, teachers' professional development is related to professional learning in natural settings. This vision, which is largely accepted in research on professional development, is rarely implemented in practice. Nowadays, most institutions are still offering traditional training programs focused on content or techniques (Webster-Wright, 2009). According to Webster-Wright, many possible reasons exist to explain this situation: 'They range from the problematic nature of a bureaucratic context for many professionals through professional issues such as time pressure and stress at work to problems in introducing changes in such change-weary time' (Webster-Wright, 2009: 704). Furthermore, these reasons also explain why such professional development programs fail. Other related reasons are that they don't take into account what motivates teachers to engage in professional development sufficiently. In recognition of these issues, the Fribourg professional development program is grounded on iterative needs analysis and offers various activities to support evaluation and enhancement of teaching practices: communities of practices, implementation or evaluation of new methods, curriculum design, peer coaching.

Professional development and organizational development

How and in which conditions are these individual evaluative practices relevant to organizational development?

A broad definition of organizational development is as a 'process by which organizations build their capacities to change and to achieve greater effectiveness' (Cummings and Worley, 2009: 22). In the Fribourg case, how could the institution develop its capacity to change and achieve greater effectiveness through these professional development evaluative practices? Our answer is based on a view of evaluative practice which contributes to a reflexive culture, i.e. one in which practice is the object of continuing adaptation and modification. In effect, evaluation becomes a 'boundary object' providing resources for evolving and improving practice (see Saunders et al., 2005).

At the end of her recent review of professional development, Webster-Wright gives other insights in answer to this question: much of the research she reports reveals most professionals as enthusiastic learners who want to improve their practice. She recommends that we listen to their experience and work to support, not hinder their learning rather than deny, seek to control, or standardize the complexity and diversity of professional learning experiences. Instead we should accept, celebrate and develop insights from these experiences to support professionals as they continue to learn (Webster-Wright, 2009: 728). In other words, evaluative practices in support of professional development need to work with the fabric of academics' realities and contexts, rather than impose artificial requirements or standards.

In the following section, we will illustrate how we have tried to put this insight into practice through the EQUAL project.

The EQUAL project: an attempt to link professional and organizational development

This project aimed at fostering gender equality in Fribourg University teaching through three related practice clusters (Dehler et al., 2009):

1 Integrating gender equality into the university's Did@cTIC teacher training program. Within the framework of the project, modules on gender-sensitive learning and teaching were offered and existing modules on university learning and teaching were revised.
2 Developing gender teaching quality criteria to support self-evaluation and suggest new teaching quality criteria for teaching evaluation conducted at the institutional level.
3 Improving articulation between professional development and organizational development through the reification of the knowledge produced by academics' communities of practice.

The third cluster illustrates how organizational and professional evaluation could be linked. First, to launch the project, we carried out a needs analysis through phone interviews addressed to 30 academics. These interviews gave us a list of their main concerns: plagiarism, academic management of students, diversity management, teaching in a bilingual university, management of a research team etc.

On this basis, at the beginning of the academic year 2009–10, we organized group meetings focused on the description, analysis, evaluation and enhancement of practices related to these themes. For some of these themes, an expert was invited to enrich the reflection by research results, references, etc. Notes were made and sent to the participants on specific topics, such as plagiarism, and further information was shared among the community through the blog of the Did@cTIC centre.

While each meeting seemed to be fruitful for those who attended, not many academics did attend. This will be taken into account in recommendations to the institution during the final board meeting of the project. In formulating these recommendations for improving practice, a key question is how these recommendations could be used by the organization to support its own development.

Formulating the recommendations in a way which will make sense both to the institution and to academic communities of practice is no easy matter. A helpful framework for keeping the recommendations contextually relevant is to develop and use all types of what Nonaka and Takeuchi (1995) call assets, as depicted in the top left hand quadrant of Table 19.1.

Experiential knowledge is an important part of professional expertise, but what is not clear is how an institution such as a university could take this knowledge into account in its organizational development. To answer this question, we need to understand better the knowledge shared in communities of practice. According to Wenger (1998), a community can share information, beliefs and ownership of meaning and practices. From the university's point of view, it could be useful to gain an understanding of academics' shared beliefs as well as shared ownership of meaning and practices. This is especially important if the university wants to innovate. For example, sharing beliefs about the main goals of a teaching program or of the development of a common research agenda could be an important condition of success and could be valuable to the institution.

Table 19.1 Knowledge assets (Nonaka, 1995: 84)

Experiental knowledge assets	*Conceptual knowledge assets*
Tacit knowledge through common experiences ■ Skills and know-how of individuals ■ Care, love and trust ■ Energy, passion and tension	Explicit knowledge articulated through images, symbols and language ■ Product concepts ■ Design ■ Brand equity
Routine knowledge assets	*Systemic knowledge assets*
Tacit knowledge routinized and embedded in actions and practices ■ Know-how in daily operations ■ Organizational routines ■ Organizational culture	Systemized and packaged explicit knowledge ■ Documents, specifications, manuals ■ Database ■ Patents and licenses

Another typology of outputs of professional development activities, either formal or informal, seems consistent with Wenger's proposal. Harland and Kinder (1997) have described outputs of formal professional development (INSET: in-service education and training) in nine categories among which institutional outcomes are acknowledged:

> Institutional outcomes acknowledge that INSET can have an important collective impact on groups of teachers and their practice. The benefits of consensus, shared meanings, collaboration and mutual support when attempting curriculum innovation in the classroom are fairly well established in the research literature. In this study, school-based INSET or the work of school curriculum leaders was often targeted at achieving institutional outcomes.
>
> (Harland and Kinder, 1997: 76)

While Harland and Kinder were talking within the schools context, their typology suggests that university leaders would do well to encourage collaborative activities between academics and to value their outputs: charters, projects, programs, products, organizational culture and routines.

Dibiaggio and Ferrary's (2003) research in knowledge management highlights other conditions for institutions to benefit organizationally from professional development. Dibiaggio and Ferrary recognize communities of practices as mediators between individuals and organizations. They highlight the roles of people who establish weak links between several communities and facilitate the negotiation of meanings and knowledge inside the organization. Furthermore, it is fundamental that institutional leaders take these meanings and knowledge into account and integrate them into an institutional vision, and in strategy operationalized in specific decisions.

One might recognize that some academics' current practices often include such negotiation. However, this can be oriented to satisfying personal interests, without enough transparency. What we call for is that these sharing and negotiation processes – as well as their results (for example, knowledge, values, decisions) – should be more explicitly communicated to all, to enable better participation, engagement and development.

As an example of this, an original initiative taken by the Derek Bok Centre for Teaching and Learning at Harvard University (Volpe Horii, 2010) offers an interesting perspective. They employ doctoral students as peer teaching mentors. Supported by the Centre, these PhD students undertake projects and teaching activities in the departments. They experience the role of change agent and the Centre supports them to reflect on their experiences and to value them as part of the university's organizational development. This type of project demonstrates how individual professional development can be related to organizational development for the benefit of all. The process is not unproblematic, but it is possible.

20

Evaluative practice and outcomes: issues at the institutional level

Veronica Bamber

> There exists a strong risk that the efforts made by universities and university systems to improve quality may end up by introducing repetitive rituals and losing sight of the contents of academic activities.
>
> (Minelli et al., 2008: 157)

Introduction

Given the range of institutional missions, cultures, priorities and theories of change, it is not surprising that the social practices of different universities should show equal variety, and that their evaluative practices should also reflect their diversity. We spoke in Chapter 1 about 'constellations of practices', and this astronomical analogy is helpful in conceptualising patterns of institutional practices which have much in common, but also present very different shapes when compared. Just as Orion differs from the Great Bear, so our case writers encapsulate the constellations of very different evaluative practices in each of their institutions. This chapter will chart some of those differences, and also note common patterns. There are a number of key issues which emerge, but the first two which I would like to concentrate on relate to the use and usability of evaluative data, and to agency. Further comments are then offered on the focus of these evaluations, and the different conceptualisations of data used in them. I use the term 'conceptualisations' rather than 'approaches' or 'methods', because methodological variations are merely the external face of fundamentally different underlying philosophies about the nature of evaluation.

Uses of evaluation

The range of underlying philosophies means, as the case writers in this section of the book demonstrate, that evaluations in different universities are put to a range of uses. We talked in Chapter 1 about evaluation framed within the quality systems of institutions, and Chapter 15 charted the increasing links between quality systems and evaluation in Higher Education (HE) since the early 1990s. While the major use and reason for evaluation is to improve quality, other agendas have emerged, as Cuthbert's chapter on league tables demonstrates (Chapter 16). These agendas may not be driven by institutions themselves, but institutions become complicit: play the game or perish.

The link between evaluation and quality does not need to be stretched too far for a further jump to be made to funding. At the national level, examples are many – the UK Research Assessment Exercise / Research Excellence Framework, cited in previous chapters, is the most obvious example. In Australia, the new quality assurance regime, with its link between university performance and funding, has led universities like Griffith to review their approach to evaluating the student experience. Universities are allocated a portion of the Learning and Teaching Performance Fund on the basis of performance against a set of key performance indicators. Evaluation outcomes are bound, therefore, to be highly political and of strategic importance to the institution. Krause makes the point that this is part of a complex, supportive process of organisational learning and cultural change – and it appears that there is a shared understanding of this across this very large institution. So, while funding–evaluation links may not be popular, there is at least explicit recognition that this is how evaluative data will be used. In this scenario, evaluative practices become a tool for organisational development. Schmidt and Rosenbusch also advocate evaluations that are committed to the 'developmental paradigm' (Chapter 18). Their use of evaluation requires, inter alia, 'special mindfulness with regard to the social dimension of organizations'. These are institutions which are taking a strategic approach in which evaluation is part of their policy framework.

However, even when it is intended to use evaluation strategically, who defines that use? While Minelli's interview respondent (below) highlights the importance of evaluation being 'useful', it would be naive to assume that such uses can be easily defined or controlled:

> The most important thing is missing, that is to say evaluation surely fails if no one is aware that it's really useful. Up to now this awareness is non-existent in the majority of universities.
>
> (Minelli et al., 2008: 167)

Policy and contextual configurations may, in fact, be contradictory, with stresses between different parts of the institution, or different initiatives – and certainly between different communities within the university. So, even in the most strategic of situations, unintended uses and consequences can ensue, and the next section deals with these.

Unintended consequences

We mentioned in Chapter 1 that impact evaluations should identify both desirable and undesirable outcomes, and should include intended, unintended and unanticipated outcomes, with an evaluation design that is responsive to each. We would also say that evaluations which are not designed to directly assess 'impact' (e.g. evaluation of an ongoing service) benefit from such lateral thinking. Charlier's links between evaluation and staff development are a case in point.

In Chapter 16, Rob Cuthbert discusses the unintended uses and outcomes of league tables. In our terms, he classifies these league tables as tightly controlled in both process and focus – which perhaps makes planning for a range of outcomes more difficult, since the institution has little discretion over how it is assessed: league table categories are not controlled by the institutions themselves. Cuthbert explains that internal interpretations of what needs to be done in order to move up the league table ladder can skew institutional priorities, and shape managerial and other social practices. In the short term, the dominant discourse within the institution is also skewed towards the league table text. Longer term, there is a danger of league tables defining what is quality, and what matters most, in universities. In another critical review of league tables, Harvey (2008) confirms that league tables are being used for a broader range of purposes than originally intended, with far greater impact than 'their arbitrary design would warrant' (Harvey, 2008: 194). Cuthbert and Harvey agree that league tables distort practices in institutions, and may even militate against good teaching, since good, transformational learning and teaching are not necessarily rewarded in the rankings. There are consequences at both the macro and the institutional level of how the sector values particular activities. I will return later to the interesting phenomenon of how evaluation is a change agent in its own right.

Agency

The Discretion Framework in Chapter 15 depicted the tensions produced in power relationships between the 'agents' in evaluative situations, and this dynamic is expressed in some of the cases. Charlier (Chapter 19) felt that the evaluative practices which had evolved at the University of Fribourg were loosely controlled in process – the word 'evolved' is indicative, since the exercise of power is usefully felt (and resisted) more when it is imposed over a short period of time, rather than growing more organically. Cuthbert describes the resistance to league table evaluations on the way down the institutional implementation staircase, when external accountability is not translated into something 'constructively meaningful for internal staff and student audiences'.

While the Discretion Framework has some validity for cases in this section, it is also clear that 'agency' within the confines of the Discretion Framework is an insufficient description for what is happening on the ground. Cuthbert cites Watson (2009: 77), who rejects the simplistic managerialist dialectic of 'unthinking resistance meets unthinking control'. The complexities of agency are teased out in Schmidt and Rosenbusch's analysis of quality and evaluation at Mainz, where the quality institute acts not only as mediator between departments and senior management, but also gives advice and consultancy and carries out evaluations. Needless to say, 'this position is not easy to maintain and is prone to conflict'. Similarly, at Griffith University, Krause aims for a whole-of-university approach to producing and using evaluative data, 'engaging all members of the university community in new practices'. While Krause mentions 'challenges' in this regard, she surely underplays the many difficulties encountered when trying to change the (social) practices of an academic community. One must assume that this, like Schmidt and Rosenbusch's case, is prone to conflict when trying to 'build bridges between the national policy context, institutional strategic plans and local actions in classrooms, online and on campuses' (Chapter 17).

Focus

Another interesting aspect of our four chapters in this section is the focus which their evaluations take. For Schmidt and Rosenbusch, their focus was obtained from a theoretical model of quality based on structures, processes and results. From the social practice perspective, this rather technical-rational view would be inadequate to capture the complexities of evaluative practices. There is also the danger of 'losing sight of the contents of academic activities', pointed out in Minelli et al.'s (2008) introductory quote for this section. However, Schmidt and Rosenbusch add that the model is supplemented by a fourth dimension focusing on the long-term goals of the social system in question. This 'social system' will bring the necessary cultural awareness and human element to their evaluations, acknowledging Alvesson's (2002: 190) advice that we should focus on specific cultural manifestations, with loosely coupled, complex meanings.

Data

The final element of our case studies which I am going to discuss is that of data (the D in the RUFDATA categorisation, mentioned in Chapter 1).

The case writers clearly appreciate that 'data' in complex evaluative situations cannot be 'scientific', and yet some level of robustness needs to be obtained. For Krause, this means avoiding 'reductive and over simplistic' performance indicators that can alienate staff and reinforce boundaries between senior management and the rest of the university. In Schmidt and Rosenbusch's case, they aim to integrate a mix of quantitative and qualitative methods. In Charlier's institution, they seek to incorporate all of Nonaka and Takeuchi's (1995) knowledge assets: experiential knowledge assets, conceptual knowledge assets, routine knowledge assets and systemic knowledge assets, as a framework for keeping evaluative data contextually relevant. This includes the difficult area of working with tacit knowledge, which could really only be used if working with communities of practice and the knowledge they hold. Again, far from simple: how does a university tap the shared understandings and beliefs of a community? For Charlier, part of the answer (and there can only ever be part answers) is through processes of sharing and negotiation, and explicit communication. There may not be complete and easy answers to these complex challenges, but the case writers all agree that 'counting what is measured' rather than 'measuring what counts' (Cuthbert, quoting Locke et al., 2008) is not one of them. 'Simple metrics for . . . narrow purposes', along with a 'proliferation of measurement, target-setting, key performance indicators and other monitoring and regulatory devices' (Chapter 16) cannot be the solution, although they might, as Krause suggests, be part of that solution if accompanied by other, more qualitative data. 'Ticking boxes in the corporate strategy' (Chapter 16) is never going to make the link between evaluative practices and the social practices of academics on the ground. 'Rebalancing the league table story' (Chapter 16) with academically-relevant evaluation – as per Minelli et al.'s (2008) opening quote – is clearly needed.

Conclusions

We have said previously, and others agree (e.g. Cheol Shin, 2009) that new accountabilities, of which evaluation forms a key part, have affected, and will continue to affect, fundamental aspects of how universities operate, in institutional management, performance and culture – although others do question how accepting university cultures are of accountability-related initiatives (e.g. Huisman and Currie, 2004). However, Cheol Shin's (2009) survey of American institutions tentatively concluded that 'performance-based accountability may not contribute to institutional performance if the new accountability is not well grounded in institutional practices'. In other words, quality and evaluative approaches which ignore the social practices of those involved risk alienating staff and introducing unsustainable initiatives. On the other hand, evaluative practices which work with social realities can offer powerful support for change, and can lead to change which exceeds what was originally planned: evaluative practices can change other social practices.

However, as this book advocates, and some of the case authors in this section emphasise, there is a need to reconceptualise evaluation. Krause and Cuthbert's chapters are illustrations of this. For Krause, this reconceptualisation means taking cognisance of the institution's wider context within national and international trends towards globalisation and marketisation. For her university to work with these new realities, they first had to work on their institutional values, and acknowledge the value of the student experience: otherwise, extensive evaluative effort made no sense. Their 'holistic approach to evaluation' meant asking questions about what the university was about, and then gaining the participation of staff and engagement of students with evaluation and the feedback loop. As Senge (1990) indicated, the aim of organisational development and organisational learning are much more likely to happen if underlying assumptions about practice are made explicit, and this is clearly the case with evaluation.

For Cuthbert, reconceptualising means thinking differently about management itself, to find social practices embodying the values needed to transcend managerialist pressures. This is partly about discourse, but also willingness to think creatively, rather than simply reacting to demands for accountability: 'managers can seize the agenda by discursively changing it', by rejecting 'either/or' approaches to evaluation, and by frequently re-affirming core educational/academic values in small ways.

In this section, we have offered some examples of how four different writers have conceptualised and reconceptualised their evaluative practices within their institutional context. We have picked out some key patterns in these cases, and we have applied conceptual tools to these patterns. In the final chapter of this book, we will draw together our analyses from each of the thematic sections, to further reconceptualise evaluation, and to support the thinking of others who are planning institutional evaluations.

Part Four

Self-evaluative practice

21

Self-evaluative practice: diversity and power

Veronica Bamber

> How a society selects, classifies, distributes, transmits and evaluates the educational knowledge it considers to be public, reflects both the distribution of power and the principles of social control.
>
> (Bernstein, 1971: 47)

Introduction

The story of self-evaluative practices can be depicted as a story of power and control. In a long period (mid-1980s onwards) of increasing levels of accountability, the extent to which academics control what, when and how their work is evaluated is one of the indications of the movement of power between different players in the Higher Education (HE) sector. The movement in evaluation is suggestive of a flow away from the individual and towards greater management decision-making. When I entered HE as a young lecturer in the early 1980s, there were no formal requirements for evaluation. In fact, I remember no talk of evaluation at all. My colleagues and I were, of course, interested in whether our classes and courses were going well, and we were aware of whom the students considered to be 'good' lecturers. Evaluative practice was intuitive and private, and no-one was required to demonstrate the value of their work. Only if students complained did management alarm bells ring, and reaction (perhaps) ensue. As a student in the 1970s I was also unaware of any attempts to assess the practice of individual lecturers, or of our lecturers seeking student opinion about our learning experiences. Elton (1987: 56) quotes Ashby (1963) as criticising this state of play:

> All over the country these groups of scholars, who would not make a decision about the shape of a leaf or the derivation of a word or the author of a manuscript without painstakingly assembling the evidence, make decisions about admissions policy, size of universities, staff-student ratios, content of courses, and similar issues, based on dubious assumptions,

> scrappy data, and mere hunch. . . . Although dedicated to the pursuit of knowledge, they have until recently resolutely declined to pursue knowledge about themselves.

What Ashby describes is, arguably, a far cry from current practice in the UK, where academic staff are constantly urged or required to evaluate their work, and 'the student voice' is actively sought at many levels: nationally, institutionally, at course level and individually. Not only are students asked for feedback about their direct educational experiences, they also participate in decision-making about almost every aspect of how the sector, the institution and their courses should operate and change.

Universities are aware of the leveraging power of 'the student voice', and student contributions are an attempt to bring a bottom-up element into an evaluation and enhancement environment which otherwise could be seen as largely top-down. Such top-down approaches to improvement use the language of business: Key Performance Indicators, Accountability, Value for Money, Fitness for Purpose and even, at one point, Total Quality Management – although that particular expression seems to have fallen into disrepute, perhaps due to an increasing awareness across the sector that such language was more likely to alienate academics than engage them in fruitful self-reflection and self-improvement processes.

What all of this means is that in order to make sense of the question of how individuals and groups attribute value to what they do – the focus of this section of the book – we need to locate these evaluative practices within the frame of the values and *practices* which they rest on, and how those practices have developed over time. For individuals in universities, this has been closely linked with the quality agenda. What Filippakou and Tapper (2008) called the 'growth industry' of quality has impinged increasingly on the lives and practices of individual academics, and the need to document and demonstrate evaluative practices at every level. This is problematic for academics because many routine practices are adopted uncritically and are part of 'the way we do things round here'. Trowler and Cooper (2002: 14) describe these as 'unreflective habitual routines which are often developed in situ and learned by newcomers during the process of secondary socialization'.

In considering this self-evaluative domain of practice within HE contexts, we will see examples of individuals and groups who have tried to unpick these recurrent practices and subject them to scrutiny. The emphasis here is not just on what academics have been obliged to do as a result of quality cultures, but also on what they choose to do in order to improve their practice, and their understanding of that practice.

It stretches credibility to talk monolithically about 'academics' practices' when we are all aware of significant differences between individuals and, for example, disciplinary groups. The ETL Project (2002) introduced the term *ways of thinking and practising* to describe the intentions of university staff in HE, related to how they see their discipline. The different ways of thinking and practising of physicists, historians and economists will condition their attitudes to evaluation, and so we must be wary here of over-simplification of complex phenomena. Having said this, some generalities do apply. For example, cultural norms in particular institutions or departments, or power differentials over time, will affect evaluation.

To illustrate this, we can refer to the Discretion Framework (Figure 21.1), which shows how differences in evaluative practices manifest themselves in terms of tight and loose control of what is evaluated and how it is evaluated. As indicated in the introduction to institutional evaluative practices (Chapter 15), this framework helps us by giving us a language to describe what goes on in evaluative practices, and might help us decide what is appropriate in different contexts. It demonstrates the pull between different political and cultural tensions; the pull towards the upper left-hand side is towards formal, top-down processes and drivers, while the pull towards the bottom right-hand side is towards informal, bottom-up processes and drivers. The specific example used in Figure 21.1 is that of module feedback.

In the bottom right-hand side are evaluative practices which are loosely controlled in both content and process: the academic has complete discretion

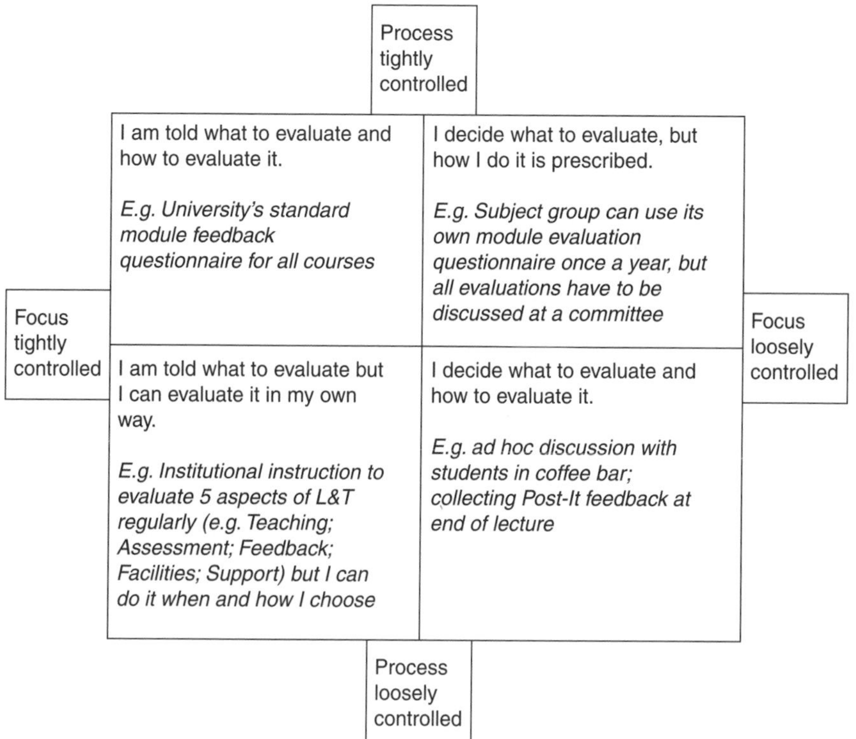

Figure 21.1 Discretion Framework for evaluative practices: example – module evaluation

over what to evaluate and how to evaluate it. This might lead to individual, informal evaluations, such as having ad hoc discussion with students in the coffee bar, or collecting brief written feedback on Post-Its at the end of a lecture. The major motivator is the academic's wish to find out more about the student experience of the module, and they are free to choose a method that suits their purpose.

The bottom left-hand quadrant holds evaluations that are loosely controlled in process, but tightly controlled in focus. This means that academics are told what to evaluate, but they can evaluate it in their own way. This might happen if the institution or department wishes to collect regular data on specific aspects of the learning experience (e.g. Assessment and feedback) but the lecturer can do it when and how they choose. Loose process control and tight focus or content control might also occur if the lecturer has obtained funding to investigate specific aspects of learning and teaching (e.g. the use of Wikis in their subject) but has freedom in how they conduct the evaluation.

In another scenario, the academic can decide what to evaluate (loose control of focus), but how they do it is prescribed (tight process control). For example, a subject group might use its own module evaluation questionnaire, but all evaluations have to be discussed and analysed at a specific committee. This would be placed in the top right-hand quadrant of the Discretion Framework.

In the final quadrant, in the top left-hand of the diagram, the lecturer is told what to evaluate and how to evaluate it, so the evaluation has both tight focus and process control. This would be the case if the university's standard module feedback questionnaire had to be used for all courses, and reporting of results was taken out of the hands of the individual member of staff.

We noted in the section on the domain of evaluative practice in institutions (Chapters 15–20), that top-down initiatives affect the activities of individual academics; the links between institutional requirements, norms and cultures and what academics do is illustrated in the module feedback example given in the Discretion Framework. In different contexts, academics will approach module evaluation according to the constraints or enablers in their context. In more regulated and managed situations, decisions on evaluative practices are more likely to reside in the left-hand side of the Discretion Framework: individuals are told what to evaluate and/or how to evaluate it. In this section of the book, we will concentrate, instead, on the types of evaluative practice in the right-hand quadrants of the Discretion Framework, which tend to be driven by academics themselves, i.e. bottom-up activities which are more likely to be intrinsically motivated. Figure 21.2 illustrates what some of these evaluative practices might be.

It is worth pausing to discuss what value has been obtained from categorising evaluative practices within a Discretion Framework. The intention is to encourage an understanding of evaluation as an activity which is strongly conditioned by cultural and political factors, and by the social practices of those involved. In the chapters which follow, we will see how these factors

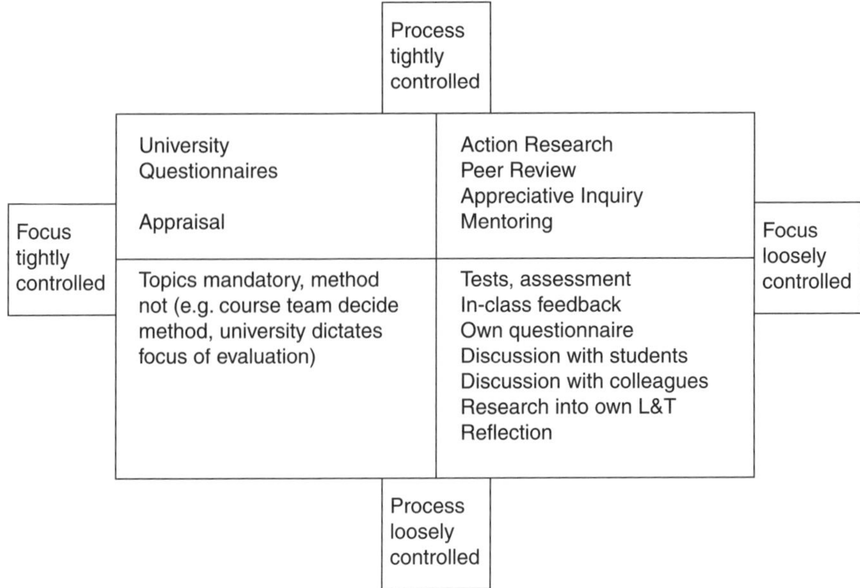

Figure 21.2 Evaluative practices within the Discretion Framework

have made certain types of evaluation work (or not). Having undertaken this analysis, individuals or groups of academics can then decide whether they are simply playing the evaluation game – tell me what I have to do and I'll crank through the motions – or whether they are making the most of what they could potentially understand better with more considered evaluative practices. This is perhaps especially important for new recruits to lecturing who, according to Henkel (2000), accept accountability and the corresponding evaluation of their performance more than those who have been in HE for longer. In the UK, new staff in most institutions have been pedagogically trained; they take concepts like 'reflection on practice' as part of their vocabulary, and they are probably familiar with the action learning cycle of plan – reflect – change – reflect (Biggs, 1999). Evaluative practices become more complex and are wider in range, because new academics do not simply inherit the long-used methods of their disciplinary colleagues.

The types of evaluative practice which academics are likely to be involved in are depicted in Figure 21.2. A disadvantage of such diagrams is that they belie the complexity of what is entailed in the different evaluative domains and, of course, these practices could take different forms depending on how they are carried out. However, the advantage of depicting evaluative practices in this way is that we then appreciate what Bernstein (1971) was so keen for us to understand: the relationship of organisational and political factors to educational practice and knowledge creation. While we can discuss the extent to which reflection is a loosely controlled evaluation activity, for example, what is beyond dispute is the contextual nature and complexity of the evaluative practices laid out in Figure 21.2.

In the next four chapters, some of these evaluative practices are explored in more depth by the case authors. In Chapter 22, Val Chapman takes us through the use of Appreciative Inquiry to evaluate the Developing and Embedding Inclusive Policies and/or Practices project. Chapter 23 covers Alison Shreeve and Margo Blythman's evaluation of a UK Centre For Excellence in Teaching and Learning; although the CETL was obliged to formally evaluate its activities as a condition of funding, they also chose to use self-driven, internal techniques to ensure that the initiative got immediate and contextually-relevant evaluation feedback. 'Tell us about it!' (Chapter 24) describes how students from diverse backgrounds evaluated their learning experiences in creative arts courses, and how academics used these evaluations. The project team avoided the deficit models often associated with non-completion of courses, and employed the students themselves to articulate their experiences, in their own voices. Finally, in Chapter 25, Harry Hubball and Marion Pearson advocate the use of scholarly approaches to curriculum evaluation, in the Canadian Context. Key issues raised by the cases are then analysed in Chapter 26.

22

Appreciative Inquiry as evaluation: enhancing and developing academic practice

Val Chapman

Introduction

In the UK, the University of Worcester's (UW) Strategic Plan (2007–12) is imbued with an unambiguous commitment to widen participation for all traditionally disadvantaged learners, including disabled people, throughout the student life cycle. Inclusion has long been championed as a central feature of University policy. Ideally, it is conceptualised as an approach to learning and teaching that avoids locating difficulty or deficit within the student, but focuses instead on the capacity of the academic department to understand and respond to individual learners requirements; but how can such an aspirational policy be translated into practice? In 2007, UW submitted a successful proposal to the Higher Education Academy's (HEA) project programme, 'Developing and Embedding Inclusive Policies and/or Practices'.

The project, Developing Inclusive Curricula in Higher Education, in its initial conceptualisation aimed to improve the learning experience of disabled students through further embedding effective inclusive practices in learning, teaching, assessment and curriculum design throughout all academic departments within the University. It was intended to achieve this through developing and delivering a comprehensive programme of staff development that would 'work with the grain of subject communities' (Trowler et al., 2003), so enabling teaching staff to meet the requirements of disabled students more successfully. However, in the very early stages of the project, it became apparent that the creation of the staff development programme was relatively unproblematic; the team's major concern was how to engage the interest and commitment of academic staff to develop further their inclusive learning and teaching practice – subsequently articulated as the project's key research question. We decided that we needed to focus on developing an effective model of engagement within one department in a pilot phase that, if successful, could later be rolled out to others.

Following a two-day residential hosted by the Higher Education Academy that included discussions with a number of 'experts', the project team chose Appreciative Inquiry (AI) as a methodology to evaluate and enhance academic practice in one of the University's departments. The Institute of Sport and Exercise Science (ISES) was selected not because its staff were least confident or able in their inclusive practice, but because the staff had a reputation for rigour, had evidenced 'following through' once engaged, and had the full support of the Head of Department.

AI has its origins in the work of Cooperrider and Whitney (1999) who propose that traditional, deficit focused, problem-solving techniques often result in conflict and negativity within teams and do not succeed in establishing or sustaining change. AI is not merely action research with a positive question at its core (Bushe, 2007: 30), neither is it a blindly optimistic Pollyanna approach that determinedly ignores concerns or difficulties – the 'shadow' in ourselves or those with whom we work (Johnson, 2008). In its broadest focus, it involves systematic discovery of what gives 'life' to a living system when it is most alive, most effective, and most constructively capable in economic, ecological, and human terms. AI involves, at its core, the art and practice of asking questions that strengthen a system's capacity to comprehend, anticipate, and heighten positive potential. It is a generative approach in which the participants co-create their reality, emphasising what is 'right' in practice and collectively envisioning what might be even better.

AI is normally conducted in four stages, as indicated in Figure 22.1, beginning with the 'Discovery' phase and completed through the 'Destiny' phase. This case study briefly describes the first three phases of our project (Sept. 2007 – Sept. 2008) that tracks the activities of the project.

The evaluative process

The project team included two academic staff, a senior manager, a disabled member of support staff, a disabled student from the Institute of Arts and Humanities, the Deputy Director of the Learning and Teaching Centre, and the Director (and project manager) of the Centre for Inclusive Learning Support. Crucially, the team included a senior member of the ISES who worked in close collaboration with the project manager throughout the project, and whose industry and support for the project were key to the project's success.

The team decided to employ disabled ISES students as researchers. Once recruited, the students were contracted to collect positive information about inclusive practice within the department using several means of data collection. A workshop was arranged (facilitated by an external expert) to train them and three members of the project team in the AI approach. Although seven students were originally recruited, due to pressures of work and domestic commitments only five engaged in the research. Prior to the workshop, the students were asked to complete a short questionnaire which offered the Tomlinson definition of inclusive practice (1996) and asked

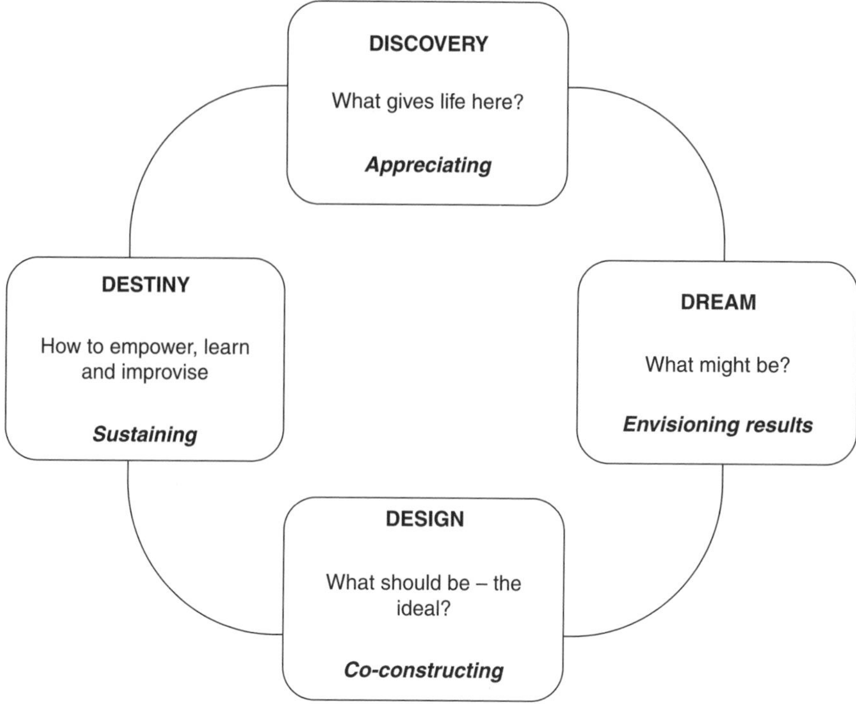

Figure 22.1 Appreciative inquiry: 4 stages

them to detail their own positive learning experiences in the ISES. The information received later formed part of the dataset.

At the workshop, one of the students struggled with the concept of AI, insisting that there were elements of practice within the department that were less than perfect. After some discussion which acknowledged his legitimate concerns and highlighted the means by which these could be reported outside the AI project (for example, through his membership of the University's Student Inclusion Group, course committee, student modular feedback forms and so on), data collection methods were agreed upon to capture the existing good practice within the department. Such appreciation of the 'shadow' (Johnson, 2008) is critical to implementing AI with authenticity, where tension is acknowledged and AI is not used to silence 'the margins' (Gergens, 1994).

Within the Discovery phase, three forms of data collection were used. Following lectures two pairs of students conducted a 'Post-it exercise' with two classes each (n = 256 students). This involved asking their peers who had attended the lecture to write down three adjectives which most accurately summed up their positive experiences of inclusive learning within their department. The blind student recorded an interview with two fellow students with visual impairments. Later, all five students contributed to a focus group interview that was led by the disabled student project team member. Prior to the interview, she had been individually briefed and also provided with a written set of guidelines on conducting focus group interviews. All interviews were recorded, transcribed and, together with the questionnaire responses, were later analysed by two project team staff members together with the disabled students to derive propositional statements that crystallised the ISES students' conceptualisation of inclusive practice within their department.

An ISES Staff/Student Research Seminar was organised as a vehicle for sharing the students' findings and a means of engaging the staff in self-evaluation regarding their inclusive practice. In order to maximise the potential impact from the students' presentation, the ISES project team member persuaded the Head of Department to instigate a three line whip, encouraging all teaching staff to attend the inaugural event. To lend even more weight to the occasion, the Learning and Teaching representatives from each of the other departments were invited, and the Vice Chancellor of the University and the Chief Executive of the British Para-Olympic Association were in attendance.

On the day, each student introduced themselves and spoke of the challenges they had faced in their educational and personal lives. This was not done with any degree of sympathy seeking; rather they gave personal accounts of what sorts of educational practices had worked really well for them. Before the results of the student Post-it activity were revealed, staff from within the Institute were themselves asked to identify three adjectives which they thought summed up the student experience. The student and staff Post-it exercise results were then compared and showed remarkable similarity.

The students then presented the seven propositional statements that had been derived from the written data. The following is an example (words in italics are direct quotes from the datasets):

> The Institute of Sport and Exercise Science offers students a *'ticket to their future'*; it gives them the opportunity to *'do things for themselves'*, *'become more independent'*, to *'reinvent themselves'* and *'be their own person'*. It offers a *'liberating'* and transformative experience.

The staff response was immediate and overwhelmingly positive: the students' presentations were extremely well received. Holding up a mirror (albeit a rose tinted one) to reflect back to the staff the student view of their inclusive practices really grabbed their attention. Staff listened with acuity heightened by the personal nature of the students' lived accounts and the direct relationship to their own practices.

To facilitate the ISES staff's self-evaluation of inclusive practice within their own department, after a short break following the student presentation, they were invited to work in groups and collectively draw a pictorial representation of their current inclusive practice. As part of the Dream phase, they were then invited to envision how their practice might become even better, using the analogy, 'If your current practice were, for example, a

Ford Focus, what would it look like if it were a Rolls Royce?'. They were asked to draw another pictorial representation to represent their thinking.

Later the following week, the project team discovered that despite being promoted as an Appreciative Inquiry event, some of the ISES staff had felt a little nervous ahead of the event and had felt anxious about the students' findings; perhaps they were too accustomed to the application of a deficit model so frequently applied in academia. Others later admitted, though hadn't shown this at the time, having felt somewhat uncomfortable when listening to positive descriptions of departmental practice. One academic commented, 'Listening to the students made me really reflect on what I do – and don't do. I had never thought of some of the enabling strategies that were mentioned, or the huge impact these can have for certain students.' Another commented wryly that the approach to gaining their interest was clearly successful as indicated by the staff's lack of reluctance to engage in drawing!

At a 'Design' phase departmental meeting, facilitated by the project manager a week later (no three line whip this time but a gratifying 75% turnout), the staff agreed, through a hermeneutic circle approach[1] (Berthon et al., 2002) a set of departmental priorities to help them envision, and find the means to co-create, their Rolls Royce version of inclusive practice. The Department's Learning and Teaching Committee was then charged with managing and monitoring the actions relating to achievement of their priorities.

One of the identified priorities was the need for staff development. In order to determine explicit areas in need of further development, the project manager circulated a questionnaire which asked staff to rate their confidence levels in a range of 16 (what might be loosely termed) 'curriculum aspects'. Not only did the use of the AI support the effective development of the focus group interviews and data collection at the Discovery stage, it also informed the development and administration of this survey instrument – demonstrating its use as an overarching approach that was able to guide the entire evaluation (Preskill and Coghlan, 2003). The questionnaire, distributed via Survey Monkey (an online survey software package), received a 78% response rate, in itself another indication of the success of the approach, which enabled the core project team to determine the most appropriate topics, formats and methods of delivery needed.

A report on the findings of the questionnaire was collated by the project manager and presented to the ISES Learning and Teaching Committee. The ensuing reflection and discussion highlighted aspects of work and collaboration that could be taken forward. Worthwhile practice that had been tacit in some areas was valued and made explicit, ways of sharing and

---

[1] 'Hermeneutic theory is a member of the social subjectivist paradigm where meaning is inter-subjectively created, in contrast to the empirical universe of assumed scientific realism.'

'growing' such practices were identified. The team also agreed the aspirational goal, 'Within the next two years, the ISES team will have an international reputation as leaders in the field of inclusive practice in sport and exercise science.' Having witnessed the embedding of a renewed commitment to inclusion within the department's core vision and action plan, the project team concluded that using an Appreciative Inquiry approach had succeeded in its aim of encouraging ISES staff to review and further improve their inclusive academic practice, and that the project had indeed supported the University to move closer towards its vision of '*being a high quality University with an international reputation for excellent, inclusive education*'.

The successful use of AI in this evaluation was rooted in several beliefs: that truth is dependent upon the context and the current reality; that planning is a process of constant re-evaluation, and that all things are interconnected. The use of AI highlighted in this case study was successful for a number of reasons, not least that the process was able to be conducted within a limited and finite time-span and with comparatively few resources; of paramount importance, however, was the fact that the process involved all key stakeholders including students as well as staff from all levels of seniority within the department. Though the department already had a reputation for its commitment to innovation and creativity, following engagement in the Design phase of the project, all key stakeholders had a clear understanding of the purpose and process of evaluation and a renewed and vigorous commitment to inclusion.

23

Evaluating a UK Centre for Excellence in Teaching and Learning: bottom-up evaluation in a top-down setting

Alison Shreeve and Margo Blythman

Introduction

This case study describes the evaluation processes used by a group of people who were obliged to undertake formal evaluation driven by funders, but were also committed to self-evaluation. The Creative Learning in Practice Centre for Excellence in Teaching and Learning (CLIP CETL) was based at the University of the Arts London (UAL) and was one of 74 CETLs funded by The Higher Education Funding Council for England (HEFCE) between 2005 and 2010. The centre was awarded significant funding, £4.85M, of which £2.35M was used on capital projects. The process designed to select centres was a competitive application in two stages. The first had to demonstrate a case for excellence in teaching and learning, with evidence to support the claims made. The second phase required a business plan setting out aims and strategies to achieve the aims.

A key aim of CLIP CETL was to engage people in enquiry into learning and teaching in practice-based arts subjects and to change the culture: we wanted to move from a position of taking teaching for granted to one that recognized, rewarded, researched and innovated learning and teaching in practice. The core CETL team developed a vision for engagement in which we saw ourselves as change agents, starting a lot of small fires and fanning the flames in order to change the culture of the university to promote and value research into learning and teaching.

In the business plan, HEFCE expected to see a process of evaluation embedded in the CETL and a self-evaluation document after 18 months. We commissioned external evaluators, the Centre for the Study of Education and Training (CSET) at Lancaster University, as an objective eye on our activities, but we also employed an internal evaluator to act as a critical friend. The internal evaluator would alert us immediately to problems with our activities, and we could respond quickly. They also understood the culture and politics of the university as an insider, bringing a different kind of evaluation to that provided by an 'objective' professional evaluation team.

Creative Learning in Practice

The CLIP CETL case for excellence was built on our links with industry and the authentic learning activities provided for students. The university is the first specialist art and design institution to be awarded university status and has an international reputation with a high research profile but, before the CETL, less obvious recognition of teaching excellence.

We used our funds for different activities. Over the five years, these included teaching excellence initiatives, an employability skills web site,[1] and research projects:[2]

- The First Year International Student Experience
- Teaching Landscapes in the Creative Arts
- Verbal Feedback Project 'Tell Us About It!' Diverse student voices of academic success.

Why did we want to evaluate CLIP CETL?

The funding body quite rightly required us to be accountable and evaluate our activities. However, as a small professional team we needed to understand what we were doing and the requirement to evaluate was concurrent with a desire to do so: self-evaluation is an integral part of our disciplinary culture, via reflection in the design process and the expectation that students will reflect through sketchbooks and writing.

Evaluation was a key component of reflective practice at all levels in CLIP CETL. Staff-initiated projects were asked to indicate how they would evaluate their activity when they submitted a bid for funding, and we encouraged student participation in that evaluation. End of project reports also prompted them to articulate what they had learned, what others could learn from their project and how their activity had improved student learning. We needed to develop the sense of critical evaluation which is fundamental both to the discipline area itself, and also to developing a culture of critique and innovation across the university. More formalized evaluation using CSET and the internal evaluator was an opportunity to ensure that we focused on specific aspects of our activity, through asking participants and key personnel how our work had been experienced.

[1] http://www.careers-creative-living.co.uk/
[2] http://www.arts.ac.uk/clipcetl-fundedprojects.htm

Internal evaluation practice

The process of internal evaluation was developed through discussion between the centre director and the internal evaluator, who was Director of Learning and Teaching at one of the constituent colleges of UAL. We wanted to know what the effect of funding for projects might be and what the CLIP CETL and the university could learn from projects. The evaluation approach was conceived of as research, allowing for the possibility of developing research outcomes from the evaluation, and reflecting the wish to promote research into learning and teaching. We therefore drew from a wide range of theoretical perspectives in our analysis. These included:

- **Communities of Practice** (Wenger, 1998) and its later critics in relation to the importance of language and power relations (Barton and Tusting, 2005).
- **Policy implementation theory** (Cerych and Sabatier, 1986), in particular how policy is mediated on the ground by 'street level bureaucrats' (Lipsky, 1980) and the operation of power relations (Hoyle, 1982).
- **School improvement critical theory**, in particular Fullan (2001), Hargreaves (1983; 1994), Harris and Bennett (2001), Bascia and Hargreaves (2000), Datnow (2000).
- **Staff development theory**, in particular Land (2004), Webb (1996) and Eraut (1993; 1994).
- **Importance of the course team in teacher learning** (Drew and Vaughan, 2002).
- **Explorations of the meso level in universities** (Clegg and McAuley, 2005; Trowler et al., 2005).

Internal evaluation was designed as an institutional conversation, focusing each year on a particular strand of the CETL activity that might be potentially problematic because of the level of complexity or the number of people involved. Data were mainly collected through semi-structured interviews. This was because we wanted to capture the lived experience of those doing the work and it aligned with our social constructivist perspective (Vygotsky, 1978; Cole et al., 1997). We wanted the evaluation to align to the social practices happening in the university, rather than impose a framework that was alien or additional to their work.

Semi-structured interviews make interviewees reflect on what they are doing and, at times, we saw this happening in the interview. This is important in a culture where there is very little thinking time/space. Although our approach was essentially that of researchers, we also intervened so that issues of concern from interviewees were immediately fed back to the CLIP CETL team to action. The research interview approach is based on capturing the stories that participants have to tell of their involvement. The analysis relies on knowledge of the university culture and structures as well as the literature around policy change and organization.

The internal evaluation changed as the projects changed and as we grew in efficiency and learned from the formal and informal evaluation process. The internal evaluation always provided a rigorous and research-informed view which resulted in a focus on actions that we should take in order to learn from activities and improve teaching and learning for the university community. The reports were presented and discussed at the CLIP CETL management group meetings, where actions were considered formally in relation to university policy and procedures, as well as being discussed within the team.

The evaluation reports provided an enormous amount of rich data, far more than we can probably cope with and act on. These formal, research-based and insightful reflections by an experienced colleague were very rigorous ways to understand both the process and effects of rewarding teaching and learning.

The success of this form of evaluation relies on:

- Funding to allocate the time and resources of an experienced researcher
- Someone who understands how to research and also the university culture
- Time and energy to work on implementing recommendations
- Networks of contacts across the university and influence at different levels
- The support of key personnel in the university.

Issues with internal evaluation

Needless to say, there were challenges in undertaking this kind of evaluation:

- Being in a position to understand the internal politics does not necessarily mean that we were also in a position to act on this or bring about change.
- Recommendations in reports were not always welcome and we learned to re-phrase these so that individuals could fashion their own actions in response to evaluation (Saunders, 2006).
- Respondents didn't appear to have many negative messages or ideas for improvement, maybe due to a reluctance to criticize those who had given them money and support.
- We didn't look at the experience of people who didn't receive funding, whose bids were rejected.
- We had too much data to be able to work on all aspects of university life that might need change.
- Formal evaluation of local projects provides a focus and link to institutional issues (see Shreeve, 2010).

Although a requirement of HEFCE's funding, evaluation has been and continues to be one of the most interesting and exciting aspects of this CETL. We learn collectively from individual engagement and seek to learn and to change as an institution. We try to benefit from research into learning and teaching and from the opportunities that having a funded centre for excellence in teaching and learning have enabled.

24

'Tell us about it!' Evaluating what helps students from diverse backgrounds to succeed at the University of the Arts London

Alison Shreeve

Introduction

This case study describes how students evaluated their learning experiences in creative arts courses and how academics have built on and used these evaluations. The outcomes were considered in a 'use strategy workshop' devised to maximise the usability of evaluation (Saunders, 2008). This led to the development of exhibitions and workshops to disseminate learning from evaluation.

Setting up 'Tell Us About It!'

This scheme was an evaluation of student learning experiences from their own perspectives and through their own voices (Saunders, 2006). Listening to and learning from students was the main reason for instigating the project. Statistical data such as the National Student Survey provides a set of predetermined questions for students but doesn't necessarily address all the important aspects of learning in the discipline. All art and design institutions fare badly in these kinds of surveys, but deeper underlying reasons for student dissatisfaction are hard to access.

In a climate of concern in the UK to widen participation to Higher Education (HE) (Lillis, 2001; Archer et al., 2005) we asked students from different backgrounds what helped them to succeed on their course. We adopted a positive model, as opposed to the deficit model so frequently used to identify non-completion and lower academic achievement of student groups (Stuart, 2000). By asking successful students what helped them and what they found challenging in their studies we avoided the stereotyping of groups of students being less able or less well prepared for study in UK universities. Through celebrating the achievements of students who were put forward by their course directors, and who received a bursary to tell us what helped them to succeed we have been enabled to learn vicariously through their voices. They have evaluated their own learning experiences and we have evaluated their stories.

Working with the unexpected

In the first year the scheme ran we expected students to write an essay, but because the disciplines have a high rate of dyslexia we also offered students a video interview or video diary option. The questions we asked were open in order to be inclusive and not pre-empt student responses:

- What helped you learn on your course?
- What kind of challenges did you face and how did you overcome them?
- What tips/strategies can you share with other students about your learning experience at the University?

The scheme was managed by an experienced study support tutor and CLIP CETL coordinator who was open to suggestions from the students and facilitated their responses, either by interviewing them or by prompting them to reflect. Her response to students' requests to create alternative formats to these questions through their own subject specialism was fundamental to the outcome of the evaluation of student learning. This was an unexpected response from students and we built on it in subsequent years.

In their own words

The students' own words were in various unanticipated formats. This was a reflection of the different subjects they had studied, from fine art through to graphics and animation. Producing artefacts and artwork had become fundamental to how they identified themselves as students and graduates in the creative arts. This was the language in which they had been learning to express themselves and through which many of them preferred to tell their stories about challenges and success. Students who were able to see examples of work from previous years probably gained in confidence to express themselves in ways that they felt at home.

This has resulted in a collection of very moving and powerful depictions in response to the three questions we asked. Artefacts include sketchbooks, artworks, artefacts such as a mouse mat illustrating the first year experience, a board game, videos made by students, animations and music, as well as essays, illustrated stories and recorded interviews. The students have told us in their own language what helped them to succeed.

Issues of interpretation

All communication through words, actions and objects are culturally situated (Holland and Valsiner, 1988; Holland et al., 1998; Vygotsky, 1978) and student artefacts are no different. For tutors in art and design a white box that contains half-obscured writing and images on leaves of paper which requires a physical act of unpacking is a metaphor for a particular students' experience. Her identity is contained within the box which some tutors have placed her in. Her African heritage and identity had been obscured until a tutor recognised how central this was to her own art practice. The message for all tutors is the importance of student identity and autonomy in learning, but tutors from other disciplines were faced with a foreign language. Whilst this presented difficulties in staff development workshops to learn from the evaluation, the ensuing discussion around the artefact was a powerful process of active dissemination and engagement on the part of the tutors learning about the student experience.

The artefacts themselves are intriguing and work at emotive levels. For example a video animation and musical score made by an international student clearly moves one to empathise with the experience of arriving in London to study. Dissemination of the messages the artefacts contained required new approaches, not simply written summaries of the points students made, though a team of academic, study support and diversity unit staff spent many hours analysing these. As well as workshops in which participants handled the objects and viewed video diaries, we have presented exhibitions of the work in local colleges. The workshop facilitator invited comments about the workshop from those involved. These took the form of Post-it notes which are collated in a sketchbook and this provided another layer of evaluation, resulting in another object in its own right which was also open to scrutiny.

Although we have summarised conditions that support and hinder students' learning, all students were of course different, with different 'life conditions' experiences and needs. What worked for some didn't work for others, for example where halls of residence were a place of 'ultra-minging kitchens' for one student they were a source of friends and a support network for another. These diverse messages serve to remind us that students need to be treated as individuals.

Issues of evaluative practice

As well as working with an unexpected physical format presented by artwork, tutors had to support and encourage students who took part. They were mentored through an introductory workshop and individual contact to ensure they met deadlines. In addition the tutor had to make sure that they addressed the questions and sometimes careful support was needed to bring this out. Students of course selected what they chose to tell us and sometimes there were key points missing in their narratives, such as being in receipt of disability allowances. Although admiration for the student succeeding in the face of severe physical challenges may have been the reason for inclusion in the scheme, we could not override the students' own evaluation of their experience that avoided reference to their disability. As an example of success in the face of major challenges, this particular example might have offered valuable insights to others, but we have no way of knowing whether the student's account incorporated the most important messages or not. This limits the objectivity of the evaluation, but also indicates that most forms of evaluation rely on second order accounts of experience, not in-process evaluation. The supporting tutor also had to verify our interpretation of the messages the work contained with the students and in some cases a short accompanying statement was added to the artwork.

Further evaluation was undertaken through a discussion group comprised of different staff expertise: academic, support and diversity. This was intended to make explicit a concern that the usability of the student evaluation might be missed by those we wanted to engage with the evaluation messages, our target audience. A bullet point list of key issues was made available through

Table 24.1 Using RUFDATA to summarise the TUAI! scheme

Reasons	To use a positive, rather than a deficit model to evaluate student experience To listen to what the students told us about success and to let them have choice in the way they told us about what helped or hindered them in their studies
Uses	To inform new and prospective students about study in art and design To inform academic and student support staff of the key messages from student voices
Focus	On experience and what helped students from diverse backgrounds to succeed academically in art and design
Data	Artefacts, artworks, video interviews and diaries, games, essays, animations, visual representations of experience
Audience	Information for academics and student services teams, and for students
Timing	Self-evaluation is a post experience reflection on students' academic success. Awarding a bursary also recognises success and rewards them for exploring and retelling the experience for others
Agency	The evaluation process and method has evolved in response to the students who took part. They have responded in the medium of their studies and their vocations in art and design. They use a language of communication based on the visual and the embodied object, not solely on verbal language. This is their choice and as academics we have to respond to their communication choices

a CLIP CETL publication (available from http://www.arts.ac.uk/clipcetl-tellusaboutitpublication.htm) and through workshops to engage with the students' experiences.

What we learned about evaluation:

- We had to devolve power and control and let the students determine what they wanted to tell us and how they wanted to tell us
- Taking a risk in this way resulted in new formats and unexpected outcomes of evaluation
- Evaluation does not always have to follow text based and verbal processes
- Dissemination or the 'usability' of evaluation is an important part of the outcome and this is dependent on the format the evaluation takes
- Acts of translation are required between different kinds of medium (words and objects) and also between different people with different previous experiences
- Evaluation is also a context dependent and cultural activity
- Arts based outcomes have more power to evoke empathy than most forms of evaluation, particularly reports
- Their messages can be conveyed quickly and more effectively than through written language, provided people are receptive to the medium

'Tell Us About It!' has given us another dimension to understanding or evaluating the student experience in art and design. It has challenged us to interpret and to find new ways to learn from the evaluation which was situated in students reflecting on their success and the journeys they made to get there.

25

Scholarly approaches to curriculum evaluation: critical contributions for undergraduate degree program reform in a Canadian context

Harry Hubball and Marion L. Pearson

Introduction

Fuelled by global concerns about rigour, transferability, and accountability of undergraduate degree programs, there has been increasing attention to curriculum evaluation in a broad array of disciplines. In North America, despite a growing body of literature in the Scholarship of Teaching and Learning (SoTL), and more recently the Scholarship of Curriculum Practice (SoCP), there have been remarkably few studies that focus on scholarly approaches to curriculum evaluation practices in Higher Education (HE) (Bresciani, 2006; Christensen Hughes, 2007; Cox and Richlin, 2004; Hubball and Gold, 2007; McKinney, 2007). A scholarly approach to curriculum evaluation is central to the effectiveness of undergraduate degree program reform, as it can identify strengths and weaknesses in existing curricula during the development stage of program reform, establish critical indicators of success for redesigned curricula, and facilitate the collection and analysis of data about program effectiveness during various stages of implementation. In practice, however, ad hoc approaches to curriculum evaluation are often used, resulting in numerous accounts of methodological shortcomings in evaluation procedures that tend to yield less useful (and less authentic) data pertaining to program development and/or effectiveness. This chapter provides critical insight for scholarly approaches to curriculum evaluation practices within and across disciplines in a Canadian context. These insights are grounded in the SoTL/SoCP literature and 15 years of curricular consultations and leadership experiences across nine different faculties at the University of Windsor and various units at the University of British Columbia (UBC), including the Faculty of Pharmaceutical Sciences, the Department of Civil Engineering in the Faculty of Applied Sciences, the Women's and

Gender Studies program in the Faculty of Arts, and the Graduate School of Journalism.

Scholarly practices in curriculum evaluation

Given the parallels between curriculum evaluation and traditional disciplinary forms of research (i.e., with processes of review of the relevant literature, selection of an appropriate conceptual framework, systematic collection of appropriate data, critical reflection, and dissemination of findings in peer-review contexts), one might expect a greater congruence, for example, for scholarly investigations that focus on program effectiveness. Despite rich opportunities for curriculum evaluation in the current Canadian context of undergraduate degree program reform, theory-practice connections have rarely occurred in the same way as faculties typically approach disciplinary research investigations (Hubball and Pearson, 2009). There are encouraging signs that curriculum evaluations in many faculties, however, are increasingly turning to scholarly approaches in order to enhance program development and effectiveness.

Scholarly approaches to curriculum evaluation are situated within a broad curriculum community context. To use a specific example, it was evident in the Faculty of Pharmaceutical Sciences at UBC, where 32 faculty members and some 300 students engaged in a 2-year process to redesign a 4-year B.Sc. (Pharm.) program, that an engaged curriculum learning community and good leadership (from internal champions and an external curriculum consultant) helped facilitate effective communications in the critical debates and complex decision-making processes required for the sustained effort involved in curriculum evaluation. Strategies that were particularly helpful included holding regular 'town hall' meetings, posting a large schematic of the curriculum in a public hallway, and ensuring that the process was inclusive of all faculty members and an array of important stakeholder groups, including students, practitioners, and practice leaders. Other mechanisms for effective communication in the curriculum evaluation process include the use of dedicated web sites, email, suggestion boxes in key locations, curriculum notice boards, and interactive curriculum committee representatives. Further, scholarly approaches to curriculum evaluation are informed by the HE literature (e.g., for guidance and contextualized evidence for useful strategies that have been successfully employed elsewhere) and internalize theory and practice through a collaborative, systematic, and cyclical process of inquiry that involves hypothesis testing, planning, observation, analysis, action, and further inquiry (Friedman, 2008; Senge and Scharmer, 2008). Essentially, scholarly approaches to curriculum evaluation have invited curriculum evaluators to consider which conceptual framework is appropriate, which research questions are important to examine, what data to gather, when and how to collect and analyse these data, how to initiate positive changes to practice, how to engage curriculum stakeholders in the process, and, finally, to consider how this curriculum evaluation might be of interest to the broader scholarly community through dissemination and peer review.

As with all forms of research (including curriculum evaluation), there are underlying assumptions about knowledge and its generation. In particular, there are three such assumptions that have been relevant for curriculum evaluations in multidisciplinary settings: knowledge is 1) personally constructed, 2) socially mediated, and 3) inherently situated (Cox and Richlin, 2004; Hubball and Burt, 2007; Hubball and Albon, 2007; McKinney, 2007; Senge and Scharmer, 2008). These assumptions are intimately related and are regularly the subject of debate within the SoTL/SoCP research community. All three have played a part in the way various universities and academic units have approached curriculum evaluation. For example, responsiveness to individual students, attention to fostering communities of practice, and a focus on relevant issues in the field of practice were critical to the process of evaluating curricular effectiveness in the 4-year undergraduate programs in both Civil Engineering and Women's and Gender Studies at the University of British Columbia. Recognizing that individuals personally construct knowledge about curriculum experiences is essential for understanding the nature and substance of curriculum evaluations. The socially mediated aspect of knowledge construction speaks to the notion of communities of practice, in particular the milieu in which curriculum evaluation takes place and the multiple negotiations (i.e., regarding competing interests such as emphases on context, process, impact, and/or long-term follow-up evaluations) that occur in these settings (Baldwin, 2008; Fraser, 2006). Further, the principle that knowledge construction is inherently situated is key to understanding the uniqueness (e.g., with regard to the faculty and students, resources, broad field of study, and pedagogical practices) and rich contextually-bound cues (e.g., historic, social, economic, political, environmental) within curricular contexts where authentic evaluations occur (Bresciani, 2006). Acknowledgement of the underlying research assumptions and a broad conceptual framework for curriculum evaluation are key foundations for enhancing undergraduate degree program reform.

A conceptual framework for curriculum evaluation

The following flexible and iterative curriculum evaluation framework (Figure 25.1, Adapted, Hubball and Burt, 2007) has been employed by educational developers and university teachers to examine curriculum contexts, processes, impacts, and long-term follow-up evaluations in various HE settings (Albon and Hubball, 2004; Hubball and Albon, 2007; Hubball and Poole, 2003; Hubball and Burt, 2004, 2007; Hubball, Mighty, Britnell, and Gold, 2007; Hubball, 2010).

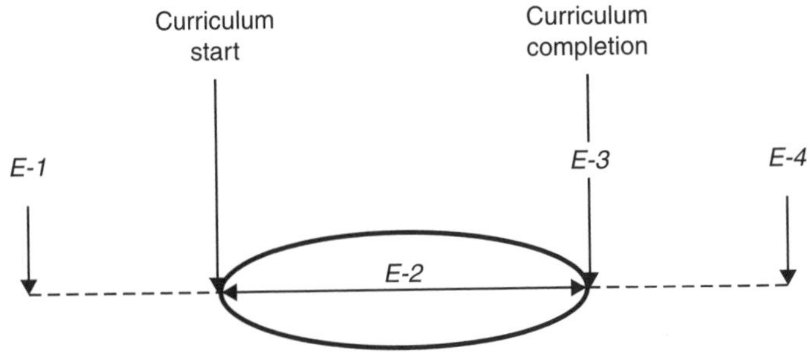

CURRICULUM EVALUATION PHASES

CONTEXT CONSIDERATIONS: Audience, Objectives, Resources for evaluation projects

E-1: Curriculum context evaluations

E-2: Curriculum process evaluations

E-3: Curriculum impact evaluations

E-4: Curriculum follow-up evaluations

Figure 25.1 A framework for conceptualising key phases of curriculum evaluation

Source: Hubball and Burt, adapted 2007.

As part of a scholarly approach to curriculum evaluation, this framework takes into account the curriculum context and enables a wide range of curriculum investigations.

Curriculum context evaluations

These address key issues such as the intended audience for the curriculum evaluation, the objectives of the evaluation, and available resources to conduct specified evaluation projects. For example, curriculum context evaluations might include: researching relevant literature; assessing the perceived needs of various stakeholder groups pertaining to curriculum context factors, processes, and outcomes; and curriculum evaluation feasibility issues. What needs to be considered, improved, why, and how?

Curriculum process evaluations

These are periodic formative evaluations that focus on issues of importance that arise throughout the curriculum. For example, to what extent are learning outcomes made explicitly clear to students through course syllabi? To what extent are individual instructors incorporating active learning methodologies and program-level learning outcomes in their own teaching practices? How do students best achieve learning outcomes? What are the strengths and weaknesses of curriculum learning experiences? What needs to be improved, why, and how?

Curriculum impact evaluations

These are summative evaluations that focus on issues of importance that occur as a result of curriculum outcomes. For example, how do students demonstrate learning outcomes? To what extent does the undergraduate curriculum serve institutional purposes? To what extent does the curriculum meet, surpass, or fall short of its goals? What needs to be improved, why, and how?

Curriculum follow-up evaluations

These focus on issues of importance which arise as a result of the longer-term outcomes (e.g., over months or years) of a curriculum. For example, to what extent are there high numbers of graduates in leadership and/or employment positions within the community? As a student and/or graduate reflects upon the curriculum and learning outcomes, what does he/she remember and value most? Generally speaking, to whom and to what extent, if at all, did the curriculum make any difference? If at all, how did the curriculum contribute to students' development as citizens in a diverse world?

As the foregoing suggests, a conceptual framework for curriculum evaluation provides a key foundation for strategic and systematic approaches to undergraduate degree program reform.

Strategic and systematic approaches to curriculum evaluation

Situated in a broad curriculum context, and guided by the HE literature as outlined previously, units such as UBC's School of Journalism (which offers a 2-year graduate program) have taken strategic and systematic approaches to curriculum evaluation planning, focussing on a comprehensive needs assessment of the curriculum context (including input from representative key stakeholders such as faculty, students, colleagues in the field, and institutional administrators); the identification of indicators of success for an effective program (e.g., achievement of program-level learning outcomes, high levels of student applications and low attrition rates, high levels of graduates in leadership and/or employment positions within the community, high levels of satisfaction by staff and students within programs, high levels of positive reputation of the program within the community, and/or program-level learning applications in the workplace or society); the selection of an appropriate research design, methodology, appropriate data sources (e.g., students, faculty, administrators, alumni, and/or employers); and an ongoing process of data gathering and analysis.

Data collection strategies, for example, have been in the form of both quantitative (e.g., numeric performance and graduation records, rating and rank-order preference scales) and qualitative sources (e.g., documents such as course syllabi, open-ended feedback forms and/or focus group interviews, interpretation of students' assignments, portfolios, etc.). Analysis of appropriate combinations of qualitative and quantitative data has yielded critical information to enhance program development and effectiveness (Gay, Mills, and Airasian, 2009; Merriam, 2002; Stake, 2005). Finally, strategic and systematic approaches have closely monitored curriculum evaluation challenges, progress, and timelines for further improvements, and have focussed on the dissemination of findings in peer-review contexts (Driscoll and Wood, 2007; Hubball and Clarke, in press). This dissemination of curriculum evaluations has taken all the usual scholarly forms, including journal publications (e.g., *The Canadian Journal for the Scholarship of Teaching and Learning*, conference presentations, Society for Teaching and Learning in Higher Education) and scholarly grant applications (e.g., Social Sciences and Humanities Research Council of Canada). It has also included curriculum leadership and documentation presentations for the academic learning community, such as a Reporting Template for curriculum evaluation. The Reporting Template covers not only the different curriculum components, but also encourages academics to consider contextual factors which influence the faculty's curriculum, and implementation strategies.

It is important to note that while several of the above issues might be of interest to evaluate, strategic decisions have always had to be made and priorities set so that the curriculum evaluation process was manageable and sustainable, and so that it provided the evidence necessary to support efforts to enhance undergraduate degree program reform (Pennee, 2007; Shavelson and Huang, 2003).

Criticisms and challenges to curriculum evaluation practices

Experiences in multi-institutional and multidisciplinary settings have shown that existing curriculum evaluation practices demonstrate a general lack of attention to scholarly approaches, including the poor use of curriculum evaluation frameworks, a tendency to sporadic rather than ongoing curriculum evaluation, and less than useful methodology for fostering engagement and change. Along with many other existing challenges as outlined, these observations suggest that many academic units are ill-equipped to conduct authentic curriculum evaluations. Of course, curriculum evaluation is shaped by many factors (social, political, economic, organizational, cultural, and individual) and can involve people at various institutional levels (administrators, curriculum development committee personnel, instructors, colleagues in the field, and students) in complex settings (Davis and Sumara, 2006;

Schnieder and Schoenberg, 1999). When ad hoc curriculum evaluation practices are used, as is commonly the case, central criticisms about the shortcomings tend to focus on provision of unhelpful data for enhancing program development and/or effectiveness; poor visibility within (and outside of) academic units; poor engagement with key stakeholders; and ill-defined timelines and lack of clarity about who was responsible for specific reporting tasks. These challenges and levels of complexity, in addition to lack of time due to already-substantial workloads, a lack of SoTL/SoCP expertise, competing institutional priorities (e.g., criteria for tenure and promotion, student grading practices), and lack of agreement on the importance of learning outcomes have posed significant methodological and organizational barriers for faculty members, administrators, and students in order to engage in effective curriculum evaluations (Grunert O'Brien, Millis, and Cohen, 2008; Roy, Borin, and Kustra, 2007; Eisner, 2004; Sumsion and Goodfellow, 2004). Adequate institutional support and scholarly approaches to curriculum evaluation have been required to overcome these significant obstacles and yield authentic evaluation procedures that enhance undergraduate degree program reform (Hubball and Pearson, in press; Knight and Trowler, 2000; McInnis, 2000).

Conclusion

Engagement in scholarly and practical rigour to evaluate curricula is vital to the success and sustainability of efforts to reform undergraduate programs. The imperative for strategic and systematic curriculum evaluations is even more compelling as ad hoc undergraduate degree program reform efforts with scant attention to scholarship gain momentum across HE institutions. To overcome inherent complexities, and to avoid ad hoc approaches to curriculum evaluation, therefore, academic units have instead (and are increasingly) focussed on theoretically-driven strategic and systematic approaches that are integral to the initial development stages, and to each phase of implementing undergraduate degree program reform. This chapter provides critical insight for scholarly approaches to curriculum evaluation practices within and across disciplines in a Canadian context.[1]

[1] **Acknowledgements:** the authors would like to express their sincere thanks to all curriculum leaders and SoTL Leadership Program graduates from multi-institutional and disciplinary settings for their critical contributions to this chapter.

26

Evaluative practice and outcomes: issues at the self-evaluative level

Veronica Bamber

> Reflective scholars are interested in helping scholars understand, question, investigate and take seriously their own learning and teaching. They argue that professional education has taken a wrong turn in seeing the role of staff and faculty developers as being to interpret, translate and implement theoretical insights. They believe instead that practitioners, including university faculty, must research their own work sites, must recognise and generate their own theories of practice rather than importing them from outside, and must develop the capacity for a kind of continuous investigation and monitoring of their efforts. Good teachers, according to this tradition, are in the habit of identifying and checking the assumptions behind their practice and of experimenting creatively with approaches they have themselves evolved in response to the unique demands of the situations in which they work.
>
> (Brookfield, 1995: 129)

Introduction

This chapter considers some of the issues which have been raised by the cases in the self-evaluative practices section of this book, all of which offer examples of groups and individuals who, to paraphrase Brookfield (1995), identify and check the assumptions behind their practice and experiment creatively with approaches to evaluation which they themselves have evolved. Six major points have become clear from these cases:

Self-evaluative practices are self-driven: agency is a key element in evaluation, and, perhaps not surprisingly, the evaluations described in the four case studies all sit in the bottom right-hand quadrant of the Discretion Framework outlined in Chapter 21. Those undertaking evaluations largely decide what they will evaluate and how they will do the evaluation.

Agency is not straightforward: while the Discretion Framework is a helpful heuristic, the complexities of agency are not fully captured by dichotomous categorisation. In fact, phrases like 'bottom-up' sometimes obscure rather than illustrate the realities of self-evaluation, where the roles of agent, audience, and other concerned stakeholders are interwoven, even in 'self'-evaluation. Outside influence is already present (from past learning, from absorbing ideas without realising it, from adapting practice based on true or false assumptions or expectations about aims and requirements of stakeholders).

Discretion does not mean free-for-all: self-evaluative practices are bounded by the cultural and social practices of the evaluative context; discretion as to what or how to evaluate does not mean a free-for-all. For example, evaluators usually aim for congruence with research cultures or disciplinary norms – i.e. the social practices of those being evaluated.

What is evaluated goes beyond the project: although self-evaluation usually tries to avoid the discourse of managerialist 'stakeholder involvement', stakeholders still form part of the evaluative focus, as does the context.

Emerging outcomes are worked with, not against: what these evaluations reveal is a philosophical commitment to acknowledge the situation of those involved, and to work not with rationality, but with the mix of possible intended, unintended and unanticipated outcomes that might emerge during the evaluation.

Self-evaluative practices are a vital part of change efforts: self-evaluative practices can provide a fertile seeding ground for changes reaching far beyond the evaluation itself and unintended (but desirable) consequences can ensue from thoughtfully designed catalysts.

Having drawn these points out from the cases, I will now consider examples of the six points from the chapters written by Val Chapman (Appreciative Inquiry); Alison Shreeve and Alison Blythman (internal evaluation of a CETL project); Shreeve (learning experiences of arts students) and Harry Hubball and Marion Pearson (scholarly approaches to curriculum evaluation).

Self-evaluative practices are self-driven

The introductory commentary on this theme (Chapter 21) suggests that the story of self-evaluative practices could be seen as a story of power. While the trajectory of evaluation from the mid-1980s on is one of increasing levels of accountability and decreasing levels of discretion as to how academics evaluate their practice, and what they evaluate – 'a flow away from the individual and towards greater management decision-making' (Chapter 21), the cases in the theme show that if this is 'the rule' then there is no shortage of exceptions to that rule – like most rules, especially in academic environments and cultures which are (still) characterised by (some) autonomy. In each chapter we see instances of academics not only choosing to evaluate their practice, but also choosing to do this in creative ways. The implementation staircase mentioned in Chapter 1 could be seen as a fairly flat one at the individual/group level where academics have been able to choose their evaluative practices: they play with and implement their evaluations, and adjust them in the light of their own social practices and needs. The implementation of evaluation is not hierarchical, although this does not mean it is unproblematic, as the case writers have shown. Nonetheless, the key point is that for these writers evaluative practices are nested in academic cultures, and influencing factors emanate from the values and pressures of academic life itself, not just from above.

The defining feature of the four cases in this section of the book, then, is Agency, one of the 'A's in the RUFDATA framework: the emphasis is on how individuals and groups of academics evaluate their *own* practice, to inform their professional activities. It is not about systems or measures of control and, as mentioned in the introductory chapter of the book, these evaluative practices are consequently more likely to be rooted in academic values and norms than other, more externally imposed evaluative practices. This improves the chance that the outcomes of such evaluations will be taken seriously, at least by the academics involved in the initiative.

While national, programmatic or institutional evaluations are (increasingly) in the public domain, the outcomes of these self-evaluative practices are not always intended to be of public interest. Self-evaluators may well decide to disseminate their outcomes, as in the cases of Shreeve, Shreeve and Blythman and, most determinedly, Hubball and Pearson. However, the primary focus of self-evaluation is generally professionals reflecting on their practices and tinkering with them – as Brookfield (1995) advocates, in the quote which opens this chapter, rather than trying to make 'big bang' changes to large scale initiatives (Knight and Trowler, 2001: 23). Neither is the key purpose of such evaluations an attempt to influence policy. So, in the self-evaluative theme, the first two chapters focus on academics evaluating to inform their own practice – what Ashwin and Trigwell (2004) refer to as personal or local knowledge, as opposed to public knowledge. Although Ashwin and Trigwell were referring to the scholarship of teaching and learning, their pyramid of the purposes of an investigation can be applied to evaluation. They outline three levels: at Level 1, academics are writing for personal knowledge, i.e. to inform themselves; at Level 2 they are writing for local knowledge, to inform a group in a shared context; and at Level 3, for public knowledge, to inform a wider audience. At the self-evaluative level of evaluation, academics are usually writing at Level 1 or, perhaps, Level 2. Writing for themselves and their peers means that they are writing for their own purposes and within their own norms – or is it that simple? Hubball and Pearson's advocacy of research-related evaluation would suggest not.

Agency is not straightforward

Hubball and Pearson's case would suggest that, while typologies (such as the Discretion Framework) are helpful in starting an analysis, they then have to be drilled through to reflect the realities of an evaluative situation. And we are all aware of the complexity of academic life in general. In matters of quality evaluation, for instance, Cheng (2009) points out the tension between university audit cultures and academics' feelings of professionalism; but the academic interviewees in Cheng's study presented a far from unanimous view of audit. An illustration of the complexity of agency among our case writers is Chapman's use of Appreciative Inquiry (AI) to engage academic staff in developing their inclusive learning and teaching practice. The prime agents of the evaluation were the change agents who wanted to make changes to the academic environment and academic practices; they – not the academics themselves – led the evaluation. So, while AI is often seen as an antidote to top-down evaluative practices (Cooperrider and Whitney, 2005), and the philosophy of AI is bottom-up, the evaluation was still being done 'to' the academics concerned – even if they turned out to be (mainly) willing collaborators. Not, then, a straightforward case of self-evaluation.

The complexity of agency is also clear in Shreeve and Blythman's evaluation of a UK Centre for Excellence in Teaching and Learning (CETL): they again aimed for bottom-up evaluation, even though a different kind of (formal) evaluation had also been mandated by the funding body. In the team's own evaluation of the CLIP CETL, they wanted to acknowledge the influence of the culture and politics of the university, and so the agent of the evaluation was an insider who was familiar with, and could incorporate, contextual factors. Nonetheless, the lead evaluators were still not the individuals who were doing the work on the ground. Where this takes us is that bottom-up, self-evaluative practices may not just be 'for the academics, by the academics': this type of evaluation inhabits a middle ground in which the ethos of the evaluation is the engagement of those being evaluated, and the construction of a participative, honest exchange between them and the evaluators.

Discretion does not mean free-for-all

The context of an evaluation forms part of the evaluation; in RUFDATA terms, the context provides important Data and evidence which, if ignored, can skew the evaluative outcomes. Following the metaphor of the implementation staircase again, it would seem that working with the local context, and locating evaluative practices clearly within the social practices in question, in observable, practical situations – a key theme of this book – makes the steps on the staircase less slippery. Achieving this is hard work, however, and requires close, iterative attention to cultural norms.

Examples are seen in each of the cases. For instance, in Chapman's AI, an underpinning belief for the evaluation was that 'truth is dependent upon the context and the current reality' (Chapter 22), and this brought 'a process of constant re-evaluation' based on that changing, dynamic context. For Shreeve and Blythman, awareness of the university culture, policy, practices and structures was central to how the insider view was obtained. Hubball and Pearson's scholarly approach to curriculum evaluation is equally 'situated within a broad curriculum community context' and depends on 'rich contextually-bound cues' (Chapter 25).

Contextual differences lead the evaluators in each case example to use a different mix of methodological approaches. What this suggests is that if the focus is on social practices, this opens doors to using evaluative approaches which can be imaginative and creative, and consonant with the norms of the group in question. This does not mean, of course, that evaluators can take off on a flight of evaluative fantasy without knowledge of methodologies and techniques: 'it is fundamental to understand and manage the organisational aspects, relationships and communication of evaluation practices' (Minelli et al., 2008: 166). In Chapman's chapter on Appreciative Inquiry, the desire for a positive focus meant reversing the common approach of asking 'What's working? What isn't?' Instead, AI led them through the four stages of discovery, dream, design and destiny – within the frame of the group and subject area in question. In Shreeve and Blythman's CLIP CETL, the evaluation focus was conceived as research, reflecting the wish, within the subject area, to promote research into learning and teaching, and draw on a range of theoretical perspectives. For Hubball and Pearson, scholarly practices were again to the fore, aiming for congruence with their research culture; there was, consequently, a clear commitment to research-type data and evidence, with hopes for 'critical insight' and 'scholarly and practical rigour'. Ironically, research-type practices did not otherwise characterise academics' general focus in curriculum review, even when the practices of these academics in their subject discipline research were deeply steeped in research norms.

Shreeve's TUAI evaluation focused on what helped students from diverse backgrounds to succeed in their studies, looking at student learning experiences from their own perspectives and through their own voices. Like Chapman, Shreeve's aim was to avoid deficit models, in this case frequently associated with non-completion and lower academic achievement. In TUAI, the student evaluators rejected text-based methods in favour of both a focus and a type of evidence, which were more congruent with their disciplinary norms of creative expression.

What we have seen in this theme is that, although the focus of each chapter is different, the ethos of the evaluation in each case strives to be authentic and appropriate for the practices of the group concerned. The methods used within this ethos are varied, and demonstrate that methodological strait jackets do not come as part of the self-evaluative package. However, there are common elements, such as reflective practice; these practitioners work to generate their own theories of practice, rather than importing them from outside, they question the assumptions behind their practice, and continuously investigate their work (Brookfield, 1995: 129). In RUFDATA terms, the Reasons and purposes for the evaluation are largely self-generated.

What is evaluated goes beyond the project

Even in self-evaluation, other stakeholders 'should form the centre of an evaluation and will yield the resources for judgement about value and worth'

(Chapter 1), and are often also part of the RUFDATA category of Audience for the evaluation. Since stakeholders are likely to have initiated or at least influenced the initiative that is being evaluated, and will have their theories of change about what was intended (Connell and Kubisch, 1999), their inclusion in the evaluation seems obvious. However, while claims about stakeholder involvement may sound glib, the reality is that this type of involvement is relatively recent (Guba and Lincoln, 1989) and putting it into practice is far from simple in the highly political world of Higher Education (HE). This is especially the case, as mentioned in Chapter 21, when the word 'stakeholder' may have immediate associations with inspection and top-down managerialism – clearly not desirable when, as in the CLIP CETL (Chapter 23), students are protagonists. The result is likely to be that, as a minimum, evaluators at this level will try to avoid the language of what could be seen as top-down 'stakeholder involvement'.

Emerging outcomes are worked with, not against

The interweaving roles of agent, audience, and other concerned stakeholders can mean that political navigation, even at this local level, can be challenging and needs to be consciously worked with. For TUAI (Chapter 24), power and control were devolved to students, so they were able to express their ideas in their own medium. Again, this is not problem-free. For example, in the TUAI case, those who were analysing the data could not impose their own subjective interpretations of student data, even when they thought key information had been omitted. So, whether the aim was to 'capture the lived experience of those doing the work' (Chapter 23) or to situate the evaluation within the knowledge world of those involved (Hubball and Pearson, Chapter 25), what these evaluations reveal is a philosophical commitment to respect the situation of those involved, and to work not with rationality, but with the possible intended, unintended and unanticipated outcomes that might emerge during the evaluation. For example, if you give students the job of being evaluators, you can prepare them for that role and support them, but if they then don't operate in the way you might have expected, you can't simply annul the evaluation. And if they don't produce the results that might have been anticipated, then the results they do achieve may still be valuable. All evaluations can give unexpected outcomes; working with this richness and creativity is risky, but necessary.

Self-evaluative practices are a vital part of change efforts

Another RUFDATA thread which is common to the cases in this theme is the Uses to which the evaluation will be put – what Shreeve (Chapter 24) calls 'usability'. These self-evaluators are clear that the evaluative practices will have an effect on whether anything happens as a result of their use. Nonetheless, even those evaluators who pay acute attention to social practices, internal politics and stakeholder needs will not necessarily find – as Shreeve explains – that change will ensue, or that evaluation outcomes will be welcome. In fact, Hubball and Pearson refer to 'significant methodological and organizational barriers' (Chapter 25) which can lead to unsatisfactory, ad hoc evaluative practices.

Conclusions

So, what have we learned in this theme about evaluative practices which are rooted in the desire of individuals or groups to assign value to their learning and teaching? We have seen that the Discretion Framework outlined in Chapter 21 has relevance in that the evaluations described in the four case studies are all located in the bottom right-hand quadrant of the framework. They are characterised by loose external control of process and focus, i.e. significant discretion by those involved to evaluate according to their own agendas. However, this seeming lack of constraint is bounded by the cultural and social practices of the evaluative context; even the most complete discretion does not mean a free-for-all. Evaluators tune in to cultural appropriateness and what is likely to be usable for everyone involved: they work hard to ensure that their evaluative practices work with the grain of social practices, whether it's the desire of Hubball and Pearson to respect scholarship in a scholarly environment, Shreeve allowing students to express themselves in their own discourse, Shreeve and Blythman using students with disabilities to research inclusive practice, or Chapman using appreciative inquiry to bring out the positives in a challenging issue. In some cases, using evaluative practices which challenge the boundaries of prevailing social practices, such as employing students as researchers, may lead to the social practices themselves adapting. This suggests that self-evaluative practices can constitute a fertile seeding ground for changes reaching far beyond the evaluation itself and that, as so often is the case in HE settings, unintended (fruitful) consequences can ensue from thoughtfully designed catalysts.

Part Five

Overview

27

The practice turn: reconceptualising evaluation in higher education

Murray Saunders, Paul Trowler and Veronica Bamber

> [Social practices are . . .] forms of bodily activities, forms of mental activities, 'things' and their use, a background knowledge in the form of understanding, know-how, states of emotion and motivational knowledge. A practice – a way of cooking, of consuming, of working, of investigating, of taking care of oneself or of others, etc. – forms so to speak a 'block' whose existence necessarily depends on the existence and specific interconnectedness of these elements, and which cannot be reduced to any one of these single elements . . .
>
> (Reckwitz, 2002: 249)

Evaluation as social practice

As we noted in our opening chapter, this book recasts the idea of evaluation by conceptualising it as a 'block' or 'cluster' of practices concerning the attribution of value to *'what we do'*, in this case, in Higher Education (HE). While this is the focus of this book, this perspective may apply equally to evaluative practice in any other public policy sphere.

Hitherto, evaluation has been associated with a relatively restricted form of activity. We have shown, through our case studies and commentaries, that the attribution of value occurs within blocks of practices that transcend conventional boundaries and moves fluidly between domains of practices from national policy arenas to small groups undertaking reflections on their own practices. The cases have also shown that the purposes, focus and use of evaluative practices have important emphases as we move from one domain to another within the sector and we comment further on that in this chapter.

So, evaluation is itself a social practice with the interconnected dimensions expressed by Reckwitz (2002). At its heart evaluation is about looking at how social practices on the ground have changed as a result of an intervention, and what the value of those changes is, if any. Thus both evaluation and the object of evaluation, its focus, are seen as social practices. Evaluation involves the systematic collection of information about changing practices following an intervention or policy in order to attribute value. However we are left with the question of *how* to attribute value from a social practice perspective. As we will see below, a practice perspective adds complexity to that question.

We saw from our case studies that practice in the various domains are recurrent, that is, they happen not just once or twice but are endemic to a particular set of activities and purposes. They are 'habitual' in the sense that they are not always consciously or reflectively undertaken. Because of this, they are often hard to change and 'engrooved' in nature, supported and framed by sets of entrenched values and assumptions about what counts as appropriate behaviour, bases for decisions and needs. Practices constitute our social reality, which is partly locally generated by our immediate frames for action (institutional contexts, cultures and assumptions) and partly structurally sourced by the constraining imperatives derived from drivers associated with the interests of the state, policy, resource allocations, and histories of difference in access, tradition and status. This has significant implications for evaluation, particularly in terms of the authority of evaluative reports in making statements about value beyond the specific sites under investigation at any given time. The attribution of value is highly situated. A practice perspective means that evaluative practice is dependent on context for its imputed meaning. We need to ask ourselves, as evaluators: where does the evaluative imperative come from? Who generated it? Who owns it? How will its outputs be used? The discourse in use reflects these nuances. If the locus of evaluative practice lies with a small group of innovative teachers within an HE institution, for example, their discursive preoccupations are with the language of improvement, with problem solving and with diagnosis. Methodologies are often informal, collaborative and optimistic. However, if the locus lies with formal government agencies concerned with effecting policy change, then we have the symbols of accountability, rubrics, formal protocols and procedures with a discourse of comparability, standards, excellence and 'impact'. The discourse within *evaluative* practices has interesting intersections and importations, often involving complicity, compliance and co-option. The language of business, for example, is deployed to evaluate academic *'product'* and where institutions are vying for position within the academic global *'market'*, they may refer to evaluative criteria as associated with the *'market position'*. These nuances are often not always 'visible', to use Barnett's formulation (Barnett, 2009).

So, discourse and the use of particular discursive repertoires is part of evaluation-as-social-practice. In the same way so is bringing to the centre stage issues of power and the way in which identities shape and constrain changes and, in particular, the propensity for the outputs from an evaluation to be used and act as a positive resource for change or as a means to control and achieve compliance. Viewing evaluation this way suggests that what the object or focus of evaluation may be is not agreed by all. Evaluators therefore must be clear about the different ways of 'seeing' the potential foci of evaluation and be aware that what may seem like a legitimate focus (for example, a policy assumption or emphasis) may not be seen by policy makers as appropriate or relevant, although they may be happy for evaluators to investigate policy 'uptake'.

Seeing evaluation as a social practice also means that we depict policy 'making' and the design of initiatives not as a technical-rational process but as one shaped by a messy evolution of compromise, accommodation and compliance. It implies that policy learning and (re-)design proceeds in a fuzzy, highly political, dynamic and sometimes illogical way. This is the main reason that evaluators should be wary of attempting to measure the 'gap' between intent and outcome, because understanding that difference as a gap is conceptually confused and over-mechanistic. It is better to evaluate a policy or initiative by focusing on a set of evolving experiences, and analysing the ensuing practices as an account of what happened in the name of a policy. Our perspective acknowledges that outcomes on the ground will have multiple manifestations, expressing conditions in different local contexts as initiatives which are received and shaped according to situated interests, priorities and power configurations. As we noted above, all this renders the attribution of value rather difficult.

Information collection methods

The push to establish unequivocally the effects, the 'impact', of interventions and policies in all evaluative domains of the HE sector is resurging in importance across the world, partly driven by financial constraints and the associated need for effectiveness and efficiency. This groundswell of concern has resulted in an imperative to find ever more reliable and valid ways of establishing *for sure* the way positive effects can be attributed to a particular source. One outcome of this push has been the seduction of apparent certainty offered by experimentalism within evaluative practice. For policy makers in particular, randomised control trials appear to offer a sound way of knowing whether an intervention or a 'treatment' is, or isn't, worth the money or produces specific effects. During the Bush administration in America, for example, this approach became the standard by which proposals for research were evaluated for government support (Anyon, 2009: 1).

By contrast, we call for a multi-method approach to evaluating effects and eschew a 'gold standard' for evaluation method. Following the guidance offered by most evaluation societies and associations on impact evaluations, *all* methods and approaches have strengths and limitations and there are a wide range of scientific, evidence-based, rigorous approaches to evaluation that have been used in varying contexts for establishing effects. But evaluating effects is complex, particularly in multi-dimensional interventions that require the use of a variety of different methods that can take into account rather than obscure inherent complexity.

This re-emergence of interest in ways of understanding the impact of interventions is valuable, even if it can lead to misguided faith in single solutions for some (Saunders, 2011). While the imperative for the resurgence of interest is driven by an increasing desire for certainty in the way we outline above, we see another potential reason for rethinking 'impact'. This lies in the need to develop improved ways of sense-making in increasingly complex and turbulent environments. Evaluations can build knowledge of the conditions for success of interventions designed to bring about improvement by developing our understanding of complexity. Karl Weick talks about sense-making in terms of 'active agents' structuring the unknown. He notes that sense-making begins

> with the basic question, is it still possible to take things for granted? If the answer is no, if it has become impossible to continue with automatic information processing, then the question becomes why is this so? And what next?
>
> (Weick, 1995: 14)

This is also reminiscent of Eleanor Chelimsky's (1997) formulation of 'evaluations for knowledge', which points to the kinds of policies, interventions and ways of doing things within HE which are likely to have positive effects. This prompts the search for ways of knowing that can realise such lofty ambitions. As the Commissioner for Regional Policy Cohesion, Pawel Samecki, suggests within the European context of HE and social cohesion:

> The more we generate evidence on the performance of the policy, the more insights we gain into not only 'what works', but also 'what doesn't work' and 'what could work an awful lot better'. We know there are some weaknesses in the policy. We have questions about what really changes in some of our regions, in our cities, as a result of expenditure of cohesion policy resources. We know that in some regions, structural weaknesses can persist over successive programme periods despite significant injections of Community tax-payers' funds. Why is this so? Insights from our evaluations suggest a need for a more rigorous design and implementation of programmes, with clear ideas of how change will be effected, greater concentration of resources and better project planning.
>
> (Samecki, 2009: 4)

So, while the social practice lens is methodologically neutral, it does mean that the evaluative environment for most policy evaluations is simply too messy to be controlled and the timescale over which fundamental change occurs often too long to grasp adequately in conventional timescales provided for evidence-gathering. This makes it very difficult to make comparisons between randomly controlled groups except in the most delimited contexts. Most policy implementation contexts (and, therefore, their evaluations) do not allow for this type of control over the conditions of a change process.

However, if we adopt a social practice perspective, informed by realist evaluation (Pawson and Tilly, 1997) and the work of Evert Vedung (1998), then we can delineate levels of focus for an evaluation (see also Chapter 10) which emphasises practice within three 'practice contexts': at the level of national policy-making; the instruments that are designed to further that policy; and the mechanisms used by those instruments to change practice on the ground. We illustrate this in Figure 27.1.

It is at the lower point (mechanisms) that it becomes possible to yield evidence of the efficacy of different 'treatments' in a policy environment, in a small scale evaluative study or within an institution. An experimental design using controlled trials in the medical modelling tradition *may* be possible at the level of a mechanism. However, this opportunity should be considered as part of the design of the programme, policy or intervention, not undertaken as an afterthought or post hoc attempt to give certainty to policy effects. It means that 'evaluability' should be part of policy or programme designs and it implies, as we will argue in a moment that evidence is primarily used to build up a case rather than establish 'proof' of worth.

The national or systemic policy

If the level of evaluative practice is national or systemic (e.g. widening participation, massification, closer HE-employment connections, improved teaching and learning, research excellence), the focus of the evaluation would consist of the logic of policy intention or the way in which, or basis upon which, resources are distributed or how the contestation of different policy options unfolded. It might examine the morality of the policy or its underlying values as well as the extent to which its assumptions and constituent parts connect together in a consistent and justifiable way.

Policy instruments

If the evaluation is addressing ***the policy instruments,*** (e.g. resource allocations to universities for widening participation, ring fenced funds for targeted developments, Subject Centre Networks, Centres of Excellence for Teaching and Learning), the focus of the evaluation might be the theory in action of those instruments i.e. what was the basis on which particular instruments were going to bring about desired changes.

Mechanism

When we examine evaluative practices at the level of ***a mechanism*** (specific strategies used to 'enact' programmes), the implication of a social practice approach would be to explore the efficacy of the theories of change embedded in specific strategies, for example how a small scale research grant worked as a way of producing wider changes within an institution.

Figure 27.1 Focus for evaluative practice in policy implementation

We indicated previously that evaluative approaches based on a technical-rational model of policy-making and implementation can be a poor reflection of what really happens in HE evaluative contexts. The social practice approach suggests that we should, instead, be looking for different metaphors to evoke the policy process, metaphors which are underpinned by the idea that practices are shaped and reshaped in different locales and over time in ways that are heavily conditioned by the past. Metaphors such as the 'implementation staircase' (which sees policy being selectively interpreted and refracted at different points in the hierarchy of implementation) and 'policy trajectories' (which depicts them as shifting over time due to the exigencies of circumstance). These emphasise the *adaptive nature of policy implementation* and are more likely to yield sensitive and authoritative evaluations of take-up or effect.

If these alternative metaphors are developed and considered, then there are implications for the process of evaluation practice. *Practice* takes place with real people, in real time in real places; this means that *evaluative practice* follows the same maxim. No matter how elaborate the modelling (and some economic models are extremely elaborate and abstract), there is a kind of reductionism in our perspective (for which we offer no apology) which is that changes, effects, focus and uses within an evaluation are reducible to different expressions of the idea of practices.

So, some of the implications of this are as follows:

- The identification of key stakeholders or 'players' within an evaluation environment becomes fore-grounded because it is what people *do* that counts.
- There is a focus on adaptation and the way people adjust expectations, modify policy or programme implications or respond to different types of evaluative practice in highly situated ways.
- There is a focus on the evolution and evaluation of policy experience over time as policies evolve, morph and creep.
- There is a clear distinction between a policy-in-text and the policy enactment process: a focus on gaps between the two. Notions like 'barriers to take-up' or 'resistance' miss the point. We argue that policy will have to be adapted, modified and reconstructed once it is let loose in the field; this is an ontological starting point that flows clearly from a social practice perspective. For evaluative practice, similar adaptation, modification and reconstruction are required.
- The evaluation evidence for adaptations and experiences of a policy, change or intervention can be various but social practice suggests an open and imaginative approach to evidence. It implies a shift from the metaphor of the laboratory to that of the court of law in which a wide range of data builds a persuasive, often inferential depiction of 'what happened or happens' in the name of a set of intended changes or a particular set of practices within HE.

- We need to be cautious, provisional and indicative in our approach to evaluation truths and understand evaluative practice outputs as creating provisional stabilities. In essence it eschews the chimera of certainty.

Discretion Frameworks in multiple domains

We have emphasised that social practices constitute a site for contestation and the flow of power. This means that those engaged in evaluative practice should be clear about the nature of the power dynamics at play. To bring the social practice into sharp relief, we explore in Figures 27.2 and 27.3 below the way in which evaluative practice is

- grounded in
- differentiated by, and
- underpinned by social location.

We have applied the term 'Discretion Framework' (see Chapters 15 and 21) to a model which depicts the relative control an institution may have over the way it undertakes its internal evaluative practice and, in turn, the relative control a practitioner might have on practices within departments. The nexus operates around control over what is evaluated (the evaluation focus) and how evaluations take place (the processes or practices undertaken, e.g. at institutional level or within departments). The Framework demonstrates

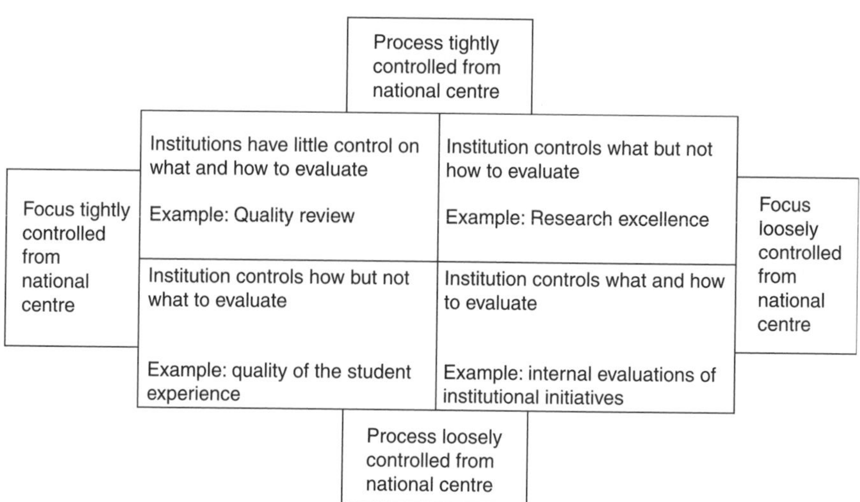

Figure 27.2 Tight and loose control of evaluative practice: the national systemic and institutional interface

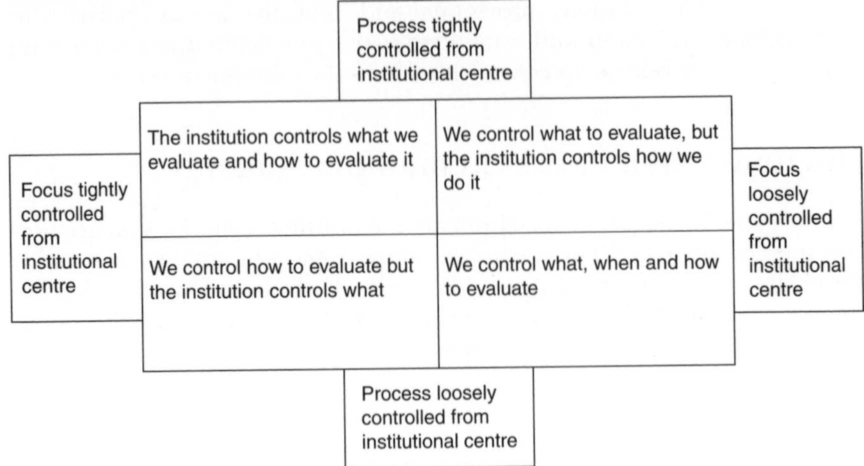

Figure 27.3 Tight and loose control of evaluative practice: the practitioner and institutional interface

the level of discretion which an institution or a group of practitioners may have in deciding how or what to evaluate in particular aspects of their activity.

The Discretion Framework matrix gives us a tool to help us understand and penetrate the nature of evaluative practice in specific contexts of 'intersection'. For example, within institutions the matrix may reveal power differentials at various levels in the same institution; in a particular institution there may be loose controls over the focus of evaluation and the way it is carried out, but different departments may have control of the focus of their own evaluative practices within that overall structure.

In Figure 27.2, we can see the pull between different political and cultural tensions as evaluation is driven by top-down, central forces (such as increasingly powerful and specialised central administrative functions), or conversely rooted in bottom-up initiatives, such as reflexive institutional questioning. In Figure 27.3, we can see how this framework plays out within institutions in the interface between institution-wide procedures for evaluation and those carried out by individuals and groups within the departments or schools.

These intersections are places where the locus of control over the function and nature of practices associated with evaluation can be contested. An important variable is the control dimension. This is not to say, however, that the practitioner evaluating her own practice or that associated with her modules does not see the national/systemic or the institutional levels as legitimate. This may or may not be the case. The important points are that the purposes of evaluative practices differ and the 'rules', history and routines that they characterise have very different meanings for national and institutional stakeholders. In addition, the evaluative impulse (why it's being undertaken) is similarly divergent.

We saw in preceding chapters the way in which the clusters of practices differ within each of the domains of evaluative practice. Figure 27.2 identifies how these clusters interface between institutions and national governments. It suggests how the autonomy of institutions is relative and regulated by national systemic requirements, with a comparatively narrow or restricted opportunity to exercise freedom to develop their own practices. The locus of control on institutions is such that only internally initiated activities are likely to be genuinely free from external controls over the process and the focus of evaluations.

Within institutions (see this dynamic in the context of a module evaluation in Chapter 21) we see a mirror image of control as institutional interests in both responding to external pressure for evaluative evidence, and their own institutional needs to regulate and manage activity within departments, connect with practitioners' desire to reflect on and develop their own teaching through evaluative practice. In the latter case, the use of evaluation is quite different to that of the institutional or the national systemic domains we have discussed. Evaluation outputs in this case are closer to 'bridging tools' (Bonamy, Charlier and Saunders, 2001), or artefacts designed to support the development of courses or other aspects of practice rather than in the provision of resources for regulation, comparison and management.

One contribution of this book, then, is our re-conceptualisation of evaluation as a social practice which is undertaken in complex political arenas, ones where the flow of power has significance for evaluative practices as well as the outcomes of innovations. We have applied this conception of evaluative practice in four domains. The metaphor of a 'domain' is not straightforward. It depicts 'sites' of evaluative behaviour within the HE sector. The cases demonstrate the rich diversity of practice within each of these domains. We demonstrate that what unifies these domains conceptually is that they are concerned with attributing value or worth to social activity, sometimes in the form of a policy working across the sector nationally, sometimes a programme or intervention, sometimes in an organisational setting within a university, and sometimes in a small group of people engaged in working within an HE environment.

This perspective goes beyond the definitional tradition associated with evaluation, by adopting a straightforward generic characterisation of evaluation that has at its core the cluster of practices associated with the way in which value or worth is attributed to HE activity within different domains.

Evaluative practice and focus

In developing a social practice approach to evaluation, we suggest there are *practice emphases* for evaluations in how the *object* of evaluations might be identified. We deliberately avoid being too dogmatic here by adopting the cautious vocabulary of 'emphasis' because this is not a world of certainties, but one of probabilities and tendencies.

We can discern two distinct ways in which the idea of an evaluation 'object' is used. The first is the use of 'object' as an 'objective' or purpose, in normal language, the point of doing something. This might involve any one or a combination of the following: extending knowledge and understanding; accounting for actions; ensuring compliance to minimum standards; making improvements; or enhancing capacity. The second is the use of evaluative object to denote the focus of the evaluation i.e. the phenomena, dimension or aspect of policy, practice, change or whatever, on which data and evidence will be collected and which will form the resource for a decision on value and worth. This dual use can cause confusion, but for us, the latter sense of the word has many possibilities and we adopt that sense here, and so we use the word 'focus' when referring to that meaning.

Patton (1997: 185), for example, discusses the way in which evaluations may arrive at a focus in one of the discussion 'menus' he offers in which he talks about 'defining questions'. He talks of the use of experimental methods to determine the relationship between a programme or intervention and the resulting outcomes. In this case *the focus* would be the effects of the intervention with *the purpose* of determining which programme or intervention works or achieves observably positive outcomes. Alternatively, in another example, *the focus* might be on the critical concerns or questions derived from the interests of various stakeholders with *the purpose* of improving practice. This is very much in Patton's utilisation-focused tradition.

The following discussion provides an extension of the idea of an evaluation focus, by arguing that the different domains of evaluative practice within HE that have structured this book, tend to be characterised by different evaluation foci which are produced by the different practice-based interests inhabiting each domain.

We can distinguish between the way in which the focus is identified in practices associated with national policy imperatives or systemic regulation (often highlighting policy implementation issues or comparisons between institutions on the basis of the quality of their performance). In the case of a programme or time-limited initiative, the focus is often embodied in an evaluation tender or specification (normally expressed through a series of questions considered to be important by a commissioner or sponsor of the evaluation). Alternatively, in a different domain, it might emerge from the quality standards that pertain within an institution or the developmental requirements of a local initiative of concern to practitioners. All examples have in common a subtle set of issues associated with the processes by which evaluative foci are identified or understood.

So, the evaluation focus operates in all the contextual domains that have structured this book and can be expressed in different ways. If we take the example of teaching and learning in the UK, we can see that the

HE environment has an evaluative shape. Beginning with teaching and learning as a policy emphasis, it uses a variety of instruments (Centres for Excellence in Teaching and Learning, the Fund for the Development of Teaching and Learning, Teaching Quality Reviews etc.) to achieve change on the ground. Each of these instruments employs a variety of specific mechanisms and these mechanisms have effects which can be assessed or identified. In each case, the way the 'focus' of an evaluation is presented, identified and exemplified is the key to starting the evaluation. This might mean, as well, what is not identified. For example the primary 'policy logics' that give rise to a particular programme are not normally accepted as a legitimate evaluation focus by commissioners. As we note in Chapter 14, this all raises issues about how we decide about what counts as an evaluative focus within, for example, programmatic evaluations in HE. Invariably, they tend to be associated with mechanisms, with a 'what works' preoccupation and a range of second order issues which do not challenge basic policy assumptions.

At the national/systemic level then it is helpful to think both about the conceptualisation, the underlying understanding, of what is being evaluated and blind spots in the evaluative gaze, in other words the foci that do not come under evaluative scrutiny, especially where it is governments and their agencies which are making choices and driving the evaluation.

To take a specific example – in the UK the new Research Excellence Framework (REF) is a periodic exercise evaluating research quality across the HE sector and allocating resources on the basis of outcomes. It has a new focus on 'impact', largely under emphasised from the preceding equivalent, the Research Assessment Exercise (RAE) discussed in Chapter 6. By 'impact' is meant the beneficial effects of research outputs on the economy, society, culture and so on. Hence within the broad evaluative focus of 'research' we have second level foci such as 'impact' and 'research environment', as well as the quality of research outputs themselves, usually publications. And associated with each of those are appropriate data sources and methods of data collection which will yield the necessary information on which to base evaluative statements.

The 'impact' metaphor used in policy documents to define this new focus carries evoked significance of a particular sort. It suggests a singular, palpable, measurable and causally simple effect of one object upon another. In making REF returns, university departments will need to demonstrate the 'impact' of their body of research work in short case studies and narratives, and the metaphor itself guides how they conceive the focus of those. Yet things are very rarely so simple: research outcomes permeate society at different levels and locales, having different effects in different places and usually have their most profound effects as part of an on-going developmental process. Causality in the social world is far more complex than the mechanical notion of 'impact'.

But governments have good reasons (from their point of view) to choose such things as impact as the foci of evaluative scrutiny, and to use discursive repertoires of that mechanical sort to depict them – even if the underlying conceptualisations and notions of causality are flawed. The drivers that propel their choices in, not only the foci for evaluation, but the ways in which those foci are conceived have both ideological and pragmatic roots. And so therefore do the absences, the possibilities for evaluation that are occluded.

Programmatic evaluations rarely have the opportunity to continue long enough to have as their focus the longer term effects of the programme. This problem has given rise to an increased interest in the meta-review or synthesis as an attempt to capture the aggregate or longer term effects of a series of programmes or interventions. As well as understanding the evaluation focus as a progressively linked continuum between policy and effects it can also be understood as a logical series of evaluation foci which flow from an initial experience of awareness through a learning process which includes the 'reconstruction' of learning in new practices.

We can see that the focus of an evaluation can be complex and the interconnectedness between these dimensions and domains should have important implications for evaluation design and how indicative evidence is understood. In this way, consideration of the evaluation focus can have effects that are not immediately apparent. For example, Young et al. (2004) explore how particular conditions associated with the focus of an evaluation influence the methodological approach. They acknowledge that the kinds of questions an evaluation might be interested in, as well as the evaluators' own values, are only part of the story; how an evaluation unfolds is also shaped by the object of study.

Indicators of changed social practices on the ground

Problematising the focus of evaluations also raises issues associated with the relationship between changed social practices, which are the heart of evaluative practice, but which are often difficult to capture, and the proxies and indicators which 'stand in' for them because they are more palpable and so can be 'collected' as data or evidence. The issue here is the nature of appropriate indicators in relation to the 'focus' of an evaluation. Building on previous work (for example Helsby and Saunders, 1993; Saunders, 2011), we can distinguish at least three versions of the idea of an indicator, each more developed than the last (see Table 27.1).

Table 27.1 Modes and uses of indicators

Mode	*Indicator*	*How does the indicator work*	*Advantages/disadvantages*
Mode 1	Indicators as a focus	This is where an indicator as an evaluation focus is interpreted as the areas, activities, domains or phenomena on which evidence will be collected. It is open and does not specify a standard or desired state. It is essentially an investigative or inquiry-based approach. In this case the focus of an evaluation is whatever it is decided to investigate. Designs would normally identify the focus as those aspects which exemplify the programme in some meaningful way. All the case studies used this notion of indicator. An example might be that the area of student participation in departmental decision-making is identified in advance in an evaluation plan as an area on which data will be gathered.	Advantages are that this approach catches unintended effects, avoids spurious or arbitrary targets, and is potentially participative and collaborative. The disadvantages, however, are that it does not control or specify desired outcomes, can include collection of irrelevant data and is expensive.
Mode 2	Indicators as evidence	This is where an indicator as an evaluation focus is interpreted as the evidence itself. It is usually post hoc and retrospective. It refers to what is actually uncovered as a result of an inquiry, not the dimension on which evidence is collected as in a Mode 1 indicator. An example might be that student participation in departmental decision making is identified 'post hoc'.	The advantages are that it can be focused, will pick up unintended effects, can be formative as well as summative and can test theories of change. Disadvantages are that it cannot be used as a management control tool, does not provide targets or objectives, it is low on accountability and cannot be used for project planning.
Mode 3	Indicators as prescriptions of good practice	This is where indicators are used as a pre-defined or prescribed state to be achieved or obtained. In this way indicators constitute desired outcomes. The focus for the evaluation therefore is phenomena that might not display desired characteristics. An example is student participation in departmental decision-making where prescribed types of participation are in place (e.g. course representative mechanisms, departmental committee representation, specified types of feedback mechanism, students' report experiences of involvement etc.) and are identified in advance as an indicator of good practice. Evaluation focuses on the 'gap' between actuality and prescription which becomes the evaluation focus. To some extent the Owen chapter (Chapter 11) is within this tradition.	Advantages are that it can be used as standard/success criteria, can focus an evaluation, can be collaboratively derived and can help with project planning. However, disadvantages are that it can be too restrictive, does not address unanticipated effects, tends to be external and control oriented, tends to reduce participation and is provider/donor driven.

We can say, then, that the focus of evaluation has profound implications for the method of inquiry as well as evaluation approach. It raises issues that centre on the capacity we have to attribute value, and ones that involve clarity on establishing the effects of an intervention or programme. For many commissioners, the most desirable yet illusive evaluation focus is the existence or not of an unequivocal causal link between what is happening and the stimulus for change provided by the programme, the intervention, or the policy.

Returning to the idea of domains which we highlighted as a structural characteristic of the HE context earlier in this chapter, we can now link the different domains to the concept of evaluative focus, and see that focus can look quite different in each domain. These nuances of how evaluative foci are played out at different levels of the HE system can be captured in diagrammatic form:

Table 27.2 Focus in the four domains of evaluative practice in HE

Evaluative domain	*Practice emphasis*	*Purpose*	*Focus*
National/systemic	Regulation	To create national comparisons and to regulate quality	Numerical ranking of research and teaching quality
Programmatic	Policy learning	To create positive changes and embodiments of good practice	Process, outputs and outcomes associated with specific programmes
Institutional	Enhancement/ assurance	Control quality for comparative purposes and ensure quality practice	Teaching and research process compliance and judgements on quality
Self	Development	To improve or strengthen practices or projects	Processes, mechanisms and outcomes from change strategies, experience of stakeholders

We can say, then, that within the social practice tradition, the way the focus in an evaluation is derived is socially located in the purposes, preoccupations and uses of evaluation in different domains within the sector. Each domain has different positional interests which are enacted out in evaluative practices in the form of *practice emphases.* The categories we identify in Table 27.2 are not intended to be mutually exclusive, but express what evaluative practices tend to focus on as evaluation foci within differing sets of positional interests.

These foci flow logically from the evaluative purposes that reflect the socially located practice preoccupations of the different domains. This means that evaluation purposes tend to be quite different from one domain to the next, and foci mean different things to different stakeholders. In some cases, the same phenomena can have quite different significances depending on where the decision to use them as evaluation foci came from, how they are going to be used and what the implications of that use may be. Using indicators successfully depends to a large extent on their levels of legitimacy and the practices associated with their use. These considerations are overwhelmingly associated with the situated power of the stakeholders within an evaluative environment; in other words, who decides what is being evaluated (the focus), why (the purpose) and how the outputs from the evaluation are going to be used.

Evaluative practices and the people involved in them

We referred earlier to the important social practice idea of creating *provisional stabilities* through our evaluations. It takes seriously the notion that we are working and learning in social conditions of chronic uncertainty, with periods of normlessness and destructive instability. Changes in HE can produce such instabilities as a transition is made across a boundary from one culture of practice to another and, for learners, from HE into new work practices. Learners and teachers in HE can be supported by constructing provisional stabilities as they seek creative solutions to problems produced by change. These provisional stabilities are produced by reflection on and developing an understanding of change, enabling choices or decisions for future action. Formative evaluations can provide the resources for such reflections and act as a bridging tool for planning and innovation.

Adopting this social practice approach to evaluation helps to identify different stakeholders and their potential connection with evaluative practice more clearly (Saunders, 2006). We normally draw a distinction between those who initiated a policy or programme being evaluated on the one hand and those on the ground whose practices are supposed to be changed by that intervention. But at the institutional and national levels it is the initiators of policy or programmes who are being evaluated – it is the value of their intentions, decisions and resource allocations, after all, that is under scrutiny. However, often, in the minds of those involved in evaluation as commissioners (usually exactly these initiators and funders of interventions), the 'evaluated' are the recipients of policy, i.e., those that provide the main source of evidence of its efficacy. Or, put another way, it is those who will experience the programme's effects, good or bad. But this perception is misleading. In an important sense the programme's 'target' or 'recipient' group constitute the main source of evidence for evaluative judgements; they should not be confused with 'the evaluated' (or, sometimes, in clumsy language, 'evaluands'). To avoid this fallacy we call this target group 'programme or policy recipients'.

We argue that the voice of recipients should be prioritised in evaluation design. Not just for equity or for socially democratic reasons, but also on the basis that their voice will authenticate and validate the provenance of the evaluation and improve and strengthen its design. Their experience should be articulated faithfully by the evaluation and it is on this basis that the evaluated, that is the policy makers and programme designers who promulgate policy, will have the best resources on which to make judgements about the effects of their policies or programmes.

So, the voice of programme recipients can be heard in four main ways:

- By involving them in identifying and using key questions, indicators or issues. This arises from a concern with participatory approaches and is exemplified most graphically in empowerment evaluation. This is at the 'strong' end of the participatory evaluation continuum (see Fetterman et al., 1996, and its critique by Patton, 1997).
- Being part of an ethically justifiable process, arising from a concern with evaluation ethics (see Simons, 2006)
- Making sure their experience is faithfully reported even under political pressure to obscure or edit parts out. This arises from a concern with authentic reportage.
- By ensuring that evaluation outputs feed a public debate. This arises from a concern with evaluation as part of a democratic process and as a way of promoting democratic participation.

Focusing on the first of these in particular, for Patton (1996) it is the commissioners' role to be involved in evaluation design, but asking the programme's recipients to identify what the key questions should be helps cut to the essence of a programme's effects on them. The process of involving recipients can be achieved through workshop designs in which representatives of the target group are provided with an opportunity to present the questions or indicators that will, in their experience, yield a good depiction of what may happen to them or will potentially happen. Undertaking this process at the outset of an evaluation also can move the evaluation design into the other three areas of 'voice' identified above.

Evaluative practices and use

We noted above that the 'object' of an evaluation can be understood as its objective – the use to which it will be put. Conventionally, use has been understood as mainly connected with the interactions between commissioners and the evaluators: commissioners determine the use to which evaluations are put. Within the social practice approach, the issue of use is much wider. We know that the practices associated with the use of evaluation outputs such as reports are concerned with the attribution of value and worth. But they are often inserted into politically charged environments. These domains have different practice emphases, and this has implications for how evaluative outputs are intended to be used, as Table 27.3 indicates:

Table 27.3 Evaluative outputs and use

Evaluative domain	*Practice emphasis*	*Use*
National/systemic	Regulation	To distribute resources and distinguish between institutional performance
Programmatic	Policy learning	To create resources for decisions on successful policy instruments and mechanisms
Institutional	Enhancement/ assurance	Practices associated with internal departmental review and institutional process checks
Self	Development	Diagnosis, problem spotting, impression management and PR, identifying good practice

In order to make 'really useful' evaluations happen, the social practice approach suggests we need to take into account the existing social milieu into which an evaluative output might be placed in our designs for use or, put another way, our engagement strategies. In summary, there are some further distinctions we might make which help this discussion to centre on the difference between use on the one hand and usability on the other. These categories refer to the interaction between the organisational environment into which an evaluation output might be intervening and the design of the evaluation output itself. Both these features interact to determine the extent to which an evaluation output or an evaluation process can create effects. An interesting distinction in this respect is between 'use' and 'usability' of an evaluation.

Use: refers to the extent to which the outputs of an evaluation are used as a resource for onward practice, policy or decision making.

The extent to which an evaluation is used depends on the capacity of the potential users to respond to the messages an evaluation might contain. The following characteristics of this 'use environment' are drawn from the cases and demonstrate the factors that seem particularly pertinent in terms of maximising use.

- The timing and nature of the 'release' of the evaluation output is embedded in decision making cycles (this requires clear knowledge on when decisions take place and who makes them).
- The evaluators and commissioners have a clear understanding of the organisational or sectoral memory and are able to locate the evaluation within an accumulation of evaluative knowledge.

- The evaluation has reflexive knowledge of the capacity of an organisation or commissioning body to respond. This requires the following dimensions:
- The evaluation output connects effectively with systemic processes. This means the messages are able to feed into structures that are able to identify and act on implications.
- Organisations that are lightly bureaucratised, sometimes called adaptive systems, are better placed to respond to 'tricky' or awkward evaluations because their practices are more fluid, less mechanistic and have a 'history' of responding to new knowledge.
- Evaluations that are strongly connected to power structures are more likely to have effects because they have champions who have a stake in using evaluations to change practices.
- Evaluation outputs that identify or imply possible changes that are congruent or build on what is already in place have a greater chance of maximising use.

Usability: refers to the way an evaluation design and its practices shapes the extent to which outputs can be used.

Prosaically, our cases refer to the form the evaluation outputs take and the extent to which they 'speak' to the intended user in an appropriate way. This refers to the design of the vehicle of the message to maximise engagement (a single, cold unresponsive text, a presentation, working in a workshop, working alongside a user to draw out practice based implications etc.) but also the way in which the design of the evaluation itself lends itself to communicability. These factors include:

- purposes that are clearly articulated and designed collaboratively,
- potential uses considered as part of the design concepts,
- the focus for the evaluation and the data that is collected coinciding with the priorities and interest of potential users.

So, a primary implication for 'use' and 'usability' in adopting a social practice approach is in evaluation design. The frames of reference of evaluators and those of evaluation commissioners are likely to be different from each other, and both differ from those emanating from practices on the ground as 'users' attempt to 'enact' policy or a programme idea. In particular, these differences mean that 'engagement strategies' with evaluation processes and outputs are best embedded in evaluation designs to a much greater extent than conventionally undertaken. These participative dimensions of evaluation design should be central, with the use of outputs at all stages *'design savvy'*. So, evaluators need to engage with the commissioners and with users from the start of the evaluative process and at intervals throughout it: simply delivering a report at the end is nowhere near enough, from a social practice point of view (we return to this issue below in considering the ways in which the voice of programme recipients can be heard).

Building on previous work (Bamber et al., 2009), we know that engagement with evaluation output can be understood in the form of a continuum (from relatively low engagement and use to relatively high engagement and use). At the low engagement end of the continuum, we have dissemination or distributive practices (reliance on written texts alone in the form of articles, reports, summaries); in the middle of the continuum are what we could call presentational practices (seminars, presentations, conferences); and at the engaged end of the continuum we have interactional practices (working alongside users to identify situated implications). These differences can be depicted graphically, as in Figure 27.4.

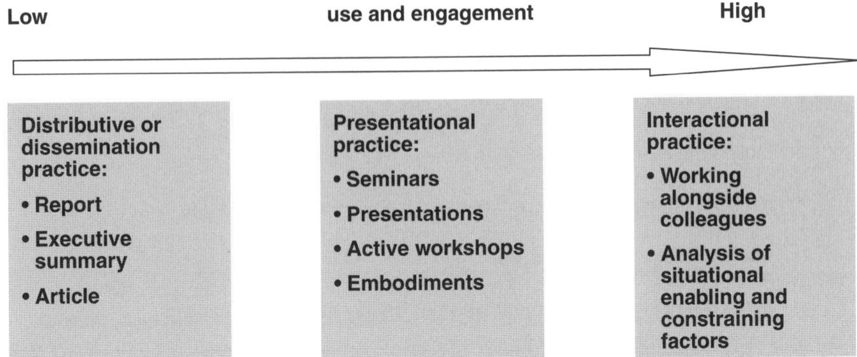

Figure 27.4 Depiction of an engaged approach to evaluation processes and outputs

The implications for evaluators of these use practices and their practice emphases, however, are not straightforward and require some demanding skills from evaluators as they attempt to chart a rout through the *use* of evaluation outputs, some of which are summarised in Figure 27.5.

Evaluators working with a social practice approach will be engaged in the following behaviours:

- balancing competing interests from different stakeholders
- brokering 'inconvenient truths'
- taking account of how different audiences respond to evaluation
- protecting vulnerable informants
- conducting 'ethical' evaluations by protecting co-constructors
- helping to make sense of the implications of evaluations.

Figure 27.5 Use of evaluation – implications for evaluators

We note that the process of establishing the voice of the user at the outset of the evaluation and building into the design a real rehearsal of the way in which an evaluation might be used tends to be both neglected and important. Alternatively, envisage a situation in which evaluators and users sit around a table and discuss what is going to happen to an evaluation report on, for example, an organisational change process. They would engage in identifying a list of specific practices of relevance to them and that process. When we look at the cases outlined in this book we see the following use or engagement practices indentified:

Evaluators working with a social practice approach will be engaged in the following engagement and use strategies:

- tabling the report at a meeting to assess its implication
- deciding on what those implications might be and acting on them
- doing so in an agreed timeline
- undertaking staff development activities on the basis of the findings
- publicising and disseminating widely
- communicating closely with commissioners throughout the period of the evaluation
- involving a range of stakeholders in key design decisions
- developing high levels of legitimacy with those implementing or working with programme objectives
- developing open and accessible interactive styles with those providing evidence or data
- exhibiting empathy with the stakeholding groups.

Figure 27.6 Engagement and use strategies

Implications for evaluation players and their practices

Throughout this book we have been building a case for understanding evaluation in HE in terms of domains of evaluative practices. The domains constitute clusters or 'constellations' of practice on the basis of different types of value and worth within very different systemic contexts.

This perspective moves away from the 'technical' boundaries between 'review', 'audit', 'inspection', and 'evaluation'. It acknowledges that between and within these traditions, concepts, procedures and assumptions have grown and developed that are conventionally seen as discrete with important differences between them. However, we assert that they are all concerned with the attribution of value to what we do in HE, and with changes to what we do brought about by policy or programme interventions. What is important is to look carefully at the way in which the evaluative imperative shifts and changes from one locus of activity to another, and how the use of these traditions is more prevalent in one domain than another, with important practice-based implications. That has formed the focus of this book and constitutes a departure from convention.

In these pages we have examined what has been *done* in the name of attributing value and worth to practices and processes within HE. This perspective is inclusive and deliberately blurs the boundaries between what are normally understood as discrete and separate professional activities, techniques and even conceptual legacies. This approach may offend specialists and 'boundary protectors' of all kinds in the fields of evaluative practice who have established discrete considerations, unique to their professional patch, or have a long and distinguished history of professional practice.

Our intention of course is not to irritate but to suggest that there are ways of seeing and researching evaluative activity within a social policy sector (e.g. education, health, criminal justice, social services) which foreground similarities, enable comparisons and depict the evaluative dimension of activity in our social policy areas as *clusters of social practices* embedded in the public domain. This perspective is grounded in what people do, as our cases demonstrate, and is concerned, in particular, with the way attributions of value and worth in public policy sectors are situated in domains of social practice. The results of taking this evaluative practice approach are that evaluations are more likely to be authentic to their context, and those involved will be more inclined to listen to and work with outcomes. In conclusion, we offer four practical tools or take-aways to help those involved in HE evaluation, in any domain, make sense of their evaluative task. Our tools include a set of generic maxims, and three sets of implications, one for stakeholders, one for evaluators and one for users of evaluations.

The social practice approach and associated evaluative practice maxims suggest the following implications for specific stakeholders who undertake, use, commission or provide evidence for evaluations.

We have attempted to range wide in the aspirations of this book and stress the shift in emphasis which a social practice approach to evaluation implies. It brings together practices that have hitherto been analysed and understood within separate discourses. Although distinctive with divergent characteristics, we have argued evaluation can be understood as situated clusters of practices that embody the way the attribution of value shifts in form and intent depending on its location within a sectoral profile. This focus emphasises how the attributions of value and worth to aspects of HE take place in four distinct domains of practice. To that extent it is worthwhile to

Remember...

- that evaluation is composed of sets of evaluative practices
- that the foci of evaluation are best understood as social practices, and changes in them, particularly when 'change' is the policy or programme objective
- that the effects or impacts of programmes or policies that often form the foci of evaluation are best understood as changes in practice irrespective of the intermediate modelling
- that the methodological stance is pluralistic but should be consistent with the ontological view that social processes are situated, messy, unpredictable and impossible to fully control. This means an open and inquisitively sceptical view of method. Multi-method is appropriate, balancing designs which require high levels of design predictability with those that are more open, adaptive and use underlying theories of change as starting points
- to acknowledge and work with the grain of complex, uncertain and multi-layered causality
- to adopt the 'truth' that the 'evaluable' i.e. what can be evaluated, is imperfect, unpredictable and often unanticipated
- to understand evaluation as a tool for creating 'provisional stabilities'.

Figure 27.7 Maxims for evaluative practice

- Policy making is a practice based on values, interests, timing and pragmatism: don't expect evaluations to be different
- Evaluations of policy should examine policy assumptions
- Policies will be subverted, adapted and reconstructed by policy 'recipients'
- Good policy allows for creative reconstruction on the ground
- Good evaluations have a clear understanding of what they can and cannot deliver
- Good evaluations run with the grain of complexity and allow for messy outcomes
- Avoid evaluations that promise certainty, it is a chimera
- Good evaluations will have clear designs for engagement and use
- Be prepared for unintended effects of regulatory evaluative practices.

Figure 27.8 Implications for policy makers and commissioners

- Don't be over-preoccupied by technique or instrument design
- See evaluative practices as multi-faceted, situated and layered
- Use robust and defendable inquiry designs
- Have an open view of what constitutes evidence
- Have an evaluation design that can respond to changing circumstances
- Focus on practice and the experience recipients have of policy, interventions, experiments and developments
- Have a well developed design for use of evaluative outputs
- Have an inclusive approach to design contributors and build in serious opportunities for consultation, participation and co-construction
- Be independent yet responsive to commissioners
- Argue for the public ownership of evaluation outputs in the public policy domain
- Expect situated responses to evaluation outputs
- Expect contestation on feedback to commissioners on issues where multiple agendas, priorities and interpretations are at play.

Figure 27.9 Implications for evaluators

- Look for opportunities to participate in evaluation commissioning
- Insist on knowing what the visible and invisible purposes of evaluation may be
- Look for clear protocols on ethics, including confidentiality and anonymity
- Look for guarantees that evaluation outputs are going to be in the public domain and connected to public policy and practice
- Look for the ways in which evaluation is connected to decision making, including the response to wicked findings and inconvenient truths
- Look for clear and transparent accounts of the uses of the evaluation outputs
- Have an idea of the range of audiences
- Look to see how your voice has been mediated and reconstructed by the evaluators
- Look for ways in which evaluations can build involvement in decision making
- Use evaluations to 'speak truth to power'.

Figure 27.10 Implications for users of evaluation, contributors to evaluation inquiry and policy recipients

develop a meta-framework that yields the possibility of comparative research into evaluative practices in other social policy domains. While the cases are indicative of variation in different domains of practice in the sector, they also suggest the richness of this vein of inquiry framework. However, while we might be focused on the heuristic mileage of this approach, we hope that the last few pages suggest that the social practice approach has practice-based implications and, in the spirit of this volume, that is probably what matters most.

References

Adams, J. (2005) Mirror, mirror, on the bench . . ., *Research Fortnight*, 28 September: 18–19.

Adams, J. and Gurney, K. (2010) *Funding Selectivity, Concentration and Excellence – How good is the UK's research?* Oxford: HEPI.

Adams, M. and Brown, S. (eds) (2006) *Towards Inclusive Learning in Higher Education: Developing curricula for disabled students*: 44–55. London: Routledge.

Albon, S. and Hubball, H. T. (2004) A learning-centred course in pharmaceutical analysis, *American Journal of Pharmaceutical Education*, 68(5): Article 114, 1–11.

Alexander, R. (1992) Floodlights, fanfares and facile factors, *Guardian*, February 11.

Alexander, R., Rose, J. and Woodhead, C. (1992) *Curriculum Organisation and Classroom Practice in Primary Schools.* London: DES.

Alvesson, M. (2002) *Understanding Organizational Culture.* London: Sage.

Antonelli, C. (2008) The new economics of the university: a knowledge governance approach, *The Journal of Technology Transfer*, 33(1): 1–22.

Anyon, J. (2009) Introduction. In Anyon, J., Dumas, M. J., Linville, D., Nolan, D., Perez, M., Tuck, E. and Weiss, J. (2009) *Theory and Educational Research: Toward critical social explanation.* New York and London: Routledge.

Archer, L. et al. (2005) *Higher Education and Social Class.* London, Routledge.

Arnseth, H.C. (2008) Activity theory and situated learning theory: contrasting views of educational practice, *Pedagogy, Culture and Society*, 16(3): 289–302.

Ashton, D.N. (2005) High skills: the concept and its application to South Africa, *Journal of Education and Work*, 18(1): 19–32.

Ashton, D.N. and Green, F. (1996) *Education, Training and the Global Economy.* Cheltenham: Edward Elgar.

Ashwin, P. and Trigwell, K. (2004) Investigating staff and educational development. In Khan, P. and Baume, D. (eds), *Enhancing Staff and Educational Development.* London: Kogan Page.

Baldwin, M. (2008) Working together, learning together: Co-operative inquiry in the development of complex practice by teams of social workers. In Reason, P. and Bradbury, H. (eds), *The SAGE Handbook of Action Research.* London: Sage Publications: 221–228.

Ball, S. (2008) *The Education Debate.* Bristol: Policy Press.

Ball, S. J. (1990) Management as a Moral Technology – a Luddite Analysis. In Ball, S. J. (ed.), *Foucault and Education: Disciplines and knowledge.* London: Routledge: 153–166.

Ball, S. J. (1998) Big policies/small world: an introduction to international perspectives in education policy, *Comparative Education*, 34(2): 119–130.

Bamber, V., Trowler, P., Saunders, M. and Knight, P. (2009) *Enhancing Learning, Teaching, Assessment and Curriculum in Higher Education: Theory, cases, practices.* Buckingham: Open University Press.

Barab, S.A. and Plucker, J.A. (2002) Smart people or smart contexts? Cognition, ability, and talent development in an age of situated approaches to knowing and learning, *Educational Psychologist*, 37(3): 165–182.

Barnett, R. (1997) Beyond competence. In Coffield, F. and Williamson, B. (eds), ,*Repositioning Higher Education.* Buckingham: SRHE/Open University Press.

Barnett, R. (2000) *Realizing the University in an Age of Supercomplexity.* Buckingham: Open University Press/SRHE.

Barnett, R. (2009) Shaping the sector. In Withers, K. (ed.), *First Class? Challenges and opportunities for the UK's university sector.* (Institute for Public Policy Research).

Barton, D. and Tusting (2005) *Beyond Communities of Practice: Language, power and social context.* Cambridge: Cambridge University Press.

Bascia, N. and Hargreaves, A. (2000) *The Sharp Edge of Educational Reform: Teaching, leading and the realities of reform.* London and New York: Routledge Falmer.

Becher, T. and Trowler, P. (2001) *Academic Tribes and Territories* (*second edition*). Buckingham: SRHE and Open University Press.

Bereiter, C. and Scardamalia, M. (1993) *Surpassing Ourselves: An inquiry into the nature and implications of expertise.* Chicago, IL: Open Court.

Bernstein, B. (1971) On the classification and framing of educational knowledge. In Young, F.D. (ed.), *Knowledge and Control: New Directions for the Sociology of Education.* London: Collier-MacMillan.

Berthon, P., Pitt, L., Ewing, M. and Carr, C.L. (2002) Potential research space in MIS: A framework for envisioning and evaluating research replication, extension, and generation, *Information Systems Research*, 13(4): 416–427.

Biggs, J.B. (1999) *Teaching for Quality Learning at University.* Buckingham: SRHE and Open University Press.

Biggs, J.B. (1987) *Student Approaches to Learning and Studying.* Hawthorn, Victoria: Australian Council for Educational Research.

Blackler, F. (1995) Knowledge, knowledge work and organisations: an overview and interpretation, *Organisation Studies*, 16(6): 1021–1045.

Blackmore, J. (2009) Academic pedagogies, quality logics and performative universities: Evaluating teaching and what students want, *Studies in Higher Education*, 34(8): 857–872.

Bleiklie, I. (2002) Explaining change in Higher Education policy. In Trowler, P. (ed.), *Higher Education Policy and Institutional Change: Intentions and outcomes in turbulent environments.* Buckingham: SRHE and Open University Press: 24–45.

Bonamy, J., Charlier, B. and Saunders, M. (2001) Bridging tools for change: evaluating a collaborative learning network, *Journal of Computer Assisted Learning* 17(3): 295–305.

Bornmann, L., Mittag, S. and Daniel, H. (2006) Quality assurance in higher education – meta-evaluation of multi-stage evaluation procedures in Germany, *Higher Education*, 52: 687–709.

Bourdieu, P. and Wacquant, L. (1992) *An Invitation to Reflexive Sociology.* Chicago: The University of Chicago Press.

Bowden, J. and Marton, F. (1998) *The University of Learning: Beyond quality and competence in higher education.* London: Stylus Publishing.

Bresciani, M. J. (2006) *Outcomes-based Academic and Co-curricular Program Review: A compilation of institutional good practices.* Sterling, VA: Stylus Publishing.

Brookfield, S. (1995) Changing the culture of scholarship to the culture of teaching: an American perspective. In Schuller, T. (ed.) (1995) *The Changing University?* Buckingham: SRHE and Open University Press.

Brown, J.S. and Duguid, P. (1991) Organizational learning and communities of practice: toward a unified view of working, learning and innovating, *Organization Science*, 2(1): 40–57.

Brown, P. and Scase, R. (1994) *Higher Education and Corporate Realities: Class, Culture and the Decline of Graduate Careers.* University of Kent.

Brown, P., Green, A. and Lauder, H. (2001) *High Skills: Globalisation, competitiveness and skill formation.* Oxford: Oxford University Press.

Bunting, I. (2002) The higher education landscape under apartheid. In Cloete, N., Fehnel, R., Maassen, P., Moja, T., Perold, H. and Gibbon, T. (eds), *Transformation in higher education: global pressures and local realities in South Africa.* Cape Town, Juta: 58–86 http://www.chet.org.za/download/3614/02_GLOBAL_PRESSURE.pdf [accessed on 11 December 2009].

Bushe, G.R. (2007) Appreciative Inquiry is not (just) about the positive, *OD Practitioner*, 3(4): 30–35.

Cerych, L. and Sabatier, P. A. (1986) *Great Expectations and Mixed Performance.* Stoke-on-Trent: Trentham Books.

Chapman, V. and Carlisle, H. (2006) *Academic Standards And Benchmark Descriptors.* In CLIP CETL (2009) http://www.arts.ac.uk/cetl.htm (Accessed 06.04.2010).

Chelimsky, E. (1997) Thoughts for a new evaluation society, *Evaluation*, 3: 97–109.

Cheng, M. (2009) Academics' professionalism and quality mechanisms: challenges and tensions, *Quality in Higher Education*, 15(3): 193–205.

Cheol Shin, J. (2009) *Impacts of Performance-based Accountability on Institutional Performance in the U.S. Higher Education.* DOI 10.1007/s10734–009-9285-y.

Christensen Hughes, J. (2007) Supporting curriculum assessment and development: implications for the faculty role and institutional support, *New Directions for Teaching and Learning*, (112): 107–110.

Clark, B.R. (1977) *Academic Power in Italy: Bureaucracy and oligarchy in a national university system.* Chicago: The University of Chicago Press.

Clark, B.R. (2005) *Sustaining Change in Universities: Continuities in case studies and concepts.* (Reprinted) Maidenhead: SRHE and Open University Press.

Clegg, S. and McAuley, J. (2005) Conceptualising middle management in higher education, *Journal of Higher Education Policy and Management*, 27(1): 19–34.

Cloete, N. and Galant, J. (2005) *Capacity Building for the Next Generation of Academics. Cape Town: Centre for Higher Education Transformation.* http://www.chet.org.za/books/capacity-building-next-generation-academics (Accessed 11.12.2009.)

Cole, M., Engestrom, Y. and Vasquez, O.A. (1997) *Mind, Culture, and Activity: Seminal papers from the Laboratory of Comparative Human Cognition.* Cambridge and New York: Cambridge University Press.

Committee on Higher Education (1963) Higher Education: Report of the Committee under the Chairmanship of Lord Lionel Robbins, CMND 2154. London: HMSO.

Connell, J.P. and Kubisch, A. (1999) Applying a theory of change approach to the evaluation of comprehensive community initiatives: progress, prospects, and problems, *New Approaches to Evaluating Community Initiatives*, (Volume 2): Aspen Institute.

Cooke Report (2003) *The Final Report of the Teaching Quality Enhancement Committee on the Future Needs and Support for Quality Enhancement of Learning and Teaching in*

Higher Education. http://www.hefce.ac.uk/learning/tqec/final.doc (Accessed 10.2.2004).

Cooperrider, D.L. and Srivastva, S. (1987) *Research in Organizational Change and Development Volume 1*: 129–169. Available at http://www.appreciative-inquiry.org/AI-Life.htm (Accessed 14.7.09.)

Cooperrider, D.L. and Whitney, D. (1999) Appreciative Inquiry: A positive revolution in change. In Holman, P. and Devane, T. (eds), *The Change Handbook.* San Francisco: Berrett- Koehler Publishers, Inc.: 245–263.

Corbyn, Z. (2009) V-c: focus research cash or 'mediocrity' awaits, *Times Higher Education,* 22 October:6.

Cox, M. and Richlin, L. (eds) (2004) Building faculty learning communities, *New Directions for Teaching and Learning* (97), San Francisco, CA: Jossey-Bass.

Crouch, C., Finegold, D. and Sako, M. (1999) *Are Skills the Answer? The political economy of skill creation in advanced industrial societies.* Oxford: Oxford University Press.

Cummings, T. and Worley, C. (2009) *Organization Development and Change.* (*Ninth edition*) Exeter: South-Western College Publishing.

Curran, P. J. (2000) Competition in UK higher education: Competitive advantage in the research assessment exercise and Porter's diamond model, *Higher Education Quarterly,* 54(4): 386–410.

Cuthbert, R. (2007) *How Can We Manage?* Professorial Inaugural Lecture, University of the West of England, 7 November 2007.

Datnow, A. (2001) Power and politics in the adoption of school reform models, *Educational Evaluation and Policy Analysis,* 22(4): 357–374.

Datta, L. (1997) A Pragmatic Basis for Mixed Method Designs, *New Directions in Program Evaluation,* 74 (Summer 1997): 33–46.

Davis, B. and Sumara, D. (2006) *Complexity and Education: Inquiries into learning, teaching, and research.* Mahwah, NJ: Lawrence Erlbaum Associates.

Day, C. (1999) *Developing Teachers: The Challenge of Lifelong Learning.* London: Falmer Press.

Dearing Report (1997) *Higher Education in the Learning Society. Report of the National Committee of Inquiry into HE (Chairman Lord Dearing).* Norwich: HMSO.

Deem, R. (2004) The Knowledge Worker, the Manager-Academic and the Contemporary UK University: new and old forms of public management? *Financial Accountability and Management,* 20, 2: 107–128.

Deem, R. and Brehony, K. (2005) Management as ideology: the case of 'new managerialism' in higher education, *Oxford Review of Education,* 31.2 (2005): 217–235.

Dehler, J., Charlier, B. and Wüthrich, A. (2009) *Conceptualization and Assessment of Gender Equality in University Teacher Training.* Paper presented at the 13th Biennial Conference for Research on Learning and Instruction (EARLI), Amsterdam, The Netherlands.

Denham, J. (2008): http://webarchive.nationalarchives.gov.uk/+/http://www.dius.gov.uk/speeches/denham_hespeech_290208.html (accessed on 23/08/10).

Dibiaggio, L. and Ferrary, M. (2003) Communautés de pratique et réseaux sociaux dans la dynamique de fonctionnement des clusters de hautes technologies. In *Revue d'économie industrielle.* 103. 2e et 3e trimestre 2003. La morphogénèse des réseau: 111–130.

Dill, D. (1998) Evaluating the 'Evaluative State': implications for research in HE, *European Journal of Education,* 33(3): 361–377.

Dill, D. and Soo, M. (2005) Academic quality, league tables and public policy: a cross-national analysis of university ranking systems, *Higher Education,* 49: 495–533.

Donabedian, A. (1980) *The Definition of Quality and Approaches to its Assessment. Exploration in quality assessment and monitoring.* Michigan: Health Administration Press.

Drew, L. and Vaughan, S. (2002) The course team as the focus for contextualised professional development, *Innovations in Education and Training International,* 39(3).

Driscoll, A. and Wood, S. (2007) *Developing Outcomes-based Assessment for Learner-centered Education: A faculty introduction.* Sterling, VA: Stylus Publishing.

Du Gay, (1996) *Consumption and Identity at Work.* London: Sage.

Easterby-Smith, M., Aráujo, L. and Burgoyne, J.G. (1999) *Organizational Learning and the Learning Organization: Developments in theory and practice.* London: Sage.

Eccles, C. (2002) The use of university rankings in the United Kingdom, *Higher Education in Europe,* 274: 423–432.

Economic and Social Research Council (ESRC) (2004) 'Memorandum from the ESRC' in evidence to the House of Commons Parliamentary Select Committee on Science and Technology (2004) *The Work of the Economic and Social Research Council.* HC13. London: The Stationery Office.

Eisner, E. (2004). Educational objectives – help or hindrance? In Flinders, D.J. and Thornton, S.J. (eds), *The Curriculum Studies Reader (second edition).* New York: Routledge: 85–92). (Original work published in 1967.)

El Khawas, E. (1998) Strong State action but limited results: perspectives on university resistance, *European Journal of Education,* 33:3: 317–330.

Elton, L. (1987) *Teaching in Higher Education: Appraisal and Training.* London: Kogan Page.

Elton, L. (2002) The UK Research Assessment Exercise: Unintended Consequences, *Higher Education Quarterly,* 54(3): 274–283.

Enders, J. (2009) Global university rankings and the academic reputation race. Presentation to a SRHE South West seminar at the University of Bath, 13 November 2009.

Engeström, Y. (1993) Developmental studies on work as a test bench of AT. In Chaiklin, S. and Lave, J. (eds), *Understanding Practice: Perspectives on activity and context.* Cambridge: Cambridge University Press: 64–103.

Engeström, Y. (1999) Activity theory and individual and social transformation. In Engeström, Y., Miettinen, R. and Punamäki-Gitai, R.L. (eds.), *Perspectives on Activity Theory.* Cambridge; New York: Cambridge University Press: xiii.

Entwistle, N. (1988) Approaches to studying and levels of processing in university students, *British Journal of Educational Psychology,* 58, 3 (Nov): 258–265.

Entwistle, N., McCune, V. and Hounsell, J. (2002) ETL Project. *Approaches to Studying and Perceptions of University Teaching-Learning Environments: Concepts, Measures and Preliminary Findings.* Occasional Report 1. (http://www.etl.tla.ed.ac.uk/docs/ETLreport1.pdf (Accessed 06.04.2010.)

Eraut, M. (1993) Teacher accountability: Why is it so central to teacher professional development? In Kremer-Hayan, L., Vonk, H.C. and Fessler, R. (eds.), *Teacher Professional Development: A multiple perspective approach.* Amsterdam: Swets Zeitlinger.

Eraut, M. (1994) *Developing Professional Knowledge and Competence.* London: Falmer.

Eraut, M. (2000) Non-formal learning and tacit knowledge in professional work, *Journal of Educational Psychology,* 70(1): 113–136.

Etzkowitz, H. and Leydesdorff, L. (2000) The dynamics of innovation: from National Systems and 'Mode 2' to a Triple Helix of university-industry-government relations, *Research Policy,* 29(2): 109–123.

EU 2010 strategy, http://ec.europa.eu/information_society/tl/research/index_en.htm (Accessed on 22.07.2009.)

EU: http://cordis.europa.eu/eu-funding-guide/home_en.html (Accessed on 21.07.09.)

European University Association (EUA) 2007. Trends V: Universities shaping the European Higher Education Area. http://www.eua.be/fileadmin/user_upload/files/Publications/Final_Trends_Report__May_10.pdf [11 December 2009] (Last accessed 11.12.09.)

Evans, M. and Lunt, N. (2010) Editorial: Understanding Competition States, *Policy Studies*, 31(1): 1–4.

Evidence Ltd (2003) *Funding Research Diversity. The impact of further concentration on university research performance and regional research capacity.* London: Universities UK.

Fähndrich, S. and Grendel, T. (2007) *Systemakkreditierung an der Johannes Gutenberg-Universität Mainz – Voraussetzungen und Ziele,* VHW Mitteilungen – Informationen und Meinungen zur Hochschulpolitik, (4): 13–16.

Fairley, J. and Patterson, L. (1995) Scottish Education and the New Managerialism, *Scottish Educational Review,* 27, 1: 13–36.

Fetterman, D.M., Kaftarian, S.J. and Wandersman, A. (1996) *Empowerment Evaluation: Knowledge and tools for self-assessment and accountability.* Thousand Oaks, CA: Sage.

Filippakou, O. and Tapper, T. (2008) Quality Assurance and Quality Enhancement in Higher Education: Contested Territories? *Higher Education Quarterly,* 62(1–2): 84–100.

Finegold, D. and Soskice, D. (1988) The failure of training in Britain: analysis and prescription, *Oxford Review of Economic Policy,* 4(3): 21–51.

Fitz-Gibbon, Carol T. and Coe, Robert (1998) School effectiveness research: criticisms and recommendations, *Oxford Review of Education* 24(4): 421–433.

Flint, A., Oxley, A., Helm, P. And Bradley, S. (2009) Preparing for success: one institution's aspirational and student focused response to the National Student Survey, *Teaching in Higher Education,* 6: 607–618.

Foucault, M. (1980) *Power/Knowledge.* New York: Pantheon.

Fraser, S.P. (2006) Shaping the university curriculum through partnerships and critical conversations, *International Journal for Academic Development,* 11(1): 5–17.

Friedman, V.J. (2008) Action science: Creating communities of inquiry in communities of practice. In Reason, P. and Bradbury, H. (eds.), *The SAGE Handbook of Action Research.* London: Sage Publications: 131–143.

Fullan, M. (2001) *The New Meaning of Educational Change* (*third edition*). London: RoutledgeFalmer.

Furlong, J. and Oancea, A. (2005) *Assessing Quality in Applied and Practice-based Educational Research. A framework for discussion.* Oxford: Oxford University Department of Educational Studies.

Gay, L.R., Mills, G.E. and Airasian, P. (2009) *Educational Research: Competencies for analysis and applications* (9th edn). Upper Saddle River, NJ: Pearson Merrill.

Gergens, K.J. (1994) *Toward Transformation in Social Knowledge* (*2nd Edition*) London: Sage.

Giddens, A. (1976) *New Rules of Sociological Method.* London: Hutchinson.

Giddens, A. (1984) *The Constitution of Society.* Cambridge: Polity Press.

Gill, A. (2008) Labour concedes that it won't deliver its 50% target on time, *Times Higher Education Supplement,* 17th April. Available at http://www.timeshighereducation.co.uk/story.aspsectioncode=26&storycode=401455 (Accessed 17.7.09.)

Gill, J. (2008) Ratings to retain peer-review base, *Times Higher Education Supplement,* 6 March 2008.

Gordon, G. and Owen, C. (2008) *Cultures of Quality Enhancement: A short overview of the literature for higher education policy makers and practitioners*. Glasgow: QAA. Scotland. http://www.enhancementthemes.ac.uk/themes/QualityCultures/default.asp (accessed 11 June 2010).

Greenaway, H. and Harding, A.G. (1978) *The Growth of Policies for Staff Development*. Dorset: SRHE.

Grendel, T. and Rosenbusch, C. (2010) System accreditation: an innovative approach to assure and develop the quality of study programmes in Germany, *Higher Education Management and Policy*, 22(1) spring.

Grunert O'Brien, J., Millis, B.J. and Cohen, M.J. (2008) *The Course Syllabus: A learning centered approach (2nd edition)*. Jaffrey, NH: Anker Publishing Company.

Guba, E.G. and Lincoln, Y.S. (1989) *Fourth Generation Evaluation*. London: Sage.

Halfon, N., DuPlessis, H. and Inkelas, M. (2007) Transforming the U.S. child health system, *Health Affairs*, 26(2): 315–330.

Hall, G.E. and Loucks, S.F. (1978) Teacher concerns as a basis for facilitating and personalizing staff development, *Teachers College Record*, 80(4): 36–53.

Hannan, A. and Silver, H. (2000) *Innovating in Higher Education: Teaching, learning and institutional cultures*. Buckingham: SRHE and Open University Press.

Hargreaves, A. (1983) The politics of administrative convenience. In Ahier, J. and Flude, M. (eds.), *Contemporary Education Policy*. London: Croom Helm.

Hargreaves, A. (1994) *Changing Teachers, Changing Times*. London: Cassell.

Harland, J. and Kinder, K. (1997) Teachers' continuing professional development: framing a model of outcomes, *Professional Development in Education*, 23(1): 71.

Harley, S. (2002) The impact of research selectivity on academic work and identities in UK higher education, *Studies in Higher Education*, 27(2): 187–205.

Harley, S. and Lee, F. (1997) Research selectivity, managerialism and the academic labour process: the future of non-mainstream economics in UK universities, *Human Relations*, 50(11): 1427–1460.

Harris, A. and Bennett, N. (2001) *School Effectiveness and School Improvement: Alternative perspectives*. London: Continuum.

Harvey, L. (2008) Rankings of higher education systems: a critical review, *Quality in Higher Education*, 14(3).

Hayward, C. R. (2000) *De-facing Power*. Cambridge: Cambridge University Press.

HEFCE (2004): http://www.hefce.ac.uk/pubs/hefce/2004/04_05/#exec (Accessed on 11.07.2009.)

HEFCE (2008) Research Assessment Exercise 2008: the outcome, RAE 01/2008. Bristol: HEFCE.

HEFCE (Higher Education Funding Council for England) (2009) National Student Survey. http://www.hefce.ac.uk/learning/nss/ (Last accessed 17.4.09.)

HEFCE (Higher Education Funding Council for England) (1999), *Research Assessment Exercise 2001: Assessment panels' criteria and working methods*. Bristol: HEFCE.

Helsby, G. and Saunders, M. (1993) Taylorism, Tylerism and performance indicators: defending the indefensible, *Educational Studies*, 19(1): 55–77.

Henkel, M. (1998) Evaluation in higher education: conceptual and epistemological foundations, *European Journal of Education*, 33(3) and in *The Evaluative State Revisited: 20th Anniversary Issue of Review of Trends in Higher Education* (Sept, 1998): 285–297.

Henkel, M. (2000) *Academic Identities and Policy Change in Higher Education*. London: Jessica Kingsley Publishers.

Hobsons (2009) *The Good Universities Guide 2010 to Universities and Private Higher Education Providers*. Melbourne: Hobsons.

Holland, D. and Valsiner, J. (1988) Cognition, symbols and Vygotsky's developmental psychology, *Ethos*, 16(3): 247–272.

Holland, D., Lachicotte, W., Skinner, D. and Cain, C. (1998) *Identity and Agency in Cultural Worlds.* Cambridge, Mass: Harvard University Press.

Hood, C. (1986) *The Tools of Government.* London: Macmillan.

House of Commons (2004) *Research Assessment Exercise: A reassessment, Eleventh Report of Session 2003–4 of the Science and Technology Select Committee, HC586.* London: The Stationery Office.

Hoyle, E. (1982) Micropolitics of Educational Organisations, *Educational Management and Administration*, 10: 87–98.

Hubball, H.T. (2010) Context-based learning impacts on team development and performance outcomes: Critical preparations for the masters/veterans futsal world cup, *International Journal of Sport and Society*, 1(1), 18 pgs.

Hubball, H.T. and Albon, S. (2007) Developing a faculty learning community: Enhancing the scholarship of teaching, learning and curriculum practice. *Journal on Excellence in College Teaching*, 18(2): 119–142.

Hubball, H.T. and Burt, H. (2004) An integrated approach to developing and implementing learning-centred curricula, *International Journal for Academic Development*, 9(1): 51–65.

Hubball, H.T. and Burt, H. (2007) Learning outcomes and program-level evaluation in a 4-year undergraduate pharmacy curriculum, *American Journal of Pharmaceutical Education*, 71(5), Article 90: 1–8.

Hubball, H.T. and Clarke, A. (in press) Diverse methodological approaches and considerations for conducting the scholarship of teaching and learning in higher education, *Canadian Journal for the Scholarship of Teaching and Learning.*

Hubball, H.T. and Gold, N. (2007) The scholarship of curriculum practice and undergraduate program reform: Integrating theory into practice, *New Directions for Teaching and Learning*, (112): 5–14.

Hubball, H.T. and Pearson, M.L. (2009) Curriculum leadership portfolios: Enhancing scholarly approaches to undergraduate program reform, *Transformative Dialogues*, 3(2): 1–16.

Hubball, H.T. and Pearson, M.L. (in press) Grappling with the complexity of undergraduate degree program reform: Critical barriers and emergent strategies, *Transformative Dialogues.*

Hubball, H.T. and Poole, G. (2003) A learning-centred faculty certificate programme on university teaching, *International Journal for Academic Development*, 8(1/2): 11–24.

Hubball, H.T., Mighty, J., Britnell, J. and Gold, N. (2007) Supporting the implementation of externally generated learning outcomes and learning-centered curriculum development: An integrated framework, *New Directions for Teaching and Learning*, (112): 93–106.

Huberman, M. (1994) Research utilization: the state of the art, *Knowledge and Policy*, 7, 4: 13–33.

Huberman, M. (1993) *The Lives of Teachers.* London: Cassell.

Hughes, M. and Traynor, T. (2000) Reconciling process and outcome in evaluating community initiatives, *Evaluation*, 6(1): 37–49.

Huisman, J. and Currie, J. (2004) Accountability in higher education: bridge over troubled water? *Higher Education*, 48: 529–551.

Huisman, J., de Weert, E. and Bartelse, J. (2002) Academic careers from a European perspective: the declining desirability of the faculty position, *The Journal of Higher Education*, 73(1): 141–160.

Jacklin, A., Robinson, C., O'Meara, L. and Harris, A. (2007) Improving the experiences of disabled students in higher education, The Higher Education Academy, February [Online] Available from: http://www.heacademy.ac.uk/assets/York/documents/ourwork/research/jacklin.pdf (Last accessed 30.12.09.)

Jacobs, C. (2000) The evaluation of educational innovation, *Evaluation*, 6(3): 261–280.

Johnston, R. (2008) On structuring subjective judgements: originality, significance and rigour in RAE 2008, *Higher Education Quarterly*, 62(1/2): 120–147.

Joint Negotiating Committee for Higher Education Staff (JNCHES) (2006) Framework agreement for the modernisation of pay structures http://www.ucu.org.uk/media/pdf/frameworkagreement.pdf (Last accessed 5.5.2009.)

Julian, D., Jones, A. and Diana Deyo (1995) Open Systems Evaluation and the Logic Model: Program Planning and Evaluation Tools, *Evaluation and Program Planning*, 18(4): 333–341.

Kahler, M. (ed.) (2009) *Networked Politics: Agency, power and governance.* Ithaca and London: Cornell University Press.

Kahn, M., Blankley, W., Maharajh, R., Pogue, T.E., Reddy, V., Cele, G. and Du Toit, M. (2004) *Flight of the flamingos: A study on the mobility of research and development workers.* Cape Town: Human Sciences Research Council Press/CSIR for the National Advisory Council on Innovation.

King, R.P. (2007) Governance and accountability in the higher education regulatory state, *Higher Education*, 53(4): 411–430.

Klapper, J.T. (1960). *The Effects of Mass Communication.* New York: Free Press: Preskill, H. and Coghlan, A., T. (eds) (2003) *Using Appreciative Inquiry in Evaluation: New Directions for Evaluation*, No. 100. San Francisco: Jossey-Bass. p. 19.

Knight, P. and Trowler, P. (2001) *Departmental Leadership in Higher Education.* Buckingham: SRHE and Open University Press.

Knight, P. T. and Trowler, P. R. (2000). Department-level cultures and the improvement of learning and teaching, *Studies in Higher Education*, 25(1): 69–83.

Kogan, M. (2002) The role of different groups in policy-making and implementation: institutional politics and policy-making. In Trowler, P. (ed.), *Higher Education Policy and Institutional Change: Intentions and outcomes in turbulent environments.* Buckingham: SRHE and Open University Press.

Kogan, M. and Hanney, S. (2000) *Reforming Higher Education.* London: Jessica Kingsley.

Kraak, A. (2004) Re-thinking the high skills thesis in South Africa. In McGrath, S.A., Badroodien, A., Kraak, A. and Unwin, L. *Shifting Understandings of Skills in South Africa: Overcoming the historical imprint of a low skills regime.* Pretoria, South Africa: Human Sciences Research Council Publication.

Kraak, A. and Press, K. (2008) *Human Resources Development Review 2008.* Pretoria, South Africa: Human Sciences Research Council Press.

Krause, K. (forthcoming) Using student survey data to shape academic development priorities and approaches. In Stefani, L. (ed.), *Evaluating the Effectiveness of Academic Development Practice.* Abingdon, Oxon: Taylor and Francis.

Kromrey, H. (2003) Qualität und Evaluation im System Hochschule. In Stockmann, R. (ed.) (2003) *Evaluationsforschung*, (*2nd edition*). Opladen: Leske Budrich: 233–258.

Krücken, G. and Meier, F. (2006) Turning the university into an organizational actor.

In Drori, G.S., Meyer, J.W. and Hwang, H. (eds), *Globalization and Organization: World society and organizational change.* Oxford: Oxford University Press: 241–257.

Kuh, G. (2001) Assessing What Really Matters to Student Learning: Inside the National Survey of Student Engagement, *Change*, 33: 10–17, 66.

Kushner (2000) *Personalizing Evaluation.* London: Sage.

Land, R. (2004) *Educational Development.* Maidenhead: SRHE/OUP.

Laughton, D. (2003) Why was the QAA Approach to Teaching Quality Assessment Rejected by Academics in UK HE? *Assessment and Evaluation in Higher Education*, 28, 3: 309–321.

Lave, J. and Wenger, E. (1991) *Situated Learning: Legitimate Peripheral Participation.* Cambridge: Cambridge University Press.

Levin, B. (1998) An epidemic of education policy: what can we learn from each other? *Comparative Education*, 34, 2: 131–142.

Lewis, J. (2002) Assessing the Research Assessment Exercise: An expensive (mad) lottery? Presentation to the AUA annual conference, April.

Lillis, T. (2001) *Student Writing Access, Regulation and Desire.* London: Routledge.

Lipsky, M. (1980) *Street Level Bureaucracy: Dilemmas of the individual in public services.* Beverley Hills: Sage.

Locke, W., Verbik, L., Richardson, J.T.E. and King, R. (2008) Counting what is measured or measuring what counts? League tables and their impact on HE institutions in England. Circular 2008/14 Report for the HE Funding Council for England. http://www.hefce.ac.uk/pubs/hefce/2008/08_14/08_14.pdf (Last accessed 2 February 2010.)

Lucas, L. (2006) *The Research Game in Academic Life.* Maidenhead: SRHE/Open University Press.

Luckett, K. (2007) Methodology Matters: What methods for quality improvement? *Perspectives in Education*, 25, 3: 1–11.

Lukes, S. (2005) *Power: A radical view.* (*Second edition*). London: Palgrave Macmillan.

Luzzatto, G. and Moscati, R. (2005) University reform in Italy: fears, expectations and contradictions. In Gornitzka, A., Kogan, M. and Amaral, A. (eds), *Reform and Change in Higher Education.* Dordrecht, Springer: 153–168.

Manathunga, C. (2005) Early warning signs in postgraduate research education: a different approach to ensuring timely completions, *Teaching in Higher Education*, 10(2): 219–233.

Mark, M., Greene, J. and Shaw, I. (2007) *Handbook of Evaluation.* London: Sage.

Marks, D. (1995) Bias in UFC research assessment exercise, *The Psychologist*, July.

Marsh, H.W., Rowe, K.J. and Martin, A. (2002) PhD students' evaluations of research supervision: issues, complexities, and challenges in a nationwide Australian experiment in benchmarking universities, *The Journal of Higher Education*, 73(3): 313–348.

Mayer, M. and Altman, M. (2005) South Africa's economic development trajectory: implications for skills development, *Journal of Education and Work*, 18(1): 33–56.

Mazzeo, C. (2001) Frameworks of State-assessment policy in historical perspective, *Teachers' College Record*, 103(3): 367–397.

McCluskey, A., Saunders, M. and Charlier, B. (2008) D.EVA.05 PALETTE evaluation framework and instruments (Part of the PALETTE Project Deliverable).

McInnis, C. (2000) Changing academic work roles: The everyday realities challenging quality in teaching. *Quality in Higher Education*, 6(2): 143–152. Retrieved 15.10.2009, from http://web.ebscohost.com/ehost/pdf?vid=2andhid=3andsid=a530695d-3c60-43d1-997b-1b55524d63d5%40sessionmgr4

McKinney, K. (2007) *Enhancing Learning Through the Scholarship of Teaching and Learning: The challenges and joys of juggling.* Bolton, MA: Anker Publishing Company.

McNay, I. (1997) *The Impact of the 1992 RAE on Institutional and Individual Behaviour in English Higher Education: The evidence from a research project.* Bristol: HEFCE.

McNay, I. (2003) Assessing the assessment: an analysis of the UK Research Assessment Exercise, 2001, and its outcomes, with special reference to research in education, *Science and Public Policy*, 30, 1: 37–54.

McNay, I. (2007) Research assessment; researcher autonomy. In Tight, M., Kayrooz, C. and Akerlind, G. (eds), *Autonomy in Social Science Research: the view from the United Kingdom and Australian universities. International Perspectives on Higher Education Research*, 4: 183–216.

McNay, I. (2009) Research quality assessment: objectives, approaches, responses and consequences. In Brew, A. and Lucas, L. *Academic Research and Researchers.* Maidenhead: SRHE/Open University Press: 35–53.

Merriam, S.B. (2002) *Qualitative Research in Practice: Examples for discussion and analysis.* San Francisco: Jossey-Bass.

Meyer, J.W. and Rowan, B. (1977) Institutionalized Organization: Formal Structure as Myth and Ceremony. *American Journal of Sociology*, 83: 340–363.

Meyer, S.E. (1996) Building community capacity with evaluation activities that empower. In Fetterman, D.M., Kaftarian, S.J., Wandersman, A. (eds), *Empowerment Evaluation: Knowledge and tools for self-assessment and accountability.* Thousand Oaks CA: Sage.

Michelson, E.S. (2006) Approaches to research and development performance assessment in the United States: an analysis of recent evaluation trends, *Science and Public Policy*, 33(8): 546–560.

Milburn, C. (2010) Why L-plate teachers miss the mark, *Education Age*, 15 February.

Minelli, E., Rebora, G. and Turreo, M. (2008) How can evaluation fail? The case of Italian universities. *Quality in Higher Education*, 14:2: 157–173.

Morley, L. (2001) Comedy of manners: Quality and power in higher education. In Trowler, P. (ed.), *Higher Education Policy and Institutional Change.* Buckingham: Open University Press/SRHE: 126–141.

Moses, I. (1988) *Academic Staff Evaluation and Development. A University Case Study.* (Publisher name and contact information, as provided by the publisher; updated only if notified by the publisher.) University of Queensland Press.

Mroz, A. (2009) Only the best for the best editorial, *Times Higher Education*, 5 November 2009.

Murphy, N., John, D., Bain, J.D. and Conrad, L. (2007) Orientations to research higher degree supervision, *Higher Education*, 53(2): 209–234.

NCIHE (1997) *Higher Education in the Learning Society* (*The Dearing Report*). London: DfEE.

Neave, G. (1998) The Evaluative State Revisited. *European Journal of Education*, 33(3): 265–284.

New Zealand Universities Academic Audit Unit (NZUAAU) 2007. 2007 Annual Report. http://www.aau.ac.nz (12.11.2009.)

Newby, P. (1999) Culture and quality in higher education. *Higher Education Policy*, 12, 3: 261–275.

Newman, M. (2010) Stop state cash for PhDs outside elite institutions, *Times Higher Education*, 7 January, p.9.

Newman, M. (2009) Funder's errors do not excuse London Met, audit finds. *Times Higher Education*, 13 August 2009.

Nonaka, I. and Takeuchi, H. (1995) *The Knowledge-Creating Company: How Japanese Companies Create the Dynamics of Innovation.* New York: Oxford University Press.

OECD (2002) Frascati Manual: Proposed Standard Practice for Surveys on Research and Experimental Development. OECD. http://browse.oecdbookshop.org/oecd/pdfs/browseit/9202081E.PDF (Last accessed 17.4.10.)

Owen, J.M. (2009) New Approaches to the Practicum in Beginning Teacher Education. Report to the Association of Independent Schools, Victoria. Unpublished.

Owen, J.M. (2007) *Program Evaluation: Forms and Approaches.* Allen and Unwin and Guildford Press. Sydney and New York. See Chapter 4.

Ozga, J. (2005) Travelling and embedded policy: the case of post-devolution Scotland within the UK. In Zambeta, E. and Coulby, D. (eds), *Globalisation and Nationalism in Education (World Year Book of Education).* London: Routledge/Taylor and Francis.

PALETTE (2006) Description of Work (DOW) in the Sixth Framework Programme, Technology Enhanced Learning (IST-2004-2.4.10). EU R&D Fund.

Parsons, T. (1971) *The System of Modern Societies.* Englewood Cliffs, NJ: Prentice Hall.

Parsons, T. and Platt, G.M. (1973) *The American University.* Cambridge, Mass.: Harvard University Press.

Patton, M.Q. (1996) *Utilization-Focused Evaluation.* Thousand Oaks: Sage.

Patton, M.Q. (1997) *Utilization-Focused Evaluation: The new century text,* (*Third edition*). Thousand Oaks: Sage.

Patton, M.Q. (1998) Discovering process use, *Evaluation: the International Journal of Theory, Research and Practice,* 4(2): 225–233.

Pawson, R. and Tilley, N. (1997) *Realistic Evaluation.* London: Sage Publications.

Pennee, D.P. (2007) Between cultures: Using curriculum assessment to develop and deliver the integrated core of an Arts and Sciences program, *New Directions for Teaching and Learning,* (112): 59–67.

Perrin, B. (2002) How to – and How Not to – Evaluate Innovation, *Evaluation,* 8(1): 13–28.

Pollitt, C. (1993) *Managerialism and the Public Services: Cuts or cultural change in the 1990s.* London: Blackwell.

Potocki-Malicet, D., Holmesland, I., Estrela, M. and Veiga-Simao, A. (1999) The Evaluation of Teaching and Learning. *European Journal of Education,* 34–3: 299–312.

Power, M. (1997) *The Audit Society: Rituals of verification.* Oxford: Oxford University Press.

Preskill, H. and Coghlan, A.T. (eds) (2003) *Using Appreciative Inquiry in Evaluation: New Directions for Evaluation,* No. 100. San Francisco: Jossey-Bass.

Primrose, P.L., Leonard, R. and Singer, K.E. (1996) The training of postgraduate engineers. IEEE colloquium on engineering education in the twenty-first century (Digest No. 1996/105: 10/1–10/3).

Prosser, M. (2005) Why we shouldn't use student surveys of teaching as satisfaction ratings (Electronic version). Retrieved 18.2.2010 from http://www.heacademy.ac.uk/resources/detail/ourwork/nss/NSS_interpreting_student_surveys

Prosser, M. and Barrie, C. (2003) Using a student-focused learning perspective to align academic development with institutional quality assurance. In Blackwell, R. and Blackmore, P. (eds), *Towards Strategic Staff Development in Higher Education.* Berkshire, England: SRHE and Open University Press.

Prosser, M. and Trigwell, K. (1999) *Understanding Learning and Teaching: The experience in higher education.* Buckingham: Open University Press.

Prosser, M., Ramsden, P., Trigwell, K. and Martin, E. (2003) Dissonance in Experience of Teaching and its Relation to the Quality of Student Learning, *Studies in Higher Education,* 28: 37–48.

QAA (1998) *Quality Assurance in UK Higher Education: A brief guide.* Gloucester: QAA.

QAA (2003) Learning From Subject Review: sharing good practice. Gloucester: QAA. http://www.qaa.ac.uk/reviews/subjectReview/learningfromSubjectReview/subjectreviewannex.asp (Last accessed 29.3.10.)

QAA (2006) Institutional audit: England and Northern Ireland. The Quality Assurance Agency for Higher Education. Available from: http://www.qaa.ac.uk/reviews/institutionalAudit/default.asp (Last accessed 17.7.09.)

Quality Assurance Agency (2008) *Themes,* http://www.enhancementthemes.ac.uk/default.asp (Accessed 10 June 2010.)

Quality Assurance Agency (2009) Mid-Cycle Follow Up. http://www.qaa.ac.uk/reviews/institutionalAudit/MCFUguidanceNotes_institutions.pdf (Accessed 24.08.2010.)

RAE (2001) *2001 Research Assessment Exercise: the outcome,* RAE 4/01. Bristol: HEFCE.

RAE 03/2005: Guidance on Submissions. http://www.rae.ac.uk/pubs/2005/03/ (Last accessed 17.11.08.)

Ramsden, P. (1991) A performance indicator of teaching quality in higher education: The course experience questionnaire, *Studies in Higher Education,* 16: 129–150.

Ramsden, P. (2002) *Learning to Teach in Higher Education,* (*Second edition*). London: RoutledgeFalmer.

Reay, D., David, M. and Ball, S. (2005) *Degrees of Choice: Class, race, gender and higher education.* Oxford: Blackwell.

Reckwitz, A. (2002) Toward a Theory of Social Practices: A Development in Culturalist Theorizing, *European Journal of Social Theory,* 5, 2: 243–263.

Reid, I. (2009) The contradictory managerialism of university quality assurance, *Journal of Education Policy,* 24:5: 575–593.

Rhoades, G. and Slaughter, S. (2006) Mode 3, academic capitalism and the new economy: making higher education work for whom? In Tynjala, P., Valimaa, J. and Boulton-Lewis, G. (eds), *Higher Education and Working Life: Collaboration, confrontation and challenges.* Amsterdam: Elsevier.

Richardson, J.T.E. (2005) Instruments for obtaining student feedback: a review of the literature, *Assessment and Evaluation in Higher Education,* 30(4): 387–415.

Roberts, G. (2003) *Review of Research Assessment: Report by Sir Gareth Roberts to the UK Funding Bodies.* Bristol: HEFCE.

Roy, D., Borin, P. and Kustra, E. (2007) Assisting curriculum change through departmental initiatives, *New Directions for Teaching and Learning,* (112): 21–32.

Samecki, P. (2009) Speech at the Sixth European Conference on Evaluation of Cohesion policy, Warsaw, 30 November 2009 as the European Commissioner responsible for Regional Policy.

Sauder, M. and Espeland, W.N. (2009) The discipline of rankings: tight coupling and organizational change, *American Sociological Review,* 74, 1: 63–82(20).

Saunders, M. (2000) Beginning an evaluation with RUFDATA: theorising a practical approach to evaluation planning, *Evaluation,* 6(1): 7–21.

Saunders, M. (2006) The 'presence' of evaluation theory and practice in educational and social development: towards an inclusive approach, *London Review of Education*, 4(1).

Saunders, M. (2008) The use and usability of evaluation feedback and research. (Keynote address) European Union DG Budget.

Saunders, M., Bonamy, J. and Charlie, B. (2004) The evaluative research of complex projects in e-learning: the case of the 'EQUEL'. In Banks, S. et al. (eds), *Proceedings of the Networked Learning Conference*, ISBN:1–86220-150–1. Lancaster: University of Lancaster 733–745.

Saunders, M., Bonamy, J. and Charlier, B. (2005) Using evaluation to create 'provisional stabilities': bridging innovation in higher education change processes, *Evaluation: the International Journal of Theory, Research and Practice*, 11, 2: 37–55.

Saunders, M., Knight, P., Machell, J., Trowler, P., Jones, C., Williams, S., Fulton, O. and Goodyear, P. (2002) Evaluating the Learning and Teaching Support Network: from awareness to adaptation (http://www.ltsn.ac.uk/for-us/index.asp?id=163).

Saunders, M., Trowler, P., Ashwin, P., Machell, J., Williams, S., Allaway, D., Fanghanel, J. and McKee, A. (2008) *The HEFCE Funded Centres for Excellence in Teaching and Learning Final Formative Evaluation Report, March 2008*, http://www.hefce.ac.uk/pubs/rdreports/2008/rd08_08/ (Last accessed, June 2009.)

Saunders, M., Trowler, P., Ashwin, P., Machell, J., Williams, S., Lent, N., (2008) *Evaluating the Scottish Further and Higher Education Funding Council's strategy for quality enhancement (Higher Education).* Tender submitted by CSET in the Department of Educational Research Lancaster University.

Schmidt, U. (2007) Requirements for a system of internal quality assurance in higher education institutions. In Hochschulrektorenkonferenz (ed.) (2007) *The Quality Assurance System for Higher Education at European and National Level.* Beiträge zur Hochschulpolitik 13/2007. Bonn: HRK: 112–121.

Schmidt, U. (2008) Aufbau, Funktionsweisen, Effekte und Wirkungsgrenzen einer systematischen hochschuleigenen Qualitätssicherung. Handbuch Qualität in Studium und Lehre (19. Ergänzungslieferung), E 9.5: 1–22.

Schmidt, U. (2009) Evaluation an deutschen Hochschulen – Entwicklung, Stand und Perspektiven. In Widmer, T., Beywl, W. and Fabian, C. (eds), *Evaluation. Ein systematisches Handbuch.* Wiesbaden: VS Verlag: 163–169.

Schneider, C.G. and Shoenberg, R. (1999) Habits hard to break: How persistent features of campus life frustrate curricular reform, *Change*, 31(2): 30–35.

Schön, D. A. (1991) *The Reflective Turn: Case studies in and on educational practice.* New York: Teachers' College Press.

Scottish Funding Council (2004) Circular HE/18/04: Public information on quality: further guidance. Available at: http://archive.sfc.ac.uk/information/info_circulars/shefc/2004/he1804/he1804a.pdf (Last accessed 17.7.2009.)

Scottish Funding Council (2006) *Review of the Higher Education Quality Enhancement Framework.* Edinburgh: Scottish Funding Council.

Scriven, M. (1991) *The Evaluation Thesaurus*, (*Fourth edition*). London: Sage.

SEDA (no date) Professional Development Framework: SEDA-PDF. (http://www.seda.ac.uk/professional-development.html (Last accessed 2 February 2010.)

Senge, P.M. (1990) The leader's new work: Building learning organizations, *Sloan Management Review* (Fall): 7–23.

Senge, P.M. (1999) *The Dance of Change: The challenges of sustaining momentum in learning organizations.* New York: Currency/Doubleday.

Senge, P.M. and Scharmer, C.O. (2008) Community action research: Learning as a community of practitioners, consultants and researchers. In Reason, P. and Bradbury, H. (eds), *The SAGE Handbook of Action Research*. London: Sage Publications: 195–206.

Shadish, W.R., Cook, T.D. and Leviton, L.C. (1991) *Foundations of Program Evaluation: Theories of Practice*. Newbury Park: Sage.

Sharp, S. and Coleman, S. (2005) Ratings in the Research Assessment Exercise 2001 – the patterns of university status and panel membership, *Higher Education Quarterly*, 59(2): 153–171.

Shavelson, R.J. and Huang, L. (2003) Responding responsibly to the frenzy to assess learning in higher education, *Change*, 35(1), 11–19. Retrieved 14.10.2009, from http://web.ebscohost.com/ehost/pdf?vid=2andhid=106andsid=3a3dfb57-f0c2-41c8-b52b-4cefd1c13031%40sessionmgr110

Shore, C. and Wright, S. (2004) Whose accountability? Governmentality and the auditing of universities, *Parallax*, 10(2): 100–116.

Shreeve, A. (forthcoming 2010) Joining the dots: the scholarship of teaching as part of institutional research. *Higher Education Research and Development*.

Sibeon, R. (1988) *Contemporary Sociology and Policy Analysis*. Eastham: Tudor.

Simons, H. (2006) Ethics in Evaluation. In Shaw, I., Green, J. and Mark, M. (eds), *The SAGE Handbook of Evaluation*. London: Sage.

Slaughter, S. and Rhoades, G. (2004) *Academic Capitalism and the New Economy: Markets, state and higher education*. Baltimore: The Johns Hopkins University Press.

South African Council on Higher Education (CHE) (2009a) Postgraduate studies in South Africa – a statistical profile. *Higher Education Monitor 7*. http://www.che.ac.za/documents/d000196/ (11.12.2009.)

South African Council on Higher Education (CHE) (2009b) The state of higher education report. *Higher Education Monitor 8*. http://www.che.ac.za/documents/d000201/ (11.12.2009.)

South African Department of Science and Technology (2009) Annual Report 2008/9. http://www.saasta.ac.za/pdf/NRF_vision_2015.pdf (11 December 2009).

South African Ministry of Education (2001) National Plan for Higher Education in South Africa. http://www.education.gov.za/Documents/policies/NationalPlanHE2001.pdf

South African National Research Foundation (2007) NRF vision 2015: the strategic plan of the national research foundation. http://www.saasta.ac.za/pdf/NRF_vision_2015.pdf

Sponsler, B.A. (2009) The role and relevance of rankings in HE policymaking. Washington DC: Institute for HE Policy Issue Brief, September 2009.

Sporn, B. (1999) *Adaptive University Structures: An Analysis of Adaptation to Socioeconomic Environments of US and European Universities*. London: Jessica Kingsley Publishers.

Stake, R.E. (2005) Qualitative case studies. In Denzin, N.K. and Lincoln, Y.S. (eds), *The SAGE Handbook of Qualitative Research*, (*Third edition*). Thousand Oaks, CA: Sage Publications: 443–466.

Stern, E. (2006) Contextual challenges for evaluation practice. In Shaw, I., Green, J. and Mark, M. (eds), *The Sage Handbook of Evaluation*. London: Sage.

Stuart, M. (2000) Beyond rhetoric: reclaiming a radical agenda for active participation in higher education. In J. Thompson (ed.), *Stretching the Academy: The Politics and Practice of Widening Participation in Higher Education*. Leicester: NIACE.

Sumsion, J. and Goodfellow, J. (2004) Identifying generic skills through curriculum mapping: A critical evaluation, *Higher Education Research and Development*, 23(3): 329–346.

Symes, C. and Mcintyre, J. (2002) *Working Knowledge: The new vocationalism in higher education.* London: Open University Press/SRHE.

Talib, A.A. (2000) The RAE and publications: a view of journal editors, *Higher Education Review*, 33(1): 32–46.

Tapper, T. and Filippakou, I. (2009) The world-class league tables and the sustaining of international reputations in HE, *Journal of Higher Education Policy and Management*, 31:1: 55–66.

Tavenas, F. (2003) *Quality Assurance: A Reference System for Indicators and Evaluation Procedures.* Brussels: European Universities Association.

Taylor, M.G. (1989) The implications of new organisational patterns of research, *Higher Education Management*, 1(1): 7–19.

Thorley, D. (1995) A Learning Curve in Change Management. In Slowey, M. (ed.), *Implementing Change from Within Universities and Colleges: 10 Personal Accounts.* London: Kogan Page.

Tomlinson, J. (1996) *The report of the Further Education Funding Council Learning Difficulties and/or Disabilities Committee chaired by Professor John Tomlinson.* London: HMSO. (Summary report available online.) Available from: http://www.csie.org.uk/publications/tomlinson-96.pdf (Accessed 30.12.09.)

Trigwell, K. and Prosser, M. (1996) Towards an understanding of individual acts of teaching. Different Approaches: Theory and Practice in Higher Education. Proceedings HERDSA Conference 1996. Perth, Western Australia, 8–12 July. http://www.herdsa.org.au/confs/1996/trigwell1.html

Trow, M. (1992) Thoughts on the White Paper of 1991, *Higher Education Quarterly*, 46, 3: 213–226.

Trowler, P. (1998) *Academics Responding to Change: New HE frameworks and academic cultures.* Buckingham: Society for Research into HE and Open University Press.

Trowler, P. (2001) Captured by the discourse? The socially constitutive power of new higher education discourse in the UK, *Organization*, 8, 2: 183–201.

Trowler, P. and Cooper, A. (2002) Teaching and Learning Regimes: implicit theories and recurrent practices in the enhancement of teaching and learning through educational development programmes, *Higher Education Research and Development*, 21, 3: 221–240.

Trowler, P., Saunders, M. and Knight, P. (2003) *Change Thinking, Change Practices: A guide to change for Heads of Department, Programme Leaders and other change agents in Higher Education.* York: LTSN Generic Centre.

Trowler, P., Fanghanel, J. and Wareham, T. (2005) Freeing the chi of change: the Higher Education Academy and enhancing teaching and learning in higher education, *Studies in Higher Education*, 30(4): 427–444.

Tysome, T. (2007) Scotland Slams QAA's Methods. Times Higher Education, 9 March. Available at http://www.timeshighereducation.co.uk/story.asp?storyCode=208104§ioncode=26 (Last accessed 31.3.10.)

UNESCO Institute for Statistics 2008. *Global Education Digest 2008: Comparing education statistics around the world.* Paris: UNESCO.

Ure, C. (2009) Practicum Partnerships. Report to the Department of Education, Employment and Training (DEEWR). Melbourne: Melbourne School of Graduate Education.

Vaira, M. (2007) Quality assessment in higher education. An overview on institutionalization, practices, problems and conflicts. In Cavalli, A. (ed.), *Quality Assessment for Higher Education in Europe.* London: Portland Press: 135–146.

Vaira, M. (2003) Higher education reform in Italy: an institutional analysis and a first appraisal, 1996–2001, *Higher Education Policy*, 16: 179–197.

Vaira, M. (2008) La valutazione della qualità dell'istruzione superiore in Europa: istituzionalizzazione, pratiche e conflitti, *Rassegna Italiana di Sociologia*, n. 2/2008: 215–244.

Vedung, E. (1998) Policy Instruments: typologies and theories. In Bemelmans-Videc, M-L, Rist, R. C. and Vedung, E. *Carrots, Sticks, and Sermons.* New Brunswick, NJ and London: Transation Publishers: 21–58.

Volpe Horii, C. Transforming teaching cultures, departmental teaching fellows as agents of change. In Nilson, L.B. and Miller, J.E. *To Improve the Academy*, Jossey-bass, San Fransisco. 28: 359–378.

Vygotsky, L.S. (1978) *Mind in Society: The development of higher psychological processes.* Cambridge: Harvard University Press.

Wagner, L. (1995) A 30-Year Perspective: from the Sixties to the Nineties. In Schuller, T. *The Changing University?* Buckingham: Open University press/SRHE.

Walford, L. (2000) The Research Assessment Exercise: its effect on scholarly journal publishing, *Learned Publishing*, 13, 1, 1 January 2000: 49–52.

Watson, Sir David (2009) *The Question of Morale: Managing happiness and unhappiness in university life.* Maidenhead: Open University Press.

Webb, G. (1996) *Understanding Staff Development.* Buckingham: SRHE/Open University Press.

Webster, B. J., Chan, W.S.C., Prosser, M.T. and Watkins, D.A. (2009) Undergraduates' learning experience and learning process: quantitative evidence from the East, *Higher Education*, 58(3): 375–386.

Webster-Wright, A. (2009) Reframing professional development through understanding authentic professional learning, *Review of Educational Research*, June 2009; 79: 702–739.

Weick, K. (1995) *Sensemaking in Organizations.* Thousand Oaks, CA.: Sage.

Weiss, C.H. (2005) Evaluation for decisions: is anybody there? Does anybody care? *Evaluation Research Methods*, Volume iv, Elliot Stern (eds): 286–299.

Weiss, C. (1997) How Can Theory-Based Evaluation Make Greater Headway? *Evaluation Review*, 21(4): 501–524.

Wenger, E. (2000) Communities of practice and social learning systems, *Organization*, 7(2): 225–246.

Wenger, E. (1998) *Communities of Practice: Learning, meaning and identity.* Cambridge: Cambridge University Press.

Whitley, R. (2008) Constructing universities as strategic actors: limitations and variations. In Engwall, L. and Weaire, D. (eds),*The University in the Market. Volume 84. Wenner-Gren International Series.* London: Portland Press: 23–37.

Williams, Sir Bruce (1991) *University Responses to Research Selectivity.* Centre for HE Studies, London Institute of Education.

Yorke, M. (1997) A good league table guide? *Quality Assurance in Education*, 5:2: 61–72.

Young, A., Tattersall, H., Uus, K., Bamford, J. and McCracken, W. (2004) To what extent do the characteristics of the object of evaluation influence the choice of epistemological framework? The case of Universal Newborn Hearing Screening, *Qualitative Health Research*, 14: 866.

Index

The Society for Research into Higher Education

The Society for Research into Higher Education (SRHE), an international body, exists to stimulate and coordinate research into all aspects of higher education. It aims to improve the quality of higher education through the encouragement of debate and publication on issues of policy, on the organization and management of higher education institutions, and on the curriculum, teaching and learning methods.

The Society is entirely independent and receives no subsidies, although individual events often receive sponsorship from business or industry. The Society is financed through corporate and individual subscriptions and has members from many parts of the world. It is an NGO of UNESCO.

Under the imprint *SRHE & Open University Press*, the Society is a specialist publisher of research, having over 80 titles in print. In addition to *SRHE News*, the Society's newsletter, the Society publishes three journals: *Studies in Higher Education* (three issues a year), *Higher Education Quarterly* and *Research into Higher Education Abstracts* (three issues a year).

The Society runs frequent conferences, consultations, seminars and other events. The annual conference in December is organized at and with a higher education institution. There are a growing number of networks which focus on particular areas of interest, including:

Access
Assessment
Consultants
Curriculum Development
Eastern European
Educational Development Research
FE/HE
Graduate Employment
New Technology for Learning
Postgraduate Issues
Quantitative Studies
Student Development

Benefits to members

Individual

- The opportunity to participate in the Society's networks
- Reduced rates for the annual conferences
- Free copies of *Research into Higher Education Abstracts*
- Reduced rates for *Studies in Higher Education*

- Reduced rates for *Higher Education Quarterly*
- Free online access to *Register of Members' Research Interests* – includes valuable reference material on research being pursued by the Society's members
- Free copy of occasional in-house publications, e.g. *The Thirtieth Anniversary Seminars Presented by the Vice-Presidents*
- Free copies of *SRHE News* and *International News* which inform members of the Society's activities and provides a calendar of events, with additional material provided in regular mailings
- A 35 per cent discount on all SRHE/Open University Press books
- The opportunity for you to apply for the annual research grants
- Inclusion of your research in the *Register of Members' Research Interests*

Corporate

- Reduced rates for the annual conference
- The opportunity for members of the Institution to attend SRHE's network events at reduced rates
- Free copies of *Research into Higher Education Abstracts*
- Free copies of *Studies in Higher Education*
- Free online access to *Register of Members' Research Interests* – includes valuable reference material on research being pursued by the Society's members
- Free copy of occasional in-house publications
- Free copies of *SRHE News* and *International News*
- A 35 per cent discount on all SRHE/Open University Press books
- The opportunity for members of the Institution to submit applications for the Society's research grants
- The opportunity to work with the Society and co-host conferences
- The opportunity to include in the *Register of Members' Research Interests* your Institution's research into aspects of higher education

Membership details: SRHE, 76 Portland Place, London W1B 1NT, UK Tel: 020 7637 2766. Fax: 020 7637 2781. email: srheoffice@srhe.ac.uk
world wide web: http://www.srhe.ac.uk./srhe/
Catalogue: SRHE & Open University Press, McGraw-Hill Education, McGraw-Hill House, Shoppenhangers Road, Maidenhead, Berkshire SL6 2QL. Tel: 01628 502500. Fax: 01628 770224. email: enquiries@openup.co.uk – web: www.openup.co.uk

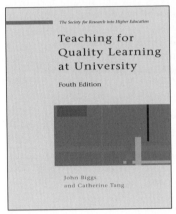

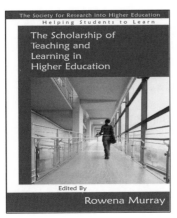

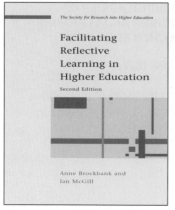

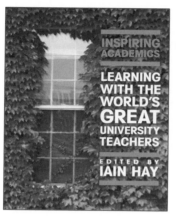

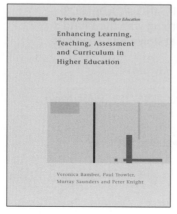